WRVS IN THE COMMUNITY

WRVS IN THE COMMUNITY

Sixty years of voluntary service
in Bolton

To Gwyneth

PAT COX

Best Wishes

Pat Cox 2003

Felton Books

First published in 2003 by
Felton Books, 16 The Highgrove, Bolton, Lancs BL1 5PX

© Pat Cox 2003

ISBN 0 9544129 1 5 *paperback*

Produced by Freelance Publishing Services, Brinscall, Lancs
www.freelancepublishingservices.co.uk
Printed in Great Britain by Lightning Source UK Ltd

Contents

Author's note

I started the book because I was afraid much of the work done by the WVS/WRVS might one day be forgotten. One can tell by reading the story that this should not happen. Members joined this service not always for the reason of 'doing good' as may often be thought, but of fulfilling a need in themselves. After choosing to join the WVS/WRVS the majority of the work members did was for the good of others, sometimes less fortunate than themselves. However, it was an inner need that proved the worth of the Service to so many, and the reason it worked so well was because of the enjoyment we all had.

It provided members with the opportunity to make friends with a common interest. This applied when some of our members working in Luncheon Clubs serving the elderly were often older than the elderly they were serving. Many times during the course of my time with the WRVS, I realised that there were people who enjoyed working for others and there were people who enjoyed having things done for them. Both were necessary, but our members were the former.

Members working in the hospitals worked in some of the most interesting places imaginable, the source for many of the television series we watch today. However not many people in those television programmes can partake of the satisfaction of presenting to the Health Authority items of comfort to sick patients and medical equipment of such great value in helping aid recovery.

In Children's Services we had members who, having enjoyed their own children, could help a child for short periods, making the involvement rewarding to both the child and the member, and make a change – however small – in a child's life. That had to be a great reward.

The work undertaken in a club for the disabled was a joy in itself and the people who came to the club were in the main jolly folk who enjoyed a laugh and meeting people and provided such fun for everyone. Time spent at these clubs was never sad, except perhaps on the death of a member.

General services for the elderly were interesting as many people coming to the clubs had lived through some difficult but very interesting times and were often very wise people who enjoyed each others' company, and of course reminiscing together.

Anyone who has had any contact with the work of the WVS/WRVS from the early days during the war years has enjoyed the work immensely, for themselves first and the recipient second; my time with the Service was one of the best I can remember. I worked hard but the rewards were great and I for one will never forget my work with the WRVS.

Acknowledgements

Thanks to all those people who sent me narratives and pictures for this book. I am particularly indebted to:

Lillian Punchaby for all the information she kept all these years;

Ann Wood, whose information was second to none and learned no doubt from Lillian, her mother. Hers was the most comprehensive report of Hospital activities during the 1990s I could have hoped for;

my thanks too for the use of the scrapbook kept by Evelyn Warr during her time as Organiser during and after the war;

to Lennie Holmes for help with information regarding changes in the WRVS;

several members for letters I have received, including those with whom I worked – thanks for all the contributions.

It has been hard to choose photographs even from my own photographs, and the ones I received from members. There obviously had to be restrictions, and in some instances photographs I needed were not available. My apology also, if, from all the many photographs included in the book there was not one of you, or your project – no offence meant. I also believe there will be discrepancies in the narrative, as I have worked mostly from my memory and other people's, and everyone knows what a memory can do.

A very special thanks to the Editor of the *Bolton Evening News* In allowing me the use of their many archive photographs and especially for the cooperation of Christine Bell, Librarian to the *Bolton Evening News* for her special help in finding photographs necessary for the story's continuity.

The WVS/WRVS has always had cooperation from the *Bolton Evening News* both in my time as Organiser and judging by the amount of photographs in their library, from the very early days of the WVS/WRVS: thank you.

Part One

Introduction to the WVS/WRVS

1

→ *The War years* ←

The Women's Voluntary Service was born out of foresight and knowledge gained from the many hardships suffered by the British public during the Great War of 1914–18. The problems experienced at that time with Germany were looming again in 1938 and memories were still vivid for many British people. The Government was aware that defence preparations would have to be in place well in advance of war breaking out. The planning for an Air Raid Precaution Unit, considered necessary for several years, was put under way. The Home Office became responsible for funding the Department and Wing Commander Olson responsible for staffing the ARP unit. By January of that year, several large towns had designated offices to help Local Authorities prepare their own ARP schemes.

The day after Hitler annexed Austria in March 1938 the Home Secretary broadcast an appeal with the hope of recruiting one million volunteers to help with the many kinds of war work the Civil Defence and ARP might need. He said 'to be effective we shall need air raid wardens, first aid parties and fire-fighters'. During the first ten days preceding the appeal 7,000 people responded, and most of the people who enrolled at that time were women. Consequently, Sir Samuel Hoare, the Home Secretary, decided that a women's organisation to help ARP could work quite well, many of the requirements were well within the capabilities of women. After much consideration he approached Stella Reading, the Dowager Marchioness of Reading, to lead the organisation. He was aware that Lady Reading was heavily involved with the Personal Service League, an organisation formed during the economic depression of the 1930s. The League's main concern was to help unemployed men and their families. The two organisations were completely unconnected, however Sir Samuel knew Lady Reading's involvement with the League would be a tremendous help when recruiting began.

Lady Reading agreed and was soon training groups of women in first aid and gas defence at her home in Chesterfield. She had relinquished her job as head of the Personal Service League to concentrate on the formation of the Women's Civil Defence Group. The Home Secretary visited Lady Reading and formally asked her to compose a memorandum to serve as a basis for a proposed new Women's Organisation for ARP. Sir Samuel Hoare said it was not long before he realised it was one of the best ideas of his life when he thought of Lady Stella Reading as Chairman for this proposed new organisation.

Stella Reading had a practical outlook and built her work on the direct contribution of women in the home. A secret of Lady Reading's success was her deep moral sense of duty and her ability to impart it to others. The Local Authorities would give training and the Home Office would pay basic expenses but general work would be unpaid. Prior to this, no voluntary organisation had ever been used as an arm of the Government.

The beginning of the WVS

The WVS began in a small cramped office in 1938 with five women who were unpaid but worked well together. They compiled a framework for the organisation and each contacted friends and associates who they believed would give their services, including part-time volunteers who were also needed.

WVS poster from the Second World War

In May 1938, an informal but confidential meeting was held of representatives from all the leading women's organisations in the country, chaired by Lady Reading. The Chairman's team for the beginning of the new service included Mrs. Priscilla Montague Norman, wife of the Governor of the Bank of England who became the Vice-Chairman; Mrs. Doreen Harris, who had worked previously on the London Regional Clothing Store and was eventually to take on the job of Regional Clothing Officer for the WVS from 1940 to 1957; Mrs. Catherine Benn as Information Officer, who would establish many worthwhile contacts abroad; Mrs. Lindsey Huxley who was Hon. Treasurer of the National Federation of the WI, and The Hon. Sylvia Fletcher Moulton.

An early consideration when forming the WVS was creating the right type of training programme that would assist the Local Authority when the time came. In due time, the WVS organised two separate courses at their new Headquarters and provided lectures for training in first aid, gas and fire fighting. The first course needed was to create trainers to train others. The second course was a basic training course for its own members. These courses relieved the strain on Civil Defence resources as many of their own personnel were now being mobilised.

The basic course taken by WVS members consisted of five short lectures in civil defence, the idea being that at least one member in each locality could help neighbours living in the same street cope with any emergencies that might arise in the years to come. Lectures were arranged in conjunction with the St John's Ambulance Brigade and the British Red Cross. Eventually a simpler set of lectures was produced for The Housewives Service.

After the Sudeten crisis, a second appeal was launched throughout the country, resulting in half a million new volunteers applying to join.

A question being asked by many was whether this new group of women was part of the forces network, and did they need a uniform? If so, what colour should it be? The decision was the uniform would be a green suit with a dark red blouse but it would not be free or compulsory. For many jobs members would wear a green overall supporting a badge which would be quite adequate.

It was to be a service without rank, but having differing levels of responsibilities. There would be no pay for the job however; key individuals working long hours and carrying much responsibility would receive only basic expenses. Being an arm of the Government and connected to The Civil Defence there would be no fundraising for the organisation either. It was decided that volunteers should be encouraged to work in their chosen fields; to feel happy and comfortable at work would enable a volunteer to do her job well, creating a phrase of Lady Reading's that would echo down the years: 'It is the job that counts'.

The WVS after being presented to the public became involved in planning for the eventual evacuation of women and children from the cities in the event that bombing should occur. The WVS accepted the new challenge and gave assurance that, given some degree of notice, they would be ready to carry out an official order from the Local Authority that made it. During the coming weeks more and more WVS centres were opened all over the country.

Creating a new centre was usually the job of a senior member of the WVS from the County Borough. An application was first made for the opening of the centre to the Town Clerk. With terms and premises agreed, the WVS took the initiative, inviting representatives from the principal women's organisations in the town to attend a meeting. The majority of the women who came to the meeting were the people most likely to be the backbone of the proposed service. During 1938–39 such centres were being formed along the length and breadth of the country. After the election of a Leader the new WVS Centre was formed. Lady Reading took a lightning tour of most the new centres, and by the end of 1938 she had spoken at 98 meetings.

After the appointment of 12 Regional Administrators, the show was on the road.

The WVS made a promise to the Government that given 36 hours' notice, the evacuation of children, teachers and young mothers from the inner cities could begin. Therefore, when Hitler invaded Poland in September, within 24 hours the Ministry of Health had alerted the new Regional Administrators who in turn contacted Centre Organisers in the regions. In the space of 14 hours, 120,000 members were alerted and another 1,700 members were ready for escort duty, preparing to help with a very large number of people evacuated from their homes.

Within a month, Her Majesty the Queen (the late Queen Mother) became President of the WVS, the largest women's organisation in any country in the world.

In the months and years to come the WVS dealt with what would be to many the most insurmountable problems, particularly in the evacuation of approximately 1,473,000 mothers, children, teachers and escorts. In towns throughout the country, members also undertook to meet every troop train both night and day that that ran through their stations.

When boatloads of people started to appear on the south coast, it was not the enemy as one might have imagined, but people from Holland and the Netherlands fleeing from the enemy as the bombing started in their respective countries.

People fled their homes without much in the way of personal possessions so clothing was needed on a massive scale. The WVS London Regional Clothing store was set up, becoming the first of many clothing stores all over the country and would be used long after the war had finished.

One stipulation had been made before the war started; that no member of WVS would be expected or allowed to carry arms of any kind. So later in the war when a narrative report was sent to Headquarters from one centre in the countryside in Yorkshire, it was obvious that on this occasion one Centre Leader had certainly used her initiative. On realising that a German was parachuting slowly down into one of the fields on her farm, the member took up a pitchfork, holding him at bay until the local police arrived, when she realised that during his fall he had sprained his ankle so could not have escaped anyway. Then, trying to revive him, as her training suggested, she had done her duty as she saw it and made him a nice cup of tea.

After the call for ships of all sizes to pitch in and help bring the stranded British Expeditionary Force home from the beaches of Dunkirk, the WVS manned canteens at the dockside, begging and borrowing items that were needed to provide comfort to injured personnel. Large jugs of hot tea were supplied for men who sat or lay injured on the dockside whilst waiting to be transported to either a hospital or back to barracks. Many of them were cold and wet and some were hurt, but being safe and back home were prepared to lie and wait. The men were given tea, sandwiches and dry clothing. Some WVS members sat and talked to soldiers, hoping in some way to aid in their recovery.

The real work, which members of the WVS had been preparing for, arrived with the Blitz on London. The story of the Blitz has been told over the years including all the hard work and bravery of the men and women that lived and died through it. By May 1941, twenty-five WVS offices in and around the major cities of Britain were destroyed during raids.

Many volunteers were wounded in the bombing and before the end of the war, 241 members had died during the course of duty. Over one million women from all occupations and walks of life had volunteered their services.

Early in the Battle of Britain, a request was made by Lord Beaverbrook to the Chairman of the WVS asking her to make an appeal to the public for their pans, colanders and anything else made from aluminium. More Spitfires and Hurricanes were needed to replace planes destroyed in the Battle of Britain. Bauxite, the ore from which aluminium is extracted, was a necessary component in the construction of planes. In the normal course of things, bauxite came from Yugoslavia but because of the war was impossible to obtain. The bauxite ore was now a valuable commodity. Within hours of the broadcast going out, the WVS centres were inundated with aluminium goods and it was estimated that following the first broadcast 1,000 tons of aluminium was collected and made available to the Government for the use of the aircraft industry.

The WVS provided the staff for the Queens Messenger Convoys, who in the height of the bombing took drinks, food and water to the bombed-out areas when all normal cooking facilities had been destroyed. The convoy consisted of mobile canteens, water carriers and supply lorries. They were able to feed 3,000 people at one time and were completely self-sufficient with their own equipment, food and kindling to start a fire for the boilers. The Ministry of Food maintained the convoys all through the war years. I enjoyed one article sent to me during my research of this fascinating subject, concerning the examination convoys. A Mechanical Transport Inspector's job was to examine the vehicles twice a year and arrange for any repairs and maintenance needed. On one of these inspection days, one MTI came into direct contact with a group of WVS members who were, in the main, from backgrounds of affluence. The women arrived at the depot in chauffeur-driven cars suitable for their station in life. Then over their rather fashionable outfits they proceeded to donn boiler suits and started cleaning and checking the vans and their contents, jobs that they would never have considered doing in their own home. When the inspector instructed members in the complicated job of changing a wheel – indeed, a job he had always thought was far too hard for women, and not one he envisaged them ever having to do, but to know how to change a tyre may be of use to them later – the Leader of the WVS group said 'Mr O'Connor, I must decline this type of work, you see it is not a suitable job for my members. I have to think of what such work would do to their hands and their nails.' No mention was made of the weight of the wheels and the tightness of the nuts holding the wheel.

When rationing came into force the WVS helped with the distribution of the ration books, one for each person; every book was written up by hand and took many long hours, it was an onerous task.

To help farmers harvest the crops with a much-depleted workforce, double summertime was introduced to enable workers to carry on working throughout the day and into the evening. Pie schemes began in several areas where members delivered hot pies to farmers, allowing the workers a much-needed hot meal at lunchtime.

WVS members worked abroad in almost every country where there were hostilities, in places as far away as India, where WVS India was set up. Within a year, India had 27 centres. As months became years there were WVS members working wherever the war was fought.

Much of what was done during the war years has faithfully been recorded elsewhere, however there was a lot done by the ordinary woman in the street and no one will ever truly know all the details. There was praise from every Government department, including one statement saying that the WVS was the Army Hitler forgot.

The WVS Role of Honour of the 241 serving members who died because of enemy action is now in its honoured place among the national treasures in Westminster Abbey.

2

⇥ *Bolton WVS during the War years* ⇤
1939–45

Watermillock

The people of Bolton were afraid of the approaching war. However, they were equally as determined that the enemy be stopped, whatever the cost. When the call came many of the town's young men and women volunteered to fight. Many women who were unable to leave families joined this new service for women, some just wanting to help in any way possible. At the height of the war, almost 2000 women in Bolton were involved with work undertaken by the WVS.

The first initiative to form a WVS Centre in Bolton probably came from the County Office in Preston (Bolton was a County Borough at that time). An open meeting was arranged and attended by the Leaders of the various charitable organisations throughout the town. Premises for the proposed centre were to be at Watermillock, a home for the elderly on Crompton Way, given for the duration of the war to Bolton's new WVS. Mrs. Clara Kay was the first Organising Secretary chosen from the first batch of volunteers willing to join the WVS. Mrs. Kay lost no time in appointing her staff. Mrs. Beresford was appointed as deputy and many other members took on some very vital roles. Some of the following members were to play a very prominent role all through the war years.

Mrs. Stones was Organiser for Bedrooms, making sure there were places available when the refugees arrived. Many of the evacuees stayed at Watermillock whilst waiting for a permanent place with a family.

Mrs. Slater was in charge of the mobile canteens and organising food for them. Mrs. Barlow was Information Officer.

Mrs. Warr, the Car Pool Organiser, took military staff to their designated places, also taking evacuees to their prospective new families when evacuation started.

Mrs. Kay, along with her volunteer staff, shouldered most of the responsibility for the work undertaken for the next five years.

The staff at WVS Headquarters in London were under tremendous pressure to pull together a nationwide team to carry the work of the WVS forward in the months to come. It was imperative to encourage and support this huge volunteer force. In the early years, members came from WVS Headquarters to the Watermillock Centre to rally members. The *Bolton Evening News* reported in January 1940 that Mrs. Montague Norman, wife of the Governor of the Bank of England and a Vice President of the WVS, paid a visit to the Watermillock WVS Centre. She came to see the work done for the people who, having lost their homes in bombing raids in other parts of the country, were now residing in Bolton. The Regional Administrator for the WVS accompanied her. Mrs. Kay welcomed them and introduced them to some of the members of the Bolton Centre. The Mayor and Mayoress, Ald. and Mrs. Beswick, thanked Mrs. Montague Norman for coming and for the all work done by the WVS at the Watermillock Centre, commenting on the appreciation of the people of Bolton for such a fine group of committed members.

However, before the new centre could open the newly formed team were scrubbing floors, painting walls, repairing mattresses and making curtains in preparation for the influx of children and mothers from cities the authorities expected to be bombed. Much work was needed in the building to make it comfortable.

Mrs. Heywood, another member, was giving lectures at Watermillock Centre to the public to help people cope in the event of gas bombs, a real threat in 1940. Everyone had gas masks provided by the Local Authority and carried them at all times.

During 1941, the Local Authority asked the WVS to take charge of rest centres in the centre of town, and with the shortage of the general workforce they were soon requested to take responsibility for the whole Borough. This was an almost impossible task. To do the job effectively it needed a person responsible for every one of the shelters. Members of the public needed to be encouraged to use the shelters after hearing the sirens. If the shelters were dirty, people were reluctant to use them, but to improve the shelters money needed spending on them. A Bring and Buy sale was arranged and the proceeds went to provide comforts and a few luxuries that would help to make them more habitable. Mayoress Tong opened the sale and commented that since the shelters had been in the care of the WVS they had improved tremendously but still much work had to be done. The Local Authority intended to add canteens to the shelters, providing refreshments during air raids. The WVS was eventually to take care of the canteens and the shelters.

Mrs. Barlow, the Treasurer of the fund, announced it was the WVS's intention to present £250 to the Mayors Comfort Fund for the Shelters at the conclusion of the sale.

The Evacuation

During 1939 children, teachers and mothers of the under-fives were moved from the cities to more rural areas for their protection. Watermillock became the Evacuee Centre for Bolton for the sorting and the distribution of the children coming to Bolton from Manchester, Liverpool the Channel Islands and many southern cities. Up to now few bombs had fallen on Bolton and nor were they expected to; it was considered a safe town for the housing of evacuees, albeit not as rural as some other places. To many householders the evacuee problem was a great one, as having a strange child or in some cases, children and mothers in the home could be difficult. Some of the children had no manners. Many were inadequately clothed, coming as they did from poor families. The evacuees themselves had even greater problems. Many were lonely, leaving family, friends and schools behind, not to mention their familiar streets with their local fish and chip shops, top of many a child's list – thankfully in Bolton that was not a problem as Bolton had chip shops on many street corners! After the children arrived and settled into their new homes it was not long before some of them were returning to the cities from where they originated, only to return later when bombing in the cities really got underway. The early part of the war became the 'Phoney War'. By the time the war was over, Bolton had accommodated more evacuees than any other town in Britain, approximately 1,600 children, also many refugees. Some families stayed in Bolton for the whole of the war years, and several families eventually made it their permanent home.

Refugees

Refugees came to Bolton from Holland and Belgium, most of them with no place to stay and knowing no one. On their arrival in Bolton, one group of refugees were housed in the classrooms of Bolton's

The portable beds for refugees, given to Bolton by the Ministry of Health

Municipal Secondary School Great Moor Street, which was hurriedly turned into dormitories by members of the WVS. The Ministry of Health gave 1,250 camp beds to the school and the Mayor of Bolton appealed for cash, food and blankets. People were generous and the fund rapidly reached £600 with hundreds of blankets donated and many bags of food.

As the enemy invaded the Channel Islands, thousands of women and children along with teachers left their homes and arrived in Britain. At a social gathering, the Mayoress of Bolton, Mrs. W Tong, presented a pink blanket to Mrs. Bailey, a Channel Island evacuee now resident in Bolton. Her Majesty the Queen had sent many of these blankets to WVS centres throughout Britain and said how much she hoped the blanket would bring comfort to the person receiving it. Mrs. Bailey was delighted and said to Mrs. Barlow how happy she was to be in Bolton, that she felt she was voicing the feelings of some 1,600 Channel Islanders in the town and what a great welcome they had received, and she wished to say a heartfelt 'Thank-you' to everyone for showing so much kindness.

Mavis Gammidge, an Islander living in Guernsey before she came to England to be with her soldier husband in Hull in 1940, provided a unique insight for us into the difficulties the islanders coped with. After Mavis's husband had volunteered for the services, Mavis left Guernsey to settle with their young son in Hull to be near her husband. As the bombing of Hull started they soon realised they were not in the safest place in Britain. At that time, the dock area was coming under heavy bombing. Sadly, under the circumstances her husband decided that Mavis and their son would be safer in Guernsey away from any falling bombs, and feeling they would be better back with family and friends they went back to the Island. Shortly after returning to the Channel Islands her husband went to Liverpool for overseas duties. Unfortunately, Mavis arrived home just three weeks before the Germans invaded Guernsey.

Evacuation began for real this time. Mavis had to leave Guernsey and come back to England, bringing her young son and her mother. Her school-aged nieces had also been evacuated with their schoolfriends and teachers, leaving their mother (Mavis's sister) and two younger siblings behind with the hope of them following later. After a difficult journey in a train full of mothers and young children, Mavis and her family were taken to a school in St Helen's that had been organised for the coming of refugees. Everyone at the school was surprised when this party arrived, expecting children from Europe not British mothers and children. Mavis was very grateful to the St Helens group, and a bonus was the children enjoyed having a playground outside, providing hours of needed fun time. Mother and son went to live eventually with a very kind family in St. Helen's and after getting in touch with her husband stationed in Liverpool awaiting embarkation, Mavis found he was able to move in with the family, so they could spend their remaining time together. He stayed with them for three months, however, Liverpool being an important port was soon to be involved in the bombing raids often lasting for twelve hours throughout the night.

During the time they were in Liverpool, Mavis heard that her nieces were billeted with their school in Cheshire so applied for, and was given permission by the Local Authority to find and claim them, hopefully to live with her. Having travelled to Cheshire, she found they had moved again. This time they were living in Warwick with their mother, Mavis's sister (who by now had been evacuated also). Mavis arrived in Warwick after being escorted there by the WVS and was overjoyed to see her sister again.

However, due to the constant bombing raids of Liverpool, Mavis eventually moved to Bolton, staying with a family in Lownds Street. Her sister moved from Warwick to be with her when Warwick was caught up in the bombing of Coventry, and as they were a family of eight people, Bolton Council offered them an empty shop as a family home. While all this was happening, Mavis's husband was on his way to fight in the war in the Middle East. By the end of the war Mavis had settled in Bolton so on her husband's return in 1945 the family made a decision to remain in Bolton, making it their permanent home.

During the mid-1950s Mavis had a friend who worked for a family living at 'Hollywood', a large house on Chorley New Road (now Beaumont Hospital) as a companion to the owner. On several occasions when visiting her friend, Mavis met several members of the WVS. They were there visiting the owner of the house. Mavis related her story of her evacuation and her gratitude to the WVS. Mavis was invited to work at the kiosk at the Bolton Royal Infirmary as a volunteer standby. She did not actually join WVS until 1986 where she worked at St Luke's Luncheon Club for fourteen years.

Mobile Canteens

In 1940, there were many problems from disruption on the railways; trains carrying troops suffered greatly. The heating on trains was at a minimum, and they were often late arriving and with little or no buffet services they were uncomfortable, to say the least. If a train came into the station, after 10 p.m., the station buffet bar was closed and there were no taxis for soldiers to get home, although they had sometimes travelled all day, often carrying heavy kit bags.

In May 1940, the *Bolton Evening News* reported that due to the generosity of the people of Bolton and the WVS, service personnel returning home to Bolton late in the evening could now find comfort in the trailer-canteen staffed and maintained by the WVS. In addition to the canteen, a car to tow the canteen was bought at a cost of £50 and used to take soldiers carrying heavy kit to their homes. Many soldiers living out of town would appreciate this, saving them a long

One of the Mobile Canteens used by the WVS during the War years

walk home late at night. Permission was given by London Midland and Scottish Railway for the mobile canteen to stand outside the station, operating every night from 10 p.m. until the last train arrived, also on Sundays. These canteens were of great value to the war effort and the WVS were not the only organisation raising funds to purchase them. Eventually it was reported that another mobile canteen was provided for the use of the Local Authority, to be used whenever the Civil Defence Services needed it, for Bolton or neighbouring towns involved in bombing raids. So useful were these canteens for mass feeding that a third one was soon on order for the fire-fighting service.

'Women on the Home Front', an article in the *Bolton Evening News*, reported in January 1941 that the third canteen acquired before Christmas by the WVS was used in Liverpool, gaining the first of its battle scars on the front line. From there, it went to help in an area in Manchester that had recently come under fire from raids, then returned home to Bolton in time to serve drinks to firemen on duty at Bolton Fire Station during the Christmas period.

The members working in these canteens often worked very late and sometimes throughout the night. They provided gallons of tea from just two urns. The urns were a godsend, as one grateful recipient of a hot drink remarked on one cold night, commenting how well they kept the tea hot. Heating and cooking was done with a paraffin oil stove, enabling ample quantities of water to be heated at the same time as soup and cocoa were being made. On occasions, the canteen provided hot water to homes where gas and electricity had been lost during some of the heaviest bombing raids. Later on in the war, American Red Cross canteens were donated to the WVS.

Appeals

Aluminium

As the 'Aluminium for Planes' appeal got under way, Mrs. Kay reported she would be happy to involve the WVS with the appeal. One problem, however, could be petrol which was as scarce a product as aluminium. She announced there would be two depots where aluminium items could be left; Victoria Square refugee depot or Watermillock Centre. If an enthusiast in each street could be encouraged to collect it, the project could be made to work. The following day Mrs. Kay received information whilst working at the Centre that

WVS members dealing with an aluminium collection

one man working alone from his immediate neighbourhood had collected 140lbs of aluminium pots and pans on the first day the appeal was announced. This convinced Mrs. Kay this appeal would be the success it eventually was. After collection, the metal went into Wellington yard to be crushed down into manageable sized pieces for transportation.

Paper

The need for salvage continued, and the WVS raised 34 tons of paper. However, with the extra publicity promised by the *Bolton Evening News*, the WVS believed it would double in the coming week. 'A mile of books' was the suggestion, a novel way of asking more waste paper to be collected. Everyone placed books along the road starting at a certain point and at the end of the day it stretched out for one mile and was quite wide in places; a simple suggestion became a great contribution.

Household Items

Roy House, on the corner of Albert Road and Chorley New Road, was used to house elderly evacuees and appeals were made for home comforts for the residents. The comfort of the home could easily be improved with small tables, cushions, ornaments and pictures, commented Mrs. Kay to the *Bolton Evening News*. 'Anyone wishing to donate articles for the home could do so by bringing them to Watermillock. We would be pleased to receive them and could arrange for collection if necessary. Come on everyone, give a cushion or a small table to help to make these old people a long way from their own home, feel a bit more at home in their new and strange surroundings', was her message.

A White Elephant Shop on Bradshawgate was opened on 11 April 1940. Requests were made for the public to dig deep yet again and bring in their unwanted oddments which the WVS could sell to someone who did need them. One person's rubbish is often greatly needed by her neighbour. All proceeds would all go to the Mayor's Infirmary Appeal and the money would be used for expansion and refurbishment of the Infirmary departments.

Manpower

The Housewives' Service was due to start soon, and was hoped to appeal to women who could not leave their homes for long periods, but were prepared to help in some small way with the war effort. Volunteers were given window cards to show they had joined the WVS and were prepared to help in emergencies. 'If we had one volunteer in each street they could take care of the people living there. It would help enormously especially should there be an incident in that vicinity. Simple training would be given, anyone can take the training, nothing too onerous will be asked of anyone'. Enrolment was at the Library Lecture Hall, Watermillock or the War Saving Depot at Churchgate. Mrs. Kay reported that the country needed this service badly, saying 'Come on ladies, we need all your help.'

Next -of-Kin Club

In September 1942, a Next-of-Kin Club started at Watermillock to help the relatives and sweethearts of prisoners in enemy hands. It met on the third Friday of every month. Members were able to exchange any news they had concerning loved ones and hopefully bring comfort to others through the exchange of news received from the circulation of letters and photographs. It was intended for relatives at home waiting patiently for news of their sons, daughters, husbands or fathers who were away. At this time there were many men from Bolton held in prisoner of war camps. The Mayor, Cllr. Booth, had been a prisoner of war during the Great War of 1914–18 and he advocated the sending of parcels to prisoners, believing it sent a strong message to Germany that Britain was capable of supplying them, providing tangible proof that Britain was not a nation starving, as the average Germans was led to believe by their Leaders. At the end of the war 160 Bolton men had been interned in prisoner of war camps behind enemy lines.

Transport

The drivers appeal was made as the WVS became responsible for the Volunteer Car Pool, whereby members using their own cars would receive mileage allowance and free licences. They drove many miles during the course of the war, taking evacuees to their new homes, people to hospital and uniformed personnel to whereever their destination required.

National Saving Scheme

Saving for the War Effort was high on the list of jobs undertaken. Funding was so badly needed it was vital to include the whole town in this scheme. To raise enthusiasm and then maintain it was a very wearing exercise. Many members working for this cause were based at 1 Churchgate, which was open to sell National Saving stamps. A target was set each week with the hope that the public would buy enough stamps to buy a tank, aeroplane or battleship. The results of their efforts were displayed at the top of the Town Hall steps when the target was reached.

The War Savings Centre on Oxford Street was another centre where Organiser, Elizabeth Ward, worked with her team. Many members worked with her including Marian McHenry, Marjorie Slater, Alice Lee, Madeline Lang, Amy Johnson, Louise Hindley, Evelyn Warr, Frances Helen Crane and Mary Hayes. These centres were in operation throughout most of the war years with many more members working in them than can be mentioned here.

An enthusiastic idea was the formation of Street Saving Groups. This proved highly successful and many were formed, raising hundreds of pounds for the effort through savings stamps being sold to individuals, priced at 6d and 2s each.

Clothing

A clothing store for refugees and evacuees coming to Bolton was introduced in 1939, again using Watermillock as the main centre. Clothing was given by the general public, then recycled and repaired by a group of members who had volunteered to do sewing and knitting for families. Eventually 7 The Arcade, off Bradshawgate, became the Children's Clothing Exchange Store, where mothers went to exchange their children's clothes for better and larger ones, returning the garments their children had outgrown. Families came as often as they needed to, but the outgrown clothes had to be returned

to the store in a good condition, clean and well repaired. It continued all through the war years, closing at the end of the war, then
being reopened when it was discovered there was still a need, in
different premises this time at 1 Silverwell Street.

In January 1942, clothing came by the ton from the USA and
Canada. A desperate appeal went out from the Bolton office asking
for one hundred volunteers to help with a deluge of new clothing
that had to be sorted. The clothing came from the USA, Red Cross,
the Lord Mayor's Air Raid Distress fund and the New Gift Fund.

During this time Bolton was the only centre able to handle bulk
distribution of these gifts and clothing. They became the receiving
and distributing centre for Lancashire, Cheshire, Cumberland and
Westmoreland. There were four other stores being formed that would
help when they were eventually up and running. The clothing consisted of 2,000 pairs of men's flannels, 60 bundles of overcoats, each
containing 30 coats, boxes of men's, women's and children's shoes
by the ton, and enough skirts, dresses, sweaters and blouses to clothe
thousands. Members worked many hours as all the goods were sorted
into bundles and eventually distributed.

February 1941: Bolton's first WVS rally

A great deal of effort had been put into the forming of the WVS and
it was equally as important that its members were kept informed of
what was happening in other cities and towns struggling with similar difficulties. There was a need to inspire and motivate members,
encouraging them to carry on the good work and assuring everyone
they were not alone in their struggles. The first Rally for the Coun-
ties was held in the Lecture Hall at Bolton Civic Centre under the
Chairmanship of Mrs. Percy Lever J.P. in February 1941.

The Mayoress, Mrs. W. Tong, paid tribute to everyone, saying she
felt that the 1,500 plus WVS women were doing excellent work, standing shoulder to shoulder with the men fighting the same enemy. For
this was a war like no other, it was a crusade against tyranny and
she believed the country owed the WVS countrywide a great debt.
Mrs. Brierley, Chairman of the Lancashire Division of WVS, congratu-
lated all the members on their great service to Bolton. She went on to
explain how other towns were coping with refugees and the evacuee
problem, commenting on the bombing taking place in London and
Liverpool and most of the southern towns. One member was heard
to say after the Rally had finished, 'I feel a lucky person to be living

in Bolton right now', as considering Bolton had only had two bombing incidents, both of them strays, the town was considered a safe place. The only bomb damage done to Bolton was in October 1941. Bolton suffered a hit when two stray 500 kilo bombs fell on Punch Street and Ardwick Street, killing 11 people and causing injury to 64 others.

Present at the meeting were the Leaders of the various branches in the locality: Blackrod, Farnworth, Horwich, Kearsley, Little Lever, Rivington and Turton. Among other speakers that day was The Mayoress of Farnworth, Miss Johnson.

At a similar rally in 1943, Mrs. Kay announced there would be a presentation of a cheque for £778 10s for the Mayor's YMCA Fund. Mrs. Barlow, Information Representative, presented the cheque to the Mayor who said it was a wonderful achievement and in keeping with the town's response to the appeal as a whole. He also announced that the appeal was for £10,000 but should now reach the huge sum of £12,000.

Mrs. Kay also reported on the many activities of the WVS members throughout the year, highlighting the Howell Croft Comforts Depot and the role of Mrs. Entwistle, the Chairman. The Depot was situated over the shops at Howell Croft and the Red Cross and the WVS had staffed it since its inception. They had made 119,437 garments and sent 4,000 parcels to many towns and countries in need.

Mrs. Kay Ormrod, Training Representative for the WVS said in her speech to the group that when the war was over the WVS should be encouraged to stay on and help the many homeless survivors she was sure there would be. The training that had been given and the many skills perfected should not go to waste, but utilised for a better and brighter future. Mrs. Davidson, Deputy Regional Administrator of the WVS, went on to give her thanks for all that was being achieved in Bolton and compared it to the work being done throughout the country. She also agreed with the previous speakers' comments on the future of the service, and said, 'Considering the many difficulties that lie ahead, the work we should be involved in after the war is over would help the country get back on its feet again. We have set a standard and after the war we shall need that stability and sense of responsibility the WVS has taught us.'

1942: the Land Army

The WVS were asked to help the young women and girls who had recently joined the Land Army to work on local farms. This was an essential part of war work, and with their effort Britain was now able to produce two thirds of its own food, far more than was ever produced in peacetime.

Land previously classed as wasteland was now being cultivated as arable farmland. Many of the girls volunteering for this work were city girls with no experience of country life. They were living away from home, missing their families and friends and often suffering. The Bolton Authorities asked the WVS to become involved with the interviewing of girls interested in entering the Land Army Service. As a result, girls were recommended for places on farms in the locality where they had been interviewed. Fortunately, the WVS members in Bolton did not just leave it at that. They realised ongoing support for these girls would be needed. They began by visiting them at their place of work, inquiring how they were getting on with their new job and if they were enjoying working on a farm: 'Just keeping in touch', they called it.

One problem for the girls was that they were not able to meet other girls doing this type of work and therefore had no opportunity of discussing any problems, which brought a feeling of isolation and loneliness, so it was decided that the Land Army girls should be invited to Watermillock for a get together on a regular basis. Eventually they formed The Women's Land Army Club where the many aspects of farming life could be discussed and lifelong friends made. Dances, table tennis and general socialising were to improve their lives considerably.

By the end of the war years in 1945–46, many women were tired from their long years of service and many decided to retire from the WVS, thinking that with the end of the war, their job was complete. Mrs. Kay also believed the need for the services of the WVS had come to an end, despite assurances from the Government that the need for volunteers would continue.

Part Two

The Organisers

3

→ Evelyn Warr, County Borough Organiser ←
1947–57

The cold post-war years

As Britain came to grips with the post-war years, trying to regain some sort of normality, the WVS began its winding-down period, watched with uncertainty by many. For women who had lost so much during the war the companionship of the WVS meant everything. At the beginning of the war, Local Authorities had provided the offices needed to carry out the job of the WVS but the offices were now needed by the Local Authorities to cope with peacetime Britain with all its new problems. This created some disillusionment among many of its members, who thought – maybe rightly so – that they had developed valuable skills in those difficult years and there should now be a place for their use in post-war Britain.

One of the difficulties that raised its head during this time was the financing of the WVS. The Local Authorities had borne the brunt up to now, providing all that was needed, but with all that about to end, the main question was who would pick up reins for this much-needed finance? About this time a question was asked in Parliament concerning the future of the WVS, resulting in the Home Secretary giving the hoped-for reassurance that the financing would be taken away from the Local Authorities and given back to the Home Office, thus assuring the future of WVS. The Home Secretary concluded his speech by saying, 'Whatever the future holds the need will continue for voluntary helpers to supplement public services both on the occasions of emergency as well as other times.' The wartime presence of the WVS was acknowledged by governments and many people worldwide and now it appeared the future of the service was assured.

1947 saw one of the coldest winters in living memory and during that time the WVS countrywide were called on to help the sick and elderly, trying to keep them warm and making sure they ate well by taking many elderly people hot meals.

Their ability to respond to disaster on a national scale was evident also in the floods of January 1953, when, without warning the sea broke through all along the East Coast and within a few hours hundreds of people had died and thousands lost their homes. During the course of one evening, the summons went out to every WVS Centre in the flooded area from the Police, the Local Authority and the Fire Service. Rest centres were set up in any kind of accommodation with a dry floor throughout the flooded area. WVS and Local Authority Officers as well as other organisations staffed the centres.

After working long hours and under difficult conditions throughout the war, it was no surprise that during August 1947 Mrs. Kay resigned as Borough Organiser of the WVS, left Bolton and went to live in Cumberland.

The fighting had finished in 1945 but the job of putting Britain back to work was to go on for years to come. Mrs. Kay felt her job was finished and there was no doubt what a great job she had done. Finally she passed the reins on to Mrs. Evelyn Warr, who was to serve as County Borough Organiser until 1957. Evelyn was destined to make huge strides in welfare work for the WVS in peacetime Bolton.

Mrs. Kay at her farewell party with a piano donated to Watermillock by the WRVS

Evelyn had worked all through the war years at the Watermillock Centre. She had helped with the cleaning of the centre for refugees and the evacuation of children, and was known as the 'mother' of hundreds of children. She sold wartime savings bonds and operated a mobile canteen. Her main job was Carpool Organiser, organising a group of members who undertook to keep their cars continually on the road and made available when needed. The job of Transport・Organiser was to provide a vehicle to take evacuees to their new homes, the sick to hospital when the need arose and members of the Government Departments to whereever their work took them.

In 1946 Watermillock, the WVS Centre throughout the whole of the war, was handed back to the Local Authority. The WVS had to find a new home and eventually settled at 1 Silverwell Street, the site of the Children's Clothing Exchange Store the second time it opened. It was an obvious and natural choice albeit a temporary one in the post-war years.

The Civil Defence and Emergency work

The Civil Defence Movement (CDM) and the WVS had worked closely together but in 1945 the CDM disbanded. People put behind them all thoughts of war, hoping the need for the movement had ended. However, by 1949 and because of the possession of the atom bomb by foreign powers and the general political uncertainty, Civil Defence was considered as important in peacetime as it was in wartime. As a result, the Civil Defence Volunteers Corps was founded. Many WVS members became members of the Civil Defence and many others joined the Women's Auxiliary Service to the Civil Defence Corps.

Their main duties were to help with welfare for children and the elderly, help with emergency feeding and build up the membership of the Civil Defence and the WVS and care for the general population in the time of any emergency. In the normal course of duty the WVS were used to helping and reassuring people in emergency and were always ready for such situations.

As Britain entered a period when threats from the Eastern Bloc were serious, the Government believed the general population would benefit from information concerning how to react in the event of nuclear warfare. As a result, the One in Five Talks started in 1956. The talks were intended for women, to educate and understand the West's dilemma over the possibility of nuclear attack. The aim was that one in five of all housewives should hear this talk. The WVS, after much training and consultation with Leaders from the Civil

Defence movement and the Home Office, prepared themselves to help with this very large commitment. By the end of 1962, over one million out of a target of three million women had heard the One in Five Talks from the WRVS and many more people heard it with other agencies.

Mrs. Ivy Roocroft, Deputy Organiser of the WVS in Bolton, was regarded as the local specialist in One in Five. It was a gigantic task to interest women in taking instruction to cope with nuclear warfare. The world was just recovering from a devastating world war, so attempting to whip up feelings concerning the possibility of another war, one even more devastating than the last one, was a daunting task. Nevertheless, interest them she did, and the majority of local organisations heard her, or one of her team, speak on One in Five for nuclear attack.

Several exercises took place in Bolton and at the Regional Office where members learned how to make outdoor ovens and how to use them. In the summer of 1957, the Annual Tourney for Civil Defence held at Bellevue took place. Each office had the opportunity to take part in the hope of a winning position. The week before the event, Bolton members of the WVS and Civil Defence, encouraged by Evelyn Warr, cooked tea and scones in a field cooker close to a member's home, 'Just as a rehearsal', she said.

Members went on to learn how best to prepare a variety of meals using these ovens. One picture in the *Bolton Evening News* in 1960 shows Madeline Wadsworth and her team laying bricks for an outside oven in case of nuclear attack. Madeline said 'If we are still here after the bomb has been dropped we will need to know what to do. We are lucky to have Mrs. Roocroft prepared to teach us how to cope.'

The Emergency plans for Civil Defence required that they and the WVS hold major amounts of bedding and clothing at offices and storerooms to be sent to whereever there was a disaster. From Silverwell Street Centre, as small as the accommodation was, clothing and bedding went to many parts of the globe.

After the Lynmouth and Lynton disaster in August 1952 when horrendous flooding caused many homes to be washed away and many died as a result, an appeal went out to clothing stores throughout the country asking for help from Local Authorities. Lynmouth was sent tons of goods from the cupboards of the WVS. After the disaster in Lynmouth and Lynton the nation heard a radio broadcast appeal from Lady Reading, saying that large amounts of clothing and bedding had been sent to the disaster areas and the WVS stocks from most of its clothing stores nationwide were sadly depleted.

Therefore, she asked everyone to dig deep into their wardrobes to refill the clothing stores for the next emergency, going on to say, 'Unfortunately these things have a habit of reoccurring and we don't want to be caught with an empty cupboard.'

The East Coast and Canvey Island floods made the Lynmouth floods pale into insignificance; such was the scale of the fierce storms of January 1953 when the sea burst over the land from Durham to the Isle of Thanet. Bolton again appealed to the town's people for their help. The Lads' Club promised their support in housing some of the goods handed in. So during the first week after the East Coast had been declared a disaster area, bedding and warm clothing were pouring into the Silverwell Street Centre, the Civil Defence Centre in Howell Croft and the Lads' Club because soon the Silverwell Street Centre was bursting at the seams. It was realised that in losing homes, many people had also lost most of their furniture, so the following week the nation was asked by the Home Secretary to collect furniture for the stricken area, also appealing to the WVS to help with the collection of it.

Help on a large scale was then organised for the battlefields of Korea and many women knitted sweaters, socks and scarves for the comfort of troops suffering in the extremely cold winters.

Bolton continued its work with the Civic Defence Movement, until the Movement disbanded for good in 1968.

Evelyn Warr still maintained an interest in the forces long after the war years and operated two Territorial Army canteens at Fletcher Street and Silverwell Street barracks two nights in every week.

On a daily basis, Mrs. Warr and her members visited 'Dunwhithins', a home for the blind and deaf situated on Chorley New Road. The home came under the auspices of the North London Homes for the Blind as one of their houses in London was bombed during the Blitz, the residents were evacuated, coming to live in Bolton and remaining there after the war ended. Each day between the hours of 2 p.m. and 4 p.m., two or three members of the WVS went to the home to read to residents or write to relatives on their behalf. In summer, local members took them on short walks around the local countryside and gardens. For their annual summer trip to Southport, the Southport WVS very kindly invited the whole coach party for tea.

In 1954, Bolton WVS began its services to the hospitals by operating its first trolley shop at Hulton Lane Hospital. Originally, it started when one member was found to be taking small comforts into the hospital for long stay patients who did not have any visitors – she

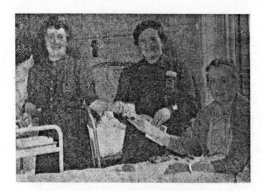

*The first WVS Trolley Shop
going around the wards at
Hulton Lane Hospital, 1954*

did this completely of her own accord. Women needed personal items like hairnets, talcum powder, hair clips and curling pins. Men needed smoking needs and shaving items. It was an unambiguous little scheme that developed like a snowball and before long a trolley was needed to carry all the requisitions around the wards. It was a great help to all the patients who were able to buy the goods they needed from the trolley. Cigarettes, chocolate and toiletries plus other items were sold on the trolley.

So popular did the Hulton Lane Trolley Shop become, that the Bolton and District Hospital Management Committee asked the WVS if they would set up similar schemes in Bolton Royal Infirmary and the Bolton District General Hospital. The first one to get under way was the Infirmary Trolley Shop, Mrs. Slater, a stalwart of Watermillock days being its first Leader.

During the next two years a tea trolley service was started in the X-ray Department at the Infirmary, later the small tea bar in the Outpatients Department was adopted, increasing the revenue and also the profit. The tea bar in the Outpatients Department was to remain open until the hospital closed some fifty years later.

There was a great upheaval when Bolton WVS moved its offices from 1 Silverwell Street to premises over the National Westminster Bank on Oxford Street in 1955. However, they were then ideally situated right in the town centre and ready for the wind of change that was about to blow through the WVS.

During Evelyn Warr's years as Organiser, the Children's Holiday Scheme was started, and needy children went to members' homes in either the countryside or the seaside for a week's break, mainly during their school holidays. In the summer of 1957, six children enjoyed a two-week holiday in the homes of WVS members living in Wallasey.

The Fylde Street disaster

In September 1957 the Fylde Street disaster became the finest hour for the WVS Emergency Team. Disasters, they say, always bring out the best in people, and there was no doubt that the disaster in Fylde Street brought out the best in the WVS.

Fylde Street is situated at Moses Gate, Farnworth, off Manchester Road, a street leading down from Manchester Road to Little Lever. On the morning of 12 September a man leaving his greengrocer's shop to go to the market saw a hole in the road. 'I only hope that gets no bigger today', he said to his wife. But on his return home about an hour later it had grown to a large fissure, and was continuing to grow. The shop he had left an hour ago before was showing signs of collapse. He roused his own family and proceeded to raise the alarm along the street. Within hours, the fronts of the houses along Fylde Street down to Hall Lane, including his shop, were beginning to crack from the floor to ceiling. The shop had fallen before lunchtime and in the early afternoon the fronts of other houses were beginning to fall. By the end of a week, more than one hundred people were homeless and 17 houses had to be demolished. It was amazing for me to see the shop in the centre of the photograph that appeared in the *Bolton Evening News* that night, for it had been my childhood home. The *Bolton Evening News* reported 'The shop in the centre of the picture was in danger of collapse, windows were breaking and walls were cracking and would no doubt have to be demolished.' The WVS

Mrs. Warr and her team serving workmen at the site of the Fylde Street disaster, 1957

were called out to set up a reception centre and kitchen, as meals would be needed for men working on the site.

For thirty-six hours after the tragedy occurred Evelyn Warr and some of her members never went home. Fifty members of the WVS worked around the clock helping to turn the Mission Hall in Corson Street into a café-cum-rest centre for the men working on the site. They worked from noon to midnight supervising and serving hundreds of meals a day to all the different services working there and dignitaries who visited the disaster site. The conditions were appalling, with mud everywhere. Many of the local people offered their services by washing dishes, dishcloths and towels. The school meal service took all the food into the Mission Hall and volunteers served it. With no water on tap, but having to be carried from standpipes or neighbouring houses, one of the most difficult tasks was keeping the hall free of mud. No washing-up or drying facilities were in place in the beginning but with dogged determination and about six weeks' hard work the WVS completed the task, as well as keeping all the other existing WVS services in place.

Within weeks of the Fylde St. disaster, Evelyn Warr had a heart attack and had to resign from the responsibility of Borough Organiser for the WVS. However for as long as I knew her the WVS was always her first love, and she continued to show a great interest in the service until her death.

4

✧ *Madeline Wadsworth* ✦
WVS/WRVS Organiser 1957–78

Madeline Wadsworth, another long serving member, became the third Organiser of the WVS in Bolton from 1957 to 1978. Madeline had begun her work with the WVS towards the end of the war and later helped to set up services in the hospitals. In her time as Organiser, the shop in the main corridor of the Bolton District Hospital started and also the trolley at Townleys branch site, the tea bar

Mrs. Wadsworth and members loading a van with clothing during the Year of the Refugee, 1954

in Maternity Department, a kiosk in Outpatients, and the Rest-a-While café in the town centre.

During 1959, the Year of the Refugee, WVS Headquarters were preparing to send abroad 1,000 tons of clothing. It all had to be collected, processed, then delivered. It was at the request of the United Nations High Commissioner for the needs of the world's refugees. If the WVS could do this, vast sums of UN money would be saved, allowing them to spend the money they had in other needy ways.

Within the WVS a change had recently taken place in the system for sending clothes abroad; it was the New Coding System which was to become an integral part of the way the WVS was to handle its clothing for years to come, eventually becoming known worldwide. Wherever clothing was packed and by whom, the use of this new code made clear exactly what the bail contained. It was very difficult persuading the volunteers of the value of this new system, but eventually they began to see the reasoning behind it. Every garment was known by a colour for the type of article, e.g. yellow for men's clothes, green for women's, but each item also had a letter of the alphabet, e.g. A for overcoat, B for skirts and C for trousers. This system carried on right down the alphabet, not an easy task with so many garments available. Therefore, a yellow ticket marked with an A was for a man's overcoat and so on. Prior to this change exactly what was in a bundle of clothing no one was quite sure, for previously on the bundle there was only the briefest of information.

Anniversary celebrations

In 1959, WVS was holding its 21st birthday celebrations and parties were held in every County Borough throughout the country, receiving encouraging support from the all the nation's Leaders. The Queen, patron of the WVS, gave a party at Buckingham Palace. The Queen Mother attended a service at Westminster Abbey. Services of Thanksgiving were held in all the Regions and County Boroughs. In the House of Lords, the Chairman of the WVS, Lady Reading, made her maiden speech as the newly appointed Baroness Swanborough in a debate on stateless persons.

Hospitals

The trolleys and tea bars maintained by the WVS had been making quite a profit over years since they opened. Wherever profit was made, it was automatically returned to that particular hospital. The gifts bought had to be comforts for the patients and not medical equipment. During the early 1950s, the guidelines for profits were strictly adhered to. In most of the wards, patients were in need of home comforts. Beds needed lockers, as well as cubicle curtains on tracks that could be pulled around the bed, covering it completely. Previously, the only privacy for the patient being examined by the doctor was by putting mobile screens around the bed; adequate maybe, but also inconvenient. There was also precious little for a patient to focus on whilst recovering, except the radio. In the 1950s television was the new entertainment, and television sets for the patients on the wards were an ideal gift.

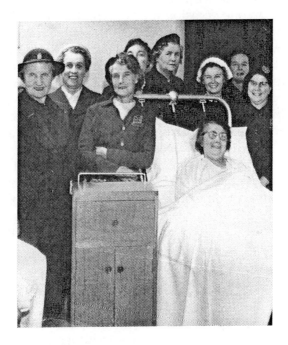

Mrs. Wadsworth presenting bedside lockers to the hospital, 1958

The WVS throughout the 1960s bought from their hospital profits many TV sets and provided miles of cubicle curtains, to all three hospitals in Bolton. Newspaper pictures appeared on a regular basis showing Madeline (and Evelyn before her) with their hospital members presenting many television sets and cubicle curtains and bedside lockers for the benefit of the patients in the hospitals.

In 1962 Madeline Wadsworth presented 200 books and a trolley to be used as a mobile library, run by the ex-service personnel society, Toc H at Bolton General Hospital, along with two self-propelled chairs. The year previously, Madeleine had donated two sets of wireless earphones to two wards at the General Hospital. The day she presented the mobile library, Madeleine on behalf of the WVS, donated earphones for another ward. Radios to listen to and books to read were a great help to patients.

The WVS became very much a part of hospital life and, in the main, members with their shops and trolley shops fitted in well, helping patients with their requisites and chatting to patients as they went around the wards, with the added bonus to the hospital from profits made from these services.

However, on one occasion the WVS had to defend their hospital welfare services when the assistant of the Confederation of the Health Service Employees stated in the Federation Journal that the 'WVS was taking the bread out of the mouths of some of the full-time workers'. This put members in an awkward position, as they were always conscious of the need never to take the job of a paid worker. As welfare work in the hospitals had grown tremendously across the country, guidelines were discussed in detail with the authorities to avoid this sort of situation. However, Mr Ernsting was the Deputy Secretary for the Bolton Group of Health and commented on this article saying, in his opinion, the WVS gave a splendid service and they were an addition to the staff, not a threat. In the Bolton hospitals, their presence in the wards gave continuity and friendship with a smile to some of their long stay patients. The WVS felt reassured by this public statement.

The WVS Long Service medal

In July 1961 the WVS Medal for fifteen years' service was struck. This happened as Headquarters were settling themselves into their new London premises, a converted nursing home at 17 Old Park Lane. These were prestigious premises with a prestigious address.

Seventeen Bolton members received this new accolade for some of the many tasks undertaken during the war years, with many of the members continuing long after the war ended. One sees the same names repeatedly, giving us an idea that during the war years, just how many hours they worked; the phrase 'How well everyone pulled together to fight a common enemy' was never more true.

The medals given for fifteen years' service to members of the WVS in Bolton were:

For work done at the Watermillock Centre: Ruth Barnes; Gladys Cleary; Florence Groves, Secretary; Clara Kay, Centre Organiser; Alice Lee; Mrs. E. Pollit; Nellie Sidney; Doris Sumner; Vera Ward.

War Savings Centre, Oxford Street: Frances Helen Crane; Louise Hindley; Amy Johnson; Madeline Lang; Alice Lee; Edith Marian McHenry, Organiser; Marjorie Slater; Elizabeth Ward, Evelyn Warr.

Mobile Canteens: Ruth Barnes; Amy Johnson; Elizabeth Ward; Evelyn Warr.

Wartime drivers: Ruth Barnes; Vera Ward; Mrs. Evelyn Warr, Officer in charge, now the County Borough Organiser.

Rest-a-while Centre Organiser: Annie Bond, Mabel Duckworth.

Infirmary Kiosk: Mabel Duckworth; Madeline Lang; Nellie Sidney; Vera Ward.

Clothing Store: Frances Helen Crane, Doris Sumner.

One-in-Five Talks: Mrs. Ivy Roocroft, the Deputy Organiser for the WVS.

Meals on Wheels: Mrs. Ruth Barnes.

Infirmary Trolley shop: Mrs. Ruth Barnes, Joint Organiser with Marjorie Slater.

Canteen Duties: Edith Marian McHenry; Marjorie Slater, Organiser; Vera Ward, Mrs. Evelyn Warr.

These were the areas of work done at the completion of fifteen years' service: there were many more members also working during those years of which no records survive.

The Beginning of Meals on Wheels

Meals on Wheels started in a simple fashion during the war and continued after the war ended. There is a distinct possibility that they came from two separate activities undertaken by the WVS. First, there was the pie scheme where members took hot pies to farm labourers working in the fields during the war. Second, an alternative idea was the British Restaurants that were introduced to help feed the refugees and evacuees coming to Britain, also helping to feed elderly folk if they were mobile enough. This was not always the case and feeding the elderly during the war years was a difficulty in itself, as there was hardly enough food to go around and cooking it was even more difficult. It was recognised that some of the infirm elderly were in dire straits so food from the British Restaurants on occasions was taken to those in need, particularly as a very bad epidemic of influenza in 1943 made it even more difficult for the elderly to cope. One member, seeing this happen, took measures into her own hands and approached the Clerk to the Council in the town where she lived and obtained the necessary rations to prepare food herself, taking the meal by car to the needy. When there was no car available, many people used bicycles with a box at the front, and also meals were often seen being delivered in prams.

It is said that on listening to Lady Reading reiterating this story, one of her American friends said, 'How wonderful, sounds rather like Meals on Wheels!' The name stuck and remains to this day.

One year after the war ended, the WVS were still taking meals out from various centres, establishing the fact that the service in itself was a sound one and needed to be extended. Rationing actually became more stringent after the war ended and coupled with the break-up of the extended family system where previously many family members lived together in the same street, life for the elderly became more precarious, and malnutrition more of a possibility. Under the new National Health Service established in 1946, the WVS realised that if anyone could push out the boat for this new service of feeding the elderly, it could be their organisation. Finding the necessary funding for this project was to be the most difficult task, as money was in short supply and a mass of factions were already crying out for whatever funding was available.

The story of Meals on Wheels is how volunteers managed to improvise, using whatever means was at their disposal until a standard pattern of cooperation was established. It was a proud day for the WVS when legislation arrived on that basis.

As petrol and equipment were two insurmountable problems, the offer of equipment that came from Canada, a country that had been of great support during the war years was a boost to morale. The Canadian authorities offered to send if needed a large amount of two-quart pails with lids. No one at Headquarters knew much about ex-army dinner pails, but as there were no better offers the pails were gratefully accepted, arriving in time for the 1947 floods, and were invaluable. At that time, thousands of meals were being delivered by the WVS nationally by a variety of methods. The Canadian Government, pleased that the pails had been of such good use to WVS, promised nine regions around the country 1,000 pails, which were used until after 1950, whilst other and better methods of utensils with improved heat retaining facilities were constantly being produced.

Other needs that arose were the equipping of vans with the necessary crockery and food containers at the cost of £35 per van, also garaging the vans and of course petrol at 1s 11d per gallon, not to mention premises to operate from.

In 1947 the National Assistance Act arrived, giving the Local Authority new powers to help any organisation willing to give assistance to the elderly; this of course included the WVS. By 1951, many of the meals for the elderly were cooked in local schools' kitchens. By 1952, charcoal heated hotlocks were in use with a great degree of success. However, weight was now a problem, and manufacturers were asked to construct lighter hotlocks more suitable for use in a car. Several of the newer hotlocks were able to rebuild the heat back into the unit each time it was opened, enabling it to comply with the 1956 food hygiene regulations that stated meals must remain at a regulation temperature. Hotlocks were still in use many years later but became lighter and easier to transport with the passing of time.

1n 1955, decisions were taken and legislation changed to allow Meals on Wheels to be delivered throughout the country. The service was invaluable to Local Authorities as well as many an elderly person, but it was still a bit haphazard and the need for more consultation was evident.

Miss Adrian Gibson had the job of travelling to find how the service was performing regionally, and several County Boroughs were chosen for special study. Throughout the 1950s many problems occurred but were dealt with, ensuring that eventually there would be a smoothly running successful Meals on Wheels Service. By 1958 and after another survey, the WVS was responsible for 77 per cent of all meals delivered. By the end of that year 1,381,654 meals were being delivered per annum, by June 1960 the total per annum was 2,118,304 of which the WVS delivered 88 per cent.

The service grew and grew: by 1976 almost 3,500,000 meals were being delivered by WRVS as well as a variety of voluntary groups and by a variety of methods. As well as cars and vans, meals were delivered in snow, on toboggans, on foot, in fog and after flooding in rowing boats and canoes.

Mrs. Wadsworth and members loading meals on to the van for delivery, 1961

Meals on Wheels in Bolton

Bolton had good welfare services, but in 1961 there were still no Meals on Wheels for the elderly, and as most towns in Britain, even the small towns around Bolton, had a thriving service it was cause for concern. The way forward was not yet clear. A sub-committee in the autumn of 1961 was appointed to look at the matter and come up with recommendations to place before the Welfare Committee. They were to look at three options to see which would best serve the people of Bolton. The decision could be a combined option or one standing alone. The Chief Welfare Officer, Mr Davies, said the committee had been looking long and hard at this problem, commenting that there had been a scheme in operation in Bolton on a voluntary basis previously but it had failed for lack of volunteers. In 1960 there had been a Bill going through Parliament enabling the Local Authority to use the general rate to buy whatever vehicles needed and to pay staff to run the service, however in recent months the Bill had fallen through. Therefore, legislation at this time meant that the Local Authority could not make purchases for this type of equipment but could provide a grant to a voluntary body such as the WVS or Old People's Welfare to operate a service on their behalf.

Mr Davies, the Chief Welfare Officer and Dr. A. I. Ross, Medical Officer of Health, did eventually approach the Bolton WVS through Madeline Wadsworth, who said she would be happy to look into the matter and considering the WVS operated most of the meals schemes in the country there was plenty of expertise around to help in organising a scheme for Bolton.

After some investigation as to how other towns coped with Meals, on Wheels. Madeline contacted Mr Davies with a proposition to organise a Meals on Wheels service in Bolton. She explained the scheme, which she felt was good one. She was confident she could recruit enough volunteers to run the service and hopefully find a good Organiser. To obtain the van and the equipment she intended to approach local companies to ask if one of them would sponsor the new Meals on Wheels Service.

Mr Davies was optimistic that the school kitchens would provide a meal for 2s a head and with a subsidy the recipient would pay only 1s 3d, with the remaining 9d and the running costs for the van being met by a grant to the WVS from the Council. It was expected that there would be around 150 elderly people living alone needing the service, some even bedridden who would be the ones in urgent need of the service. The district nurses, home helps and health visitors did a tremendous job but did not have the time to cook meals.

However, one veteran council member was not convinced and said in committee that the scheme sounded all right in theory, but might not work so well in practice. For a start he said, 'Volunteers cannot be relied upon to turn up on every occasion and we have three hundred miles of streets and would need approximately ten to twenty vans to cover the whole area. If we were to serve only part of the community's elderly it would cause endless discontent. I would like to see a "Good Neighbours Scheme" implemented, and I am sure there are many women who do this service already', he expounded, 'and it works well. There must be someone in every street that will put in an extra potato or a bit more meat and vegetables when cooking their own meals. We could pay the householder for the meal say two shillings and ask the elderly for one shilling – we would just need to appeal for volunteers to help in this small way. I feel sure we could recruit as we did for wardens during the war, make no mistake, there is plenty of neighbourly spirit still left in Bolton.'

This kind of discussion went on, but in the end largely to do with experience gained from operating Meals on Wheels in other towns, the WVS did organise Bolton's Meals on Wheels Service, with a starting grant of £350 for capital costs. The number of meals delivered was to be 25 each day, not to the same people, but most people would receive at least two meals per week. In the near future, the number of meals to be delivered would rise to 34 per week.

Meals on Wheels arrived in Bolton in 1962 and Mrs. Ann Partington was the first Organiser. She advertised for teams of new members, then trained them solely for the Meals on Wheels scheme.

A van was given to the WVS from fundraising by Littlewoods Warehouses, Dove Mill. The keys were given to The Mayor, Ald. Childs and he gave out the first meal to a Mrs. Ryley on the first delivery day. Within a very short time the number of meals increased and new vans were bought creating a need for even more drivers and helpers, which was a constant problem for Mrs. Partington. Being quite desperate, she made an appeal to the *Bolton Evening News* to help, which they did by printing an appeal highlighting the serious condition of some of the needy folk needing a meal. Mrs. Partington told the reporter that one morning after looking at the Meals on Wheels file she realised there were more and more people waiting to go on the list for a meal. The list was increasing every day, 'It is a sad situation', she said, 'We have the transport and the food – all we need are more drivers and mates to help us.

'Mr C. is eighty-six, lonely, quite depressed, has made several attempts at suicide, has a tendency not to eat if he has to prepare his own food, but with a meal twice a week, he would manage quite well.

'Miss J. is physically handicapped and lives with her 80-year-old invalid father so meals for them would be a godsend.

'Mr H. is also eighty, he is blind with Parkinson's Disease and cannot get about, relying solely on his neighbours.

'Unfortunately, these are the people we do not take meals to. Needy people come on the present list but seldom do we take them off. We have four vans now but at the minute can only use three through a shortage of volunteers. Please come and help us to help these elderly folk.'

·This article brought in twenty new drivers: the power of the Press!

Many elderly people are too independent to ask for help but will often take a meal from a WVS member which in turn helps to establish a much needed and only contact with the outside world.

A picture in the *Bolton Evening News* showed Mrs. Helen Collier of Breightmet, one of the first women to deliver meals round to some of her elderly neighbours in need of a hot meal, she delivered them by a most unusual method. The meals were brought to her home in a hotlock and she delivered the meals using a pram as her transport. It was Mrs. Collier's own idea and she took a dozen meals a day with the help of friends and neighbours. There was another person who expressed an interest in doing the same, making WVS at Headquarters realise that if this was done around the country what a difference it would make to the many older people needing a meal.

Sadly, at the end of 1964, Ann Partington gave up her WVS work on health grounds. Joan Harris, her deputy, took over. Joan had worked as a driver, going out with meals every other week as well as training new members and planning new routes. Routes increased with the demand for more meals. Joan was to be the Meal on Wheels Organiser for the next ten years. When I spoke to her of the joys and difficulties she experienced, she said there were many: frantically looking for a house where a meal was due was a constant trial, planning routes was another. However, she commented that she had far more pleasure than trials. Having enough volunteers was her biggest problem. Nevertheless, she still did a wonderful job.

Marjorie Taylor joined the WVS in the late 1960s, as a mate/driver for Meals on Wheels, always feeling the job she did was a worthwhile one. She has shared a few memories with me. She joined the WVS specifically to do Meals on Wheels and continued until it finished in Bolton. She worked every Friday with Betty Taylor (no relation) so this is the tale of two Taylors together. Having picked up the van from the welfare offices at Queen Street and collecting meals in containers from the school kitchens in Pilkington Street, their distribution area was in the upper reaches of Breightmet. They took turns with the driving and Betty, being quite tall, had no trouble with the awkward seat in the van, but Marjorie, being a petite lady, had to prop herself in with the aid of her shopping bag and a cushion to enable her to see out of the windscreen. At Christmas time, they would be loaded up, having to juggle floral arrangements (no doubt created by them for the old people), Christmas food parcels, a main course and dessert in two separate containers and with the added problem of a tight timeframe. Their enjoyment came from the good rapport they both had with some of their elderly recipients. One blind woman would sometimes ask Marjorie to read her letters. She received a huge cornflower cutting from a keen gardener. The plant has moved house with her twice since, continuing the nice memory of the old gentleman who listened as she ran down his path thus christening her 'Fairy Feet'. After one Christmas she remembers going into the office where a letter had been handed to the secretary but unfortunately it was written on a bag that had previously held cream cakes. It said 'Thank you to the lovely ladies for all their kindness throughout the year'. The writer of the letter was a sweet old Irishman who oozed blarney but his charm far outweighed his housekeeping virtues, 'We all loved him though', she said. One of the Meals on Wheels vans was an Austin A35 and quite a challenge to drive. Nobody liked it, to say the least. Marjorie became the toast of the WVS when one day as she was driving it they were in collision with another car. The impact was sufficient to write off the blessed van and we were all so thrilled it would now be going to the grave-yard for cars. Fortunately no one was hurt but nevertheless an am-bulance was sent for 'Oh, I have still two meals to deliver!' cried Marjorie 'Ee love,' the ambulance man said, 'you won't be deliver-ing them now, I think you will find they are all down the back of your dress'.

That night as she undressed for bed there was gravy in her hair and sprouts in her bra. But with the promise of a new van, she thought that every cloud has its silver lining.

Luncheon Clubs

During the course of discussions concerning Meals on Wheels a sug-gestion was made that the Welfare Service should look at creating venues where the more ambulant elderly could go out for a reason-ably priced lunch at a place convenient to their home. The meal would be at the same cost as a Meals on Wheels lunch and provided from the same source. This service eventually came into operation in 1964, two years after Meals on Wheels had started. By the late 1960s, there were five Luncheon Clubs with about sixty members each, open once a week, each one on a different day, which meant that providing they would travel a person could get a good hot meal every day of the week: ideal for a man on his own.

On 10th March 1964 the WVS Chairman, now Baroness Swanborough the Dowager Marchioness of Reading, came to Bolton for her first visit. She came mainly for the launch of the new Lun-cheon Clubs. Members from the surrounding areas were invited. She spoke to three hundred members from eleven County Boroughs in the area. In her speech, she announced that the previous year the WVS had delivered over five million meals to the elderly, one mil-lion more than the previous year.

Lady Reading said that she thought Luncheon Clubs were the way forward and enjoying meeting friends would encourage people to get up and get dressed, bringing more of a purpose to their day. The Baroness went on to talk of other services where the WVS excelled. One of the main areas was clothing. She gave an instance of the effi-ciency of a new WVS clothing supply system, since adopted by the

Red Cross and various other agencies throughout the world. The Baroness said it was because of the new system that the WVS could now respond immediately: when the WVS received an unexpected call asking for one and a half tons of clothing for Mauritius early one Thursday morning the clothes were able to be ready for dispatch the following day. In total last year, stores around the country had clothed twenty five thousand people using over one million garments.

She talked about the other services, including children's holidays and care for overseas personnel in Germany, the Middle East and North Africa.

In September of that year the WVS was honoured by the Queen adding the royal insignia to the name, so 'Women's Voluntary Service' became 'Women Royal Voluntary Service'.

The WRVS in 1966

I joined the WRVS in September 1966. At that time, I lived on Crompton Way, Bolton and found myself at home with four young children and in need of some adult stimulation. I looked up the WRVS office in the phone book and decided to pay a visit to Oxford Street where I enrolled. The only type of work I knew of was Meals on Wheels, mainly through coverage in the *Bolton Evening News* during the early 1960s. I really quite fancied taking out meals to the elderly and infirm and knew they needed voluntary drivers. However, I had not allowed for Madeline Wadsworth's brimming enthusiasm for work done in the hospitals. After hearing me explain I would like to be involved with Meals on Wheels she took me by surprise when she said,

'Oh no, you would like it much better working at the hospitals. We have a team at the Infirmary, and also that would be convenient to you, wouldn't it?'

'Well yes, it would be convenient. I had never thought of the hospitals', I replied, amazed by her response.

'Oh yes, the people that work there are so nice, you will enjoy it, I'm sure. I will ring Miss Crosbie right now – she will be so pleased to have you.'

Madeline was a delightful lady who made you feel very welcome and duly rang someone I became to know as Miss Crosbie. I overheard her say, 'Yes, and she can start any time and she is so young.'

I wasn't that young, except in the line of WRVS work! I had already explained that I had four quite young children and could not give too much time, but to Madeline that was not a problem. I rather gathered that not too many 28-year-olds unexpectedly walked into her office. The result was, I was to appear at the kiosk at Bolton Royal Infirmary the following morning to meet a Mrs. Phythian who turned out to be another sweet lady who I worked with for several years. The kiosk at that time was on the left hand side of the Outpatients Department as I walked through the main door. It was very small, just about big enough for two people at a squeeze, one filling the trolley and one person staying to serve patients waiting for appointments.

After leaving the kiosk with my trolley, which held a variety of sweets and biscuits loaded from the kiosk cupboard, I stopped to collect an urn of tea from the hospital kitchens on my way to my first call at the Accident and Emergency Department.

A & E at times would be very busy, however Plaster Clinic on a Monday morning in winter after a fall of snow was busier. There might be a queue a dozen deep waiting for a cup of tea. Signs were everywhere warning of the dangers of giving a drink to a patient who might need anaesthetics. From there I went to the X-ray Department, then down in the lift to Physiotherapy. Often it was quieter there and I would take a break for a drink of tea from the trolley. When I started, we could have one drink only during our duty, but were told never to eat anything from the trolley without first paying for it; I never did forget that gem of information. However, the thought did cross my mind: if I was caught taking an extra drink, would I get the sack? I doubted it very much. At around 11.30 a.m., I was usually heading back to the kiosk to cash up my morning takings. The kiosk would take in the region of £5 to £6 while the trolley took £4 to £5. The money would be recorded, then bagged and taken to the night safe and collected by Miss Crosbie on Thursdays. She counted it at her home, then banked it the following day. Joyce Whittle, another member who was the Leader in a Luncheon Club did the accounts for the BRI.

I enjoyed my duty, particularly seeing people I knew, which I did on most of my duty days, and I realised very soon that everyone comes to the hospital at some time. Miss Crosbie, I was to find out later, was in her late seventies and quite a remarkable lady. She lived with her four sisters in Park Street close to the hospital. She was the Organiser for the kiosk, also doing the rota for both operations. It took twenty-five members to staff the kiosk and trolley for a week, three people in a morning and two in the afternoon.

It was a special day in March 1969 that we opened the doors to a larger new kiosk in Outpatients. Originally having no room to site a new tea bar there a decision was made to partly enclose a large stairwell, giving sufficient space for the kiosk and still allowing ample accesss to the stairs. It was extended twice but remained on the same site until the hospital closed in 1997 when all the departments moved up to what became the Royal Bolton Hospital towards the end of the 1990s.

Appreciation from Joe Public

Madeline Wadsworth had been right when she had said I would enjoy working in the hospitals. I did. I felt I got more out of it than I gave. However, that was proven different one day as we were packing up to go home. I was working at that time with Dorothy Wolstenholme who I'd met whilst on duty and who also lived on Crompton Way just a few doors further up the road from myself. We travelled together and shared the work, alternately doing the kiosk or the trolley. On the way home, we would call in at the office in town, collecting a sandwich on the way. By doing this, we got to know a lot of the staff and all that was happening. That Thursday we were locking up for the morning when a reporter from the *Bolton Evening News* came to the kiosk. 'Oh dear' we were thinking, we had a latecomer just as we had cashed up, fortunately we had not drained the teapot so if he wanted a drink we could oblige him. However, it was not tea he wanted, but a photograph of the two women who worked on the kiosk and the trolley on a Thursday morning. A letter had been sent to their office extolling all the good we did and with a smile too. The picture, he said, would appear a few nights later in the then 'Town Topics'. We were thrilled, and on arriving back at the office with our sandwiches we were bursting to tell Madeline all about what had happened, thinking that it would be quite a feather in the cap of WRVS and it would not do us any harm in the eyes of the hierarchy either. However, true to form, Madeline promptly said

'Were you wearing the green WVS overalls, the ones in the locker?'

'Oh no, Madeline they are dreadful', we replied indignantly.

'In that case, we cannot send the picture to HQ, a pity though.'

Still, the picture was in the *Bolton Evening News*.

The green overalls we were supposed to wear were bought initially to fit everyone so in reality they fit no one and had hung in a cupboard for years. I asked Madeleine at one time why we could not have an overall each. 'You can,' Madeleine replied, 'but make sure it is dark green, and do not forget you have to pay for it.' Sadly, we did not fully realise the significance of the green (green and red being the colours of the WRVS uniform nationally), thinking we would look much better in pale blue, which was the colour I wore for a whole year.

Also at BRI was a trolley shop that went around the wards twice a week, run by Mrs. Brotherton and her team. They bought goods from the wholesaler, selling them to patients on the wards. They were wiser than I was as they always wore dark green.

I worked for a short time at Rest-a-While, a large wooden building that provided exactly what the name suggested, a place for the elderly to have tea, coffee, toast etc. and a sit down when either going to or returning from the open market on Ashburner Street. They could meet friends and stay as long as they liked. It was on the site of the old bus station, behind Newport Street, within easy reach of the open market, a place popular with everyone. I did not work there very often as I had to be home for the end of a school day so the timing did not work so well for me, preferring the work in the hospitals for the morning duty. Later the site of Rest-a-While was enlarged and eventually taken over by Age Concern, before their present building on the site opposite the open market.

I also worked in the Clothing Store on the odd occasion. Clothing took up most of the space in the office building, which was over the National Westminster Bank. The bank was on the ground floor and we were on the first floor of the building.

The store was open three mornings a week and clothing was issued to anyone bringing a letter from Social Services or the Probation Service, and occasionally from the headteacher of a school. The majority of requests for clothes came from men and families. The men that came to us were often down on their luck, and requests for a suit for a job interview were common. Members sometimes were asked for a suit for a wedding. The members serving bridegrooms-to-be went to a lot of trouble to get things to match so he would look good for his wedding day, even down to bringing a pair of hubby's shoes should there be none in the store that were suitable. The largest proportion of other requests was for good clothing for children and often as many as three to four families would be in the department at the same time, particularly at the start of the school holidays and again as they were returning to school after the long holiday in the hope of having their children kitted out.

Christmas presents for children were parcelled during December to be collected just before Christmas. All the clothes and children's toys we received were donated by the public. For a period, I collected clothing from various houses to deliver to the office for sorting. Overall I visited some very nice people, mainly women disposing of their husband's and children's clothes. Sometimes I would listen to stories of a husband who had died, and the lady would be reliving the memory of him wearing that special suit, bought in past times. Over the years, we collected some excellent goods and some of it very interesting. However, on one occasion I went to what turned out to be a most peculiar man. He asked me into his house, wanting to chat about anything and everything, and eventually he suggested I go upstairs to help him bring down the clothing. I did not think that was a good idea. I quickly replied that I was not allowed to and if he would bring it down, I would be opening the car door while he carried it out. It got me outside the house, and what I expected to be a large amount of clothing in fact turned out to be two only half-filled black bags.

On another occasion, after collecting clothing we parked at the back of the offices opposite Whitaker's department store. There was a back entrance to the bank with a communicating door to the WRVS offices. Because of the precinct area at the front of the office, we had to park at the back, dragging the bags up a flight of steep stone steps and into the office. There were yellow lines on the road even then, but Madeline had always assured me that the traffic wardens were very good and wouldn't bother me, 'They know what you are doing, just put your WRVS card in your car window', and she was right, until one day when my load was particularly heavy and I was having to do several journeys. On my second journey not a traffic warden but a policeman was waiting for me 'You can't park here', he said.

'But I'm not parking,' I said, reaching to my full height, 'I am on WRVS service.' 'Madam, if you were the Mayor of Bolton you would not be able to park there.'

I went away with my tail between my legs. However, I still had goods left in my car. What was I to do?

Another time in the Clothing Store, a man being thrilled with the new trousers he had received, dropped his own, forgetting he had no underclothes on and putting us all in a near panic. On occasions we handled the smelliest of bags, which for safety reasons had to go straight down to the tip. Often we found items in pockets including false teeth, money and odd bits of food. However, there were times we had designer items and brand new items. Also some clothes in excellent condition were brought into the store.

When appealing we requested used clothing in good condition

which then required sorting and sizing and when that was done the members tied them in bundles of five, with special knots for easy access and put them on the Clothing Store shelves to be issued as and when needed. Books and magazines were also sent to servicemen in several countries overseas on a regular basis.

I had never worked at the General Hospital and only heard of the projects there from Madeline. Apparently we had a kiosk in the Outpatients Department and a shop in the main corridor, a trolley shop going around the wards and another one that went around the wards at the side of the hospital we called Townleys Branch, and another tea bar in the Maternity Department.

There was a social side to the WRVS too; they held Whist Drives, albeit infrequently, in the office – all very cosy. The first time I was asked to go, I went back home to Frank, my husband, asking him 'Can you teach me how to play whist for next Wednesday? I have been asked to play in a Whist Drive at the office.'

He did his best, and when I returned from the event with the news I had won a prize he looked so pleased, but his face fell somewhat when I disclosed it was the booby prize.

We had coach trips out occasionally, usually to a factory for a tour of the plant, then a meal afterwards. This all helped people to get to know one another, and meet other members who, because of the nature of the work, one would not otherwise meet.

I spent almost a year and a half with the WRVS before becoming pregnant with our youngest son. I went in to the office explaining to Madeline that I would be finishing in a month's time due to being pregnant. It did cause something of a stir: everyone was very pleased for me but I was in no doubt that the reason for my absence was quite unusual. No one could remember anyone who had asked for maternity leave in the WRVS before.

In the September after our youngest son Martyn had been born in February, I picked up my old threads again, and went to the Fortieth Anniversary Dinner of the WRVS held at The Smithills Coaching House later in the year.

I started working at Bolton Royal Infirmary again but this time I was permanently on the trolley, continuing for the next three years, working mainly with two people who became very firm friends, Alice Williams and Miss Margaret Hall.

It was a shock to everyone when on 18 May 1971 Lady Reading, the founder of the WVS/WRVS collapsed very suddenly and subsequently died on 22 May. She would be missed tremendously, having done a brilliant job for so many years. Tributes poured in from all

Lady Reading, founder of the WVS

over the world from all the people whose lives she had touched. Mrs. Charles Clode, later becoming Dame Frances Clode DBE, the Vice Chairman, was to succeed her.

In 1972 our youngest daughter Cathy was born. I left the WRVS, returning in early 1974. Our family was now quite a large one and we realised it was time to move from our family home on Crompton Way and find a new one. We eventually went to live on Chorley New Road. When I returned to work at Bolton Royal Infirmary after the house move, little did I imagine how WRVS would change my life in the years to come. In 1973, Madeline had been County Borough Organiser for 16 years, and in the service for 21 years. She received her MBE for service to the community.

Reorganisation in 1974

During April 1974, there was Government reorganisation throughout the country, involving many boundary changes. Bolton became a Metropolitan instead of a County Borough and during this time Miss Mary Mason became Director of Social Services for the New Metropolitan of Bolton and was to continue until 1983.

Since 1962 the success of Meals on Wheels was evident, as many more meals were in demand. Alongside the WRVS, Social Services did extra rounds and the need for even more meals was obvious. By 1974, Meals on Wheels reverted to Social Services who were equipped to make the necessary increases needed. WRVS Meals on Wheels had worked very well for so many years, but it had taken all Joan Harris's cajoling abilities to cope with existing rounds. Bolton WRVS ran 4 vans and had more than 50 volunteers, however it was not enough to serve the ever-increasing number of meals required throughout the town. The WRVS ceased to operate the service and would not do so again for another 18 years. It was a big decision handing the meals service back to the Social Services Department but we took some solace in having started it and kept it going for so long. Volunteers were getting harder to recruit and Joan felt it was as much as she could do to keep it going without any expansion, which by 1974 was needed.

A party was arranged for all the 50 members who had worked so hard, with a special thanks to Joan Harris for coordinating the service as well as taking meals out on a fortnightly basis.

In July of the same year Frances Clode CBE, now Dame Frances Clode DBE, retired from the Chairmanship of WRVS and was succeeded by The Baroness Pike of Melton.

5

→ *Margaret Sydall* ←
WRVS Organiser, 1979–80

I was happy to be involved again working at BRI but whereas in my early days in the WRVS when working at the hospital I would make a day of it by calling into the office for a quick lunch and a chat, now I was so busy at home that I had no time to go into the office, so was unaware of the changes that were taking place. In the early part of 1979, I was training a new member, Mrs. Jane Whitehead, for work on the trolley; we enjoyed working together and soon became firm friends. One day she arrived at the hospital asking if I would like to go to an open meeting at the Town Hall for the WRVS, it was on Tuesday 9 March 1979. I thought about it, but I was not that interested, I'm afraid. Whilst I did enjoy working on the trolley, I had often seen a negative side to the service in so much that it didn't always move with the times. I had no idea what the theme of the meeting was to be, but the Fylde Street Disaster, which had happened in 1957, was to me still very fresh in the minds of many WRVS personnel and whilst I knew what a splendid job had been done, I'd heard the story told many times and didn't relish hearing it again. When I said I was not that interested, Jane then said, 'The meeting is to introduce a new Organiser in Bolton, she started as I joined.'

'Really, I didn't know that, has Madeline retired?' Jane of course did not know who Madeline Wadsworth was. Madeline had been Organiser since 1958. During her service of 21 years, she had seen some tremendous changes. Much of the work done at the hospital was because of her efforts. She had started Luncheon Clubs, Meals on Wheels and many other projects, and had wanted to retire for a while but had not been able to find a replacement, but apparently it had now happened. Jane and I went along to the meeting with many WRVS members, most of whom I had never met – I realised then how out of touch with the WRVS I was. On the platform was Margaret Sydall, the new Organiser, who spoke about her new job and her ambitions for the Service, explaining amongst other things that WRVS intended to open a tea bar in the Magistrates Court but we would need more volunteers for this new venture.

The next speaker was Margaret Spriggs, the new Area Organiser. She explained her new job and her ideas for a service to cope with the needs of the present day. She told us of the job she had done as Metropolitan Organiser for Trafford and explained about the reorganisation that had taken place in 1974 and how it affected the role of the WRVS. She was a very enthusiastic person and I was impressed. She then introduced Evelyn Barrett, the Area Emergency Organiser, and she explained what the Emergency Team did and the role it played in the community. She explained the training given and the fun everyone had whilst taking it, also there was no exam at the end thus causing no pressure or worry for anyone. They would require about ten people prepared to sign up for the first course which would take 6 half-day sessions at the office.

As I sat there on that day in March, I looked around to see mainly elderly women; still the WRVS was made up of mainly elderly women. These members were the backbone of the service. What I didn't see but realised later was viewed from the platform where Margaret Spriggs sat, was that Jane and I were by far the youngest there.

Jane and I sat together and listened to all this; it was probably what Jane expected but to me it was a revelation and I was very interested. During a cup of tea after the talks were finished, Margaret Spriggs came and spoke to both of us, extracting a promise from me that I would go into the Bolton office the following day to see Margaret Sydall. I went into the office the following day with considerably more confidence than when I joined the Service in 1966. She told me that they needed a Hospital Organiser and eventually a Local Organiser. Margaret Sydall, the newly appointed Metropolitan Organiser, introduced me to her secretary, Hilda Barlow. Also working in the office was Phyllis Burgess who eventually took charge of the court tea bar and Susan May who did the hospital accounts.

Court Tea Bar

My position then was the designate Hospital Organiser but I was interested in all facets of the WRVS so in 1978, after Mr Dawson,

Clerk to the Courts, had invited the WRVS to open a tea bar in the Magistrates Court, Margaret had asked me if I would accompany her to a meeting with him. There was no facility for anyone appearing in the court to buy refreshments and as they spent a long time waiting this made a difficult situation worse for the people unfortunate enough to be there. Before the meeting we visualised there would be at least a room where we could set up the tea bar and be able to store our goods.

However, rooms in the courts were at a premium, and there would not be a room to use as a tea bar nor space available to store the goods needed. We came out of that meeting bemused, asking ourselves how could we open a tea bar with no facilities at all?

Eventually, in 1979, we did open the Courts Tea Bar in a corner of the main hallway with a tiny cupboard in the cloakroom for storage and a small tabletop boiler for water, heated in the cloakroom and placed on the table we used as a counter top. No one to my knowledge ever received a burn from this but it was a dangerous way to operate. I offered to set up a rota from our existing members to staff the tea bar. It was the first new project the WRVS had opened in a long time so we were keen for it to be a success. I remember spending ages talking to various members and doing lots of cajoling. It was good experience and stood me in good stead for the coming years. Eventually the Court Tea Bar opened every morning with two members on duty each day and Phyllis Burgess as the Leader. Finally Connie Ricker was to take it over and remain its Leader until the end of the 1990s. The profits from the sale of goods were not to be used by the courts, but for the comfort of people using the courts. It was a strange phenomenon but we had to adhere to it. Some of the items we bought over the years included new chairs in the foyer, and we provided money for children's holidays, had a new storage counter made and provided a donation to Motor Aid for young offenders. This charity provided cars for young men to work on, hoping to teach them how to care for a car rather than steal one and crash it. The tea bar at the courts continued almost into the next century, providing gifts for various projects the WRVS were involved with.

Emergency

We had been recruiting members to join us to form the new Emergency Team, which was to start its training sessions under the auspices of Evelyn Barrett, the Area Emergency Organiser. We met every week for six weeks learning how to cope should we ever get called upon to help in an emergency in the community. We had been told at the beginning of the first session that we would enjoy ourselves and we did, it was great fun, and most of us were sorry when it ended.

Every Friday morning Susan May came to do the accounts for the hospital projects. She had also taken the Emergency training course and became the new Emergency Organiser. Approximately ten members became the founder members of the new Emergency Team in 1979 for WRVS in Bolton.

Emergency, we were told, was not a job we ever were likely to get a lot of practice at, so being called out to the hospital for an emergency was not something we ever envisaged. The Hospital Authorities were in a very difficult position when the cleaning staff went on strike in April 1979 and the WRVS were asked to help in trying to keep the wards looking tidy and helping out at meal times. That was not something the WRVS could do long term so after two weeks we ended that particular service. I only remember going once; I was in the Psychiatric ward, and never having been in one before I was not very sure of myself, but it was an interesting morning. I know there were several other members who went to the hospital more often than I and had some quite funny stories to relate.

After this call-out I thought it could be ages before it happened again, if indeed it ever did. One can imagine our delight when Margaret Sydall received a letter asking if we were interested in taking part in an emergency training exercise on Monday 22 October 1979. It said that the exercise was to test the recently produced Bolton

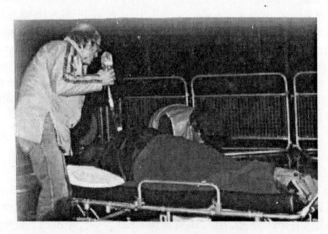

The mock emergency, stretcher patient

Health Authority Major Incident Procedure supervised by Mr Andrew Dillon. It was primarily designed to test their communications efficiency and how well the emergency services of Bolton would cope in the event of a major incident. After many planning meetings, the mock emergency was to be as realistic as possible and to include the police, fire and ambulance services. The WRVS were invited by Mr Dillon to be a part of the team by opening the kiosk at Bolton Royal Infirmary for the many 'injured'.

At the designated site, the scenario had been set for a petrol tank and a light van to crash in the centre of a busy Bolton street causing the death of 8 people and injuring 27 others. It was amazingly realistic, with volunteer victims arriving at the site early to be made up with fake blood resembling people badly injured. Some displayed a red cross, denoting they were dead.

The site for the make believe busy street where the accident took place was the car park of Warburton's bakery, created to look like a main street. Everyone thoroughly enjoyed the exercise and the atmosphere was electric. After the 'patients' arrived at the hospital, a doctor in Outpatients saw them. Many of the walking wounded were served with drinks and light snacks from the kiosk. We were kept busy all evening with most of the WRVS remaining at the kiosk until everything was finished.

Margaret Spriggs and Evelyn Barrett from our Area Office were present, observing how we performed. We served many people who had seen the doctor or needed an ambulance. Two men arrived at the kiosk towards the end of the evening, one asking for two coffees and the man who was with him was laughing as he said 'You can't

Emergency services at the mock emergency

serve him; he's been dead for two hours'. As he turned around we realised he had a big red cross on his back, denoting him 'dead'.

Another man came in covered in blood, but this time it was the real kind; he had been a fake accident victim, sent to see the doctor in Outpatients but on his way to the kiosk he had tripped in the corridor and burst his nose, creating a real patient.

At the debriefing on the Thursday following every possible action was gone over by all the services concerned and all agreed that the exercise had been a success with everyone responding well, and many valuable lessons learned.

It was at the first training meeting that I first met Betty Taylor, who was eventually to become Emergency Organiser. She was a stalwart member of the WRVS, a colleague and friend for years to come.

Hospitals

At my next visit to the office, within a short time, I became the Hospital Organiser. I asked Jane Whitehead to become Deputy Hospital Organiser, which she did. I felt quite confident with the position, believing I knew a lot about the hospitals and would be able to cope, but soon realised how little I did know. Miss Hall and Mrs. Williams were supportive and pleased about my appointment. After I found someone to take over my duty on the trolley, Miss Hall said, 'Don't forget us at the Royal, will you?' I thought it a strange thing to say.

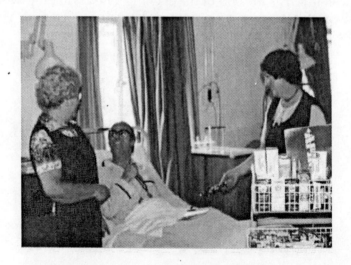

The Ward Trolley at BGH with the Leader, Miss E. Bryan, 1978

My first thought was to get to know some of the members working at the General Hospital. Fortunately, my length of service with the WRVS did stand me in good stead particularly when introducing myself to the project Leaders. Each project had at least one Leader and sometimes two. One member would take care of the rota and the other looked after the financial side arranging for the money to be counted each week. At the end of each opening the member on duty would cash up her takings, bag the money and put it into the night safe. At the end of the week the Leader would collect it from the administration office, count and bank it, then send a copy of the amount into the office each week where it would be dealt with by Susan May, producing end of year accounts for auditing by the treasurer of the Area Health Authority.

Getting around all the projects took me longer than I had anticipated. My brief was to look at each project through fresh eyes to ascertain where, and if, any improvements might be made. During the course of the next few weeks, I arranged to visit and meet all the Leaders.

I met Anne Mather who looked after Princess Anne Tea Bar in Maternity along with Mary Hesketh who both seemed to know what they were about, but needed more lockable cupboard space. An open-fronted kiosk did look good even if it was not very secure.

My meeting with Edith Bryan and her team who operated the ward trolley shop taking sweets, chocolate, toiletries, and stationery and other needs was productive. It helped me understand what they did and in time I was able to go on a trip around the wards to see how it worked at first hand. They needed more space and their stockroom

The original Main Corridor Shop at BGH, 1979

was small and inconvenient but apart from that, the trolley was very
well organised, even to having a back-up member in case one of them
was sick.

Out Patients Tea Bar was run by Dorothy Longman, helped by
her husband, and opened for three hours in the morning and two
and a half in the afternoon, much like the tea bar at BRI.

Townleys Branch Trolley Shop had five members who collectively
took care of the project, opening for two hours each morning except
Thursday when it opened all day, taking comforts around to the patients. Comforts were parcels ordered by long stay patients through
the nurse on the wards, shopped for individually by the WRVS, made
up and then delivered. The cost of the goods we purchased were
paid for by the Health Authority, extracted from the patient's pen-
sion and then a cheque for the amount we spent was sent to the
WRVS office. It was a good system and it worked very efficiently.

The Main Corridor Shop was the busiest project, opening afternoons and evenings and generating the highest income and profit.

However, unlike other projects, there did not seem to be any one
member in charge. One member appeared to be in charge of the stock,
but who did the rota was a mystery. On one of my first visits to the
shop, the member on duty that day told me she would be going on
holiday for the next two weeks and would I report it to the office?
Looking surprised, I asked, 'Who did the rota, wouldn't that be the
person to inform?' They said they did not have anyone who did the
rota; it might be in the office but there was no copy of a rota in the
shop. I was quite sure this was not how Margaret Sydall understood
it. I went back to the office to report my finding, asking if we had a
rota for the Main Corridor Shop. No one had ever seen one. I rang
another member only to be informed 'Well, I think it was done in
their head, we don't have to bother them really, we stand in for each
other – it's only when Mrs. Harriet goes on holiday do we need help.'
But on Monday morning of the following week I got a call at home
asking why I hadn't fixed up Mrs. Harriet's duties.

'But she is not off until Thursday – I saw her last Thursday and
she told me distinctly she would be off next week.'

'Ah, well you see she does six duties a week', the caller said and
my heart sank, realising that this was why they needed help when
she went away.

I had one piece of advice given to me as I started which was, even
if you have to talk on the phone all day, you never do the duty yourself. You could be running from duty to duty, exhausted and never
organising anything. Good advice, I realised, as I spent most of the

day on the phone looking for replacements for 12 duties for two weeks. I made a mental note never to have a person do more than two duties on the same project in a single week.

Despite the low price of drinks, the Hospital Projects together made quite a large profit for the benefit of patients. However, as time went by it became evident that the trolley shop had a problem with the man who took papers around the wards, because he also took sweets and chocolates, the very thing we were selling on Tuesdays and Thursdays. This had caused a rift between the members of the trolley shop and the paper man. Margaret Sydall organised a meeting at the Area Health Office in Bolton to try to deal with this problem. Margaret Sydall, Margaret Spriggs, Miss Bryan, Leader of the project and I represented the WRVS, the Chairman and Treasurer for the Health Authority representing the need to have the man deliver the papers. After much discussion and each side putting their case, it was agreed that the WRVS could not do the job the paper man did so therefore the Authority could not be too demanding of him. They promised to approach him and asked him to refrain from selling sweets on the days the WRVS went into the wards. Sadly, nothing changed; a difficult problem, and one that was not solved for years. The patients needed the morning and evening papers and as an extra line to supplement his takings, he took in the same type of goods we did. Yet, the WRVS members going into the wards provided something different to the paper man, as they had the opportunity to spend a little time at the patient's bedside, as well as offering certain goods the paper man didn't carry. Understanding and compromise would be needed and we would have to work it out somehow. The bottom line was the Health Authority received all the profits from the hospital projects, which they did appreciate, and we remembered one of Lady Reading's famous sayings, 'It's the job that counts'. As we walked back to the office and pondered on the difficulties relating to the trolley shop, we realised that in order to keep harmony, we had to keep a necessary balance between patients and all the services.

Towards the end of 1979 from profits made during the past year, we presented two defibrillators to the Bolton General Hospital at a cost of £5000. These machines stabilised patients who had undergone a heart attack. The hospital had invited all the members involved in the projects to the presentation. Phillip Scully, the Administrator for the Hospital, and the newly appointed Chairman for the Bolton Health Authority, Mr Geoffrey Redgate, were there to thank members for their efforts and we invited Margaret Spriggs, knowing she would appreciate being there.

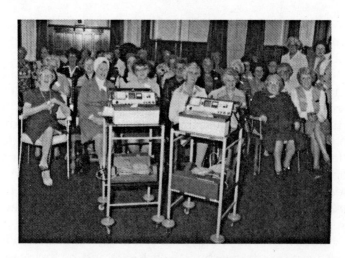

The presentation of two defibrillators to BGH, 1979

Later in the year, Margaret Sydall organised a get together for all our members at the Age Concern Centre – a *conversazione* was what she called it in her invitation to everyone. Margaret had also invited members from the Health Authority and Social Services and it was a good opportunity to meet these people, particularly the Treasurer from the Health Authority whose advice I was to seek on many occasions in my years with the WRVS.

The object of this gathering was for us to meet both WRVS members and the authorities we worked with. Three Community Service Officers were there from Social Services, each expressing interest in the WRVS working in their areas, and members from the Health Authority were offering the WRVS their support for our work in the hospitals. We were to provide the members attending the *conversazione* with tea and biscuits and wine was set aside for the dignitaries. Some of our members were quite a pesky bunch and as I was chatting to several of them during the course of the evening one member asked who the wine was for. 'Why, for the guests', I replied.

'Well, why can't we have wine, it's us as does the work?'

I did not quite know what to say but thought later she was quite right.

During the course of the evening, Margaret Spriggs presented three Long Service awards.

It was a great opportunity to get to know the problems that Leaders of the various projects had and the support they needed and in addition, any changes that needed to be made. I was soon aware that the General Hospital was to take up a lot my time. Maybe Miss Hall in her wisdom had realised something like this would happen when she said 'Don't forget us at the Royal, will you?'

Publicity was our life-blood – if we were seen to be performing well and were successful this helped enormously when recruiting volunteers, of which we needed a constant stream. The *Bolton Evening News* was kind enough to publicise our achievements throughout the year and help us with recruitment.

During 1979, we had pictures in the *Bolton Evening News* showing the defibrillators being presented and also the new cubicle curtains at BGH. At the Infirmary, we had presented several special beds, including one that would tilt and turn, helping a patient with serious burns to recover sooner, and we also had medal presentations for members at both hospitals.

1980

During the war years and for quite a period after, WRVS members generally did not take expenses, very commendable but in the light of many people's financial status this was not so reasonable in 1980. To pay members their expenses, Area Office said, was an incentive to recruitment. We should not be asking people to come and work for nothing and not be prepared to recompense members for bus fares and telephone expenses, particularly to project Leaders. To the majority, this was a positive step forward, to others a retrograde one. I was to spend many hours convincing members that it was the right thing to do: we could not expect our husbands to continue financing the WRVS. As time went by, I came to realise that many of the objectors to the scheme did not catch a bus, living close enough to the hospital to walk there. The reason for the objection to expenses by some members was, we were 'robbing the hospital profits for the benefit of the bus companies', I was once told, however one had to admire their spirit and dedication to the particular hospital they worked for.

Another of the comments I heard regularly was the shortage of variety in the drinks we sold, just tea, coffee and soft drinks, and with the choices of drinks now available, we should try harder to give some variety. The problem with brewing tea in a large teapot was if you were not very busy and selling the tea quickly, we were a victim or the customer was, to some of our very frugal members hated to waste anything, including stewed tea. I have to say this was not the norm but we certainly had a few members very keen on their profit margins for the hospital.

Therefore, before long we introduced the Klix system. I had a call from one of their salesmen, who promised to replace the tea trolley at BRI Outpatient's Clinic free in return for the WRVS purchasing Klix drinks. The drinks came in sleeves of cups containing the ingredients for the required drink. We had a new trolley in Outpatients at BRI that sold black tea and tea with milk, with a similar choice for coffee, also hot chocolate and soup – a big improvement in variety. The shops and kiosks that sold drinks had fixtures on the wall with each type of drink in a separate container, keeping everything neat and tidy. The big problem was tea; they never seemed to perfect the taste of a freshly brewed cup of tea and the argument that it was better than stewed tea somehow did not count. The best answer we found was to buy the sleeves of black tea, adding fresh milk ourselves, but the quality of the other drinks was excellent and consistent.

The profits from the tea bar in the Outpatients Department at Bolton Royal Infirmary had built up over a period. It was the policy that any monies made in the hospital were for the benefit of the hospital. During this year we purchased £6,000 worth of equipment, of which most of the items were special beds.

Twice in the course of a year the WRVS made visits to women who had been made widows during the war; there must have been many more in the days following the end of the war but in 1980 in Bolton we visited just 6 widows.

We assisted at sessions for Blood Donors in different venues at various times in the year, we made tea and occasionally did record keeping. Between all the Districts in Bolton, we attended about 70 different sessions. The secretary found members willing to do this job.

Twice a year we held training sessions for the Emergency Team, primarily to increase the size of the team but also to retain members' interest.

During 1980, my title changed and I became Local Organiser for Bolton and Jane became the Hospital Organiser. It was at this time we opened a club for the disabled in Farnworth named the Wheelers and Wobblers (see Part Three).

The National Westminster Bank had given us six months' notice of the ending of our lease earlier in the year and we had just a few months to find new offices. Being mobile enabled me to go and look at any premises that came up at short notice. Premises on the edge of town would be a better proposition, as premises in the town centre were too expensive. Headquarters' policy at that time was, if we could get reasonably priced offices in good condition it was a better investment to buy than pay rent. This only applied to a Metropolitan office, not to local offices. Headquarters dealt with all premises buying and renting, so every time we saw something that we thought might be suitable, HQ were informed, then made the journey north to view them. We asked them to look at various premises including one on Lions Brow, but all were deemed unsuitable. However, then an office came for sale in St George's Road and I rang Area Office, asking if someone from the Premises Department would come and see it quick. Margaret Spriggs sighed and said 'They won't like coming up north again so soon.'

'It is a good location and it's reasonably priced – they have to come', was my reply.

A representative from Premises Department at HQ did come quickly, and after seeing the offices they agreed it was very suitable and close enough to the town centre. The cost of the building in 1980 was £8,000 and some alterations to the building were necessary, costing approximately £2,000, so at a cost of £10,000 our office at St George's Road was opened.

We all helped to move the WRVS into the new offices in St George's Road in Sept 1980, taking with us three wagon-loads of clothing. Just before we left Oxford Street Margaret Sydall, the Organiser, gave one month's notice and left the WRVS. Margaret Spriggs came over and asked a group of us working in the office to continue to look after Bolton together, organising the work between the five of us. After a meeting together it was decided Jane would look after the hospitals; Betty the Emergency Team (Susan by now had given up as Emergency Organiser but continued as bookkeeper for the hospitals); Connie Ricker continued to take responsibility for the Court Tea Bar (following the resignation of Phyllis Burgess); Edna Foweracker was Clothing Organiser and Kathleen Clarkson was our main stay, as our new secretary.

I helped wherever there was a need, my main role being looking at possible new work in all fields of the service. Before leaving that day, Margaret Spriggs had said 'One of you will emerge as your Organiser, you'll see'.

I found myself adopting the role of Metropolitan Organiser and it was an easy move from Local Organiser so at the end of the year my appointment was made official, along with Betty Taylor as Deputy Organiser with special responsibilities for Emergency Services. Everyone holding responsibility became our Metropolitan staff. Kathleen Clarkson started as secretary after Hilda Barlow left. Kathleen was to stay with us into the mid–1980s and really put the

The Metropolitan Office Staff, 1980
From left, top row: Edna Foweraacker, Doreen Pilling, Joan Walsh,
Kathleen Clarkson, Connie Ricker. Bottom row: Pat Cox, Betty Taylor

office on a businesslike footing; she got along with everyone and
members warmed to her.

At the end of 1980 we had new offices with a new Clothing Store,
a trained Emergency Team, a Tea Bar in the Magistrates courts, a
club for the disabled in Farnworth (the Wheelers and Wobblers with
45 members), we had 7 hospital projects, all doing well and 4 Luncheon Clubs. The office staff were all working enthusiastically, and
looking forward to the next decade.

6

→ *Pat Cox* ←
Metropolitan Organiser, 1980–90

During my period in office there were many changes and much new work was started. To cope with this phenomenal expansion the number of volunteers increased at the same rate. In this section covering the 1980s each of the different areas of WRVS work will be covered separately.

Offices and Membership

After the move to our new offices in St Georges Road in September 1980 we realised the many advantages that this office would bring. To be on the ground floor was a huge help, particularly when bringing in clothing after a collection. The rooms were light and airy, just having received a fresh coat of paint. We had a new kitchen, albeit a small one. There was space at the rear of the premises for the parking of two or three cars, also a cellar plus an attic for storage. We relished the amount of space we now had. However, we had not been in our new offices for very long before a directive arrived from Area Office explaining how we were to use the accommodation. After reading it we realised changes would have to be made in the Clothing Store, which along with all other departments in other offices was not to exceed one third of the premises. Clothing, we were aware, could unless controlled, take over every bit of space we had. One is inclined to hoard, thinking 'It may come in useful' – we all do it, even in our homes. In addition, we had to make provision for a Local Office as well as a Metropolitan Office. We realised also the premises were going to have to be arranged quite differently. At the Oxford Street office, clothing had taken up much of our space and we only had one room designated as the WRVS office. This had never been a problem and it had always worked well. To bring us in line with government changes in 1974, Headquarters decreed that the office in the Metropolitan area would look after any local offices in its town. However, at that time, Bolton WRVS had no local offices, so it would be our brief for the next few years to expand the work to all areas, and if possible open offices in nearby towns. Following this premise, we would start by creating a Local Office for Bolton first. The Local Office was meant to take care of all the work in the Bolton area. Following on from this, we would create a Metropolitan Office upstairs, which would include a separate office for the Metropolitan Organiser. The Local Office and Clothing Store would be situated downstairs, complying with the instructions issued by Area Office.

The first room situated on the right as you came into the building through the front door would eventually be the Local Office and the next room along the corridor, the Clothing Store. Beyond that was the kitchen, which would double as a staff room. Upstairs we had three rooms; the large one at the front would eventually be the Metropolitan Office, the middle room the Organiser's Office and the small room at the back would be a storeroom for clothing, with the attic for extra storage. The cellar would hold our emergency equipment. However, these changes could not happen until we had appointed a Local Organiser for Bolton – for the present, the jobs of Metropolitan and Local Organiser were combined.

Before reorganisation of Local Government in 1974, Bolton's WRVS Office was a County Borough Office with the County Office being in Preston, but after becoming a Metropolitan Office it would incorporate some of the old Lancashire Districts such as Farnworth, Horwich, and Westhoughton and Turton. After the changes, Bolton was to expand its work to include Horwich and Farnworth and the other surrounding areas. We were expected to open outlying offices where there would be work for WRVS members. That was to be my job for the next few years. The changes in positions at that time did not come easily – no one ever takes kindly to change. Several power bases were lost for some, and gained by others; Preston went from a major County Borough office to a Local Office – quite a change. After the Fortieth anniversary of WRVS in 1978, the decision to change from a Regional Organisation to Areas was that it would be smaller and hopefully easier to maintain. Initially North West Area was divided into two sections but after proving unworkable Margaret Spriggs became Area Organiser for the whole of the north west.

By the end of 1981, I had attended my first National Conference where I met the Chairman of WRVS, Baroness Pike of Milton, who had officially appointed me. She was, as I remember, very down to earth with little or no airs and graces and excellent with people, making everyone feel at home and comfortable.

Starting an Office in Farnworth, 1981

The staff at Farnworth WRVS Office, 1983

At the meeting we had with the Local Authority and the hospital authority at Age Concern in 1979 I was Local Organiser and my brief was to open new work in the area. The Development Officer for Farnworth that evening had suggested we might open a club for the disabled in Farnworth. We eventually did and it became known as the Wheelers and Wobblers. This club was proving to be very successful. However, to carry out more work we needed a volunteer force from the Farnworth area and in particular a Local Organiser. During the war years there had been a thriving group working there and why it had disbanded, I had no idea. I also realised from recruiting for the club that there was always going to be a shortage of volunteers in Farnworth. Recruiting had not been easy and many volunteers were brought from Bolton. However, as there was no

Leader in the area and no premises to work from, both issues needed addressing first. We needed to advertise for someone interested enough and able to commit the time a Local Organiser needed to give. I knew that we would succeed with the right person. An advertisement went into the *Bolton Evening News*, receiving only one reply. Mrs. Shaw came for an interview the same week, showing great enthusiasm for the job. She took up the challenge in February 1981 with enthusiasm and had of ideas of her own.

Premises in Farnworth were not going to be easy to find either, particularly anywhere around the centre. Ian Hilton, Development Officer for Farnworth, knowing we were looking for a suitable office contacted us one day saying the old Civil Defence Building in Queen Street might make a good office if we were interested. I was prepared to look at anything that might be suitable as a Local Office for Farnworth.

After a viewing, I saw it was very small but adequate. We could rent two rooms at the front of the building, with their own entrance and the icing on the cake was we were able to rent a much larger room behind the office, also with its own entrance, but the big room would be on a daily basis as and when we needed it. This room would be a great bonus when we were ready to start looking at premises for any clubs Mrs. Shaw intended to open. We could rent the big room for a day for a club or any other meetings.

I contacted Margaret Spriggs again, asking her to come and look at the premises we had found in Farnworth. She was as pleased as I was, particularly when I told her we may have a Local Organiser as well. Mrs. Shaw became the Organiser for Farnworth and Dorothy Ellison became the Deputy Local Organiser for Farnworth. Dorothy had previously worked in Luncheon Clubs in Bolton.

Dancing at Farnworth Blind Club

Dominoes at Farnworth Blind Club

Within a very short time, they gathered about them a small but dedicated group of hardworking members. One of the write-ups they had in the *Bolton Evening News* referred to them as the Magnificent Seven!Between them, they opened another club for the disabled in Farnworth, this time a Club for the Blind and Partially Sighted. The new club opened in April 1981 and had a great atmosphere. They played Bingo using Braille dominoes and had afternoon tea, and the club opened every week. Over the course of several years, they enjoyed many trips out and at least two holidays. Dorothy managed to recruit John Oxford and his wife Hilda. John drove for both disabled clubs in Farnworth and stayed with the WRVS, driving in all sorts of capacities, for years to come. Prior to the ambulances being available, John Oxford drove the WRVS car to bring in disabled club members. Both John and Hilda worked at the Farnworth Office and worked in a number of other clubs in the coming years. Several of the members that came to the Blind Club brought along their guidedogs, cheering almost everyone up. Eventually a founder member at Farnworth, Phyllis Greenhalgh, became its Leader. This club was most successful and continues today although in 1995 its premises changed to Highfield House.

Farnworth WRVS, despite having only a few members, opened yet another project in 1981, a Library service in Farnworth. A group of members went to Bolton Library every Thursday to choose books to deliver, mainly to sheltered housing units, every Friday. In the lounges of the housing complex, the books were laid out on tables and occupants from their flats came in to choose a book and return the one they had borrowed the previous week. They also took books to several individual people. Dorothy and her team had to return the books back to the library on Monday which was quite a labour intensive project and with few members to call on it must have been difficult at times, however they managed to deliver approximately 400 books every week

Later that year Farnworth were able to offer a clothing service albeit on a small scale from the office during office hours.

Later in their first year, using Dorothy Ellison's childcare qualifications, Farnworth WRVS opened a Mother and Toddler group, which in its time was one of the best in the area, catering for around 50 children and opening once a week using the same premises.

The Farnworth Mother and Toddler Group, 1982

Opening an Office in Horwich, 1981

Lillian Rawlinson, on seeing Farnworth taking off so well, asked me if it was my intention to open an office in Horwich, to which I replied that eventually it was, however, it would be some time in the future.

'Would you consider me for Organiser?' she said. She was not a young woman but she was a woman of tremendous energy and spirit. I of course agreed and when the time came, Lillian proved to be ideal. I did not have to do anything to start Horwich other than give Lillian

The staff at Horwich WRVS Office, 1981

support. We realised there were no premises but those could come later. From her first mentioning it, Lillian got underway, preparing the groundwork and developing volunteers. The first venture, she informed me, was to open a Luncheon Club with the recipients staying on for entertainment and trips out during the summer. In no time, she had an Organiser and a venue for the club. The Organiser for the club was to be Emily Lomax who had been Lillian's deputy at the Infirmary kiosk. The venue she proposed for the new club was the Hilton Centre, Horwich. Together we visited the premises and found it was ideal, with a large kitchen and an even larger room to have lunch and spend their afternoons. Within a few weeks, Lillian and her team opened their doors at the Hilton Centre for a Luncheon Club every Monday, run by Emily and her team.

During this very active period, a member working at the hospital by the name of Irene Wignall came in to the office to ask if she could start a club for the elderly in Westhoughton. She did not want to start a Luncheon Club, but a dance club. I was extremely doubtful of the possibility of a project like this. 'Where do you propose to hold it?' I asked.

'At the Carnegie Hall', was her answer, she had certainly done her homework and I began to see she had it all planned out. I was still very sceptical about the idea of a club with dancing as its main feature and I asked if she was completely happy about it, explaining that we had tried to get other clubs interesting in dancing but without success.

Her reply was 'You haven't tried starting one in Westhoughton

have you? The people of Westhoughton really enjoy sequence dancing. It will be okay, you'll see.'

'Well, if you think it will work out, and you can get the room, I
don't have a problem with it.'

Irene found a number of new members to help her run the club,
then asked Linda Mason to be her deputy. In October, the club opened
its doors to about 35 people. Irene had spread the word around
Westhoughton and organised two people who would lead and teach
the dancing, leaving her volunteers to organise refreshments. I was
so surprised to see so many people on the first day and it was encouraging for the future. However, I was even more surprised when
they all became members on that first day, and even more amazed
when after approximately one month the Mayor and Mayoress of
Bolton, Cllr and Mrs. Handscombe, officially opened the Leisure
Hours Club. By then there was a membership of over 80 people, which
they retained for years. The Over-Sixties Club in Westhoughton now
boasted a membership of 110, and I had said they could not make a
dancing club work. How wrong can one be?

It was never Irene's intention to open an office, for which I was
grateful, knowing that Lillian Rawlinson was working hard to find
an office in Horwich. Three Local Offices and a Metropolitan Office
were as much as I could manage right now.

Kathleen Clarkson ran the Metropolitan office well; she did jobs
for all the Organisers requiring any form of administration. During
the week, the Bag came from Area Office with memos and any instructions for us. We always sent a copy to Area Office of every trans-
action we made. Every bill received and any expense we incurred,
be it postage, window cleaning, everything, Kathleen wrote in the
famous Day Book, also recording every letter, phone call, and visitor.
The book gave a complete picture of everything that happened in the
course of the day. All accidents and incidents were recorded and it
was a mine of information. It meant when a different person was running the office she had only to check with the book to see the previous
day's events unfold before her. Kathleen ensured the books were ready
for audit time and delivered them to the Health Authority.

When writing to Headquarters a copy of the letter went to Area
Office for their information. Kathleen also looked after the interests
and needs of the local offices, as well as doing several rotas, contacting members for extra duties when needed. Kathleen typed anything
we required on an oldfashioned typewriter and when copies were
needed, they were made with carbon paper. When multiple copies
were needed, we had a machine, the like I had never seen before.

The ink was painted on a roller, then the master letter typed on special paper, which raised the type, making it stand out, so when the master was fixed to a roller and she turned the handle the raised typeface caught the ink, transferring the print on to a sheet of paper. As the handle was rotated, several copies could be produced before the ink had to be renewed on the roller. It was often a messy job and meant Kathleen would go home with her hands covered in ink. However, that oldfashioned copier served us well for all the years I was there.

Probably the one most important thing Kathleen did was to look after any volunteers who came into the office during the course of a week, understanding that at times volunteers needed support and reassurance. She answered members' queries and dealt with complaints. On so many occasions what had seemed like a problem, after discussing it in depth with someone sympathetic, was proved not to be.

Volunteers came from all lifestyles and for a variety of different reasons. One of our main concerns was that if a person took the trouble to come in to join we should be able to find her not only a job, but also a job she enjoyed. Overall, it worked very well but I have to admit that there were some volunteers who slipped through the net. In the course of a year, there were only a few, but one was too many and we all tried hard not to let this happen.

1982

The Local Organiser for Bolton, May Fielding with her Deputy, Freda Clunie, 1982

During 1982, a Local Organiser for Bolton had been appointed. May
Fielding worked in the hospital Main Corridor Shop for several years.
Several months previously, there had been quite a serious problem
at the shop involving loss of stock, and May had very kindly worked
on the problem, helping to sort it out.

May moved into her newly created Local Office downstairs and
the Met Office moved upstairs. She eventually asked Freda Clunie
to become her Deputy. To divide the work up between the Met Office and the Local Office was not going to be the easiest thing we had
ever done, seeing none of us had ever worked this way. A compromise was worked out in that new work that came into the Local Office was done by the Local Office. When a new contact was made, it
was usually passed to the Local Office. The problem was the existing
work that had been done by the original team before Bolton became
a Metropolitan Office had to remain that way; for instance Hospitals
had to be organised by the Hospital Organiser, and the Luncheon
Clubs organised by the Food Organiser. Farnworth and Horwich
Local Offices were easier as the Local Organisers undertook work
that came to them via whichever body made the request. Bolton Office was more difficult but everyone worked at it and a reasonable
compromise was made.

We had three members in Farnworth who worked together very
well; Mrs. Dearden, Mrs. O'Hara and Mrs. Lawrence. Part way
though the year under the auspices of Mrs. Shaw and Dorothy Ellison,
the Farnworth Organisers, these members found themselves working at a new Over-Sixties club in sheltered accommodation at
Campbell House, Campbell Street, Farnworth. Dorothy had been
approached to organise this club, mainly because many of the people
living there did not know their neighbours; although the lounge was
a very comfortable place they needed encouragement to socialise.
The idea was to provide some entertainment in the afternoon and
possibly days out and parties at Easter and Christmas. The occupants of the flats were slow at coming down to the lounge at first,
wondering what would happen, and what would be expected of them
but eventually one or two came to have a look, and they then told
others, then more came and enjoyed the afternoon and eventually it
turned out to be a very comfortable club. One woman came for the
first time, hardly speaking to a soul for the whole afternoon and
Dorothy soon realised she never went out of her flat either. Eventually, as her confidence built up, she even went to the local
hairdresser's to have her hair done. In the long term, the club had a
warm atmosphere and was a great success. The Farnworth team took

a group on holiday to Sussex later that year and many day trips out were enjoyed.

About every two weeks, Lillian Rawlinson called in to talk over her plans for Horwich. She was interested in opening a club for both the partially sighted and the disabled. She had been offered the use of Horwich Leisure Centre. Her intention was provide a meal after which the members would stay for the afternoon, going home about 3 p.m. Entertainment would include activities and trips out and the number of members eventually reached 30.

Lillian rang one morning, asking if I would meet her at Flockton Court, a sheltered housing complex in Horwich. The manager of the complex had contacted Lillian asking if anything could be done to encourage the residents to use the lounge, just as had happened in Farnworth. The manager of the complex was a caring person and realised how lonely some of the people in her facility were, explaining how nice it would be if she could get them to be friends with each other, meeting on a regular basis. These complexes were excellent homes for elderly people, however, after spending a large part of their lives in one house with neighbours and friends nearby when the time came for them to move out and a make a fresh start, many found that shyness at making new friends difficult to cope with. The kitchen in the complex, whilst very nice, was too small to make a full lunch, so I suggested a mini Luncheon Club where she might serve soup, a variety of sandwiches and a simple dessert. It could be run on exactly the same lines as a regular Luncheon Club with less work. Lillian had

Members of the Horwich clubs going on a trip

Luncheon Club, Horwich

already thought along these lines so instead of making a six-week menu for meals she did the same for soup and sandwiches. It worked extremely well.

Lillian's mini lunch club was so successful during the course of 1982 that the idea caught on and she was asked by managers of two more housing associations to open a club for them. One was in Greenbank and the other in a new complex, Rivington House. After the meal, members of all these clubs stayed and enjoyed bingo or some other entertainment. During the course of the year, the Organisers of these clubs arranged parties and trips out and even a holiday to the Isle of Wight.

Recruiting enough volunteers was a constant problem and appeals for them went on throughout the year. Lillian found many of her volunteers from members living on the Horwich side of Bolton. When Lillian was Organiser at the Bolton Royal Infirmary she was in touch with many volunteers working there, so recruiting was a bit easier in Horwich than it was in Farnworth.

Barry Sharpley, a Development Officer for Bolton Social Services, visited me one day, asking if we might be interested in looking at a variety of sites, mainly in the Horwich area. The Director of Social Services had brought to Barry's attention that there were places in and around the Horwich side of the Borough that could be utilised as meeting places for elderly and children's services. We arranged a time and place to meet for the following week. It was his intention we should visit The Brazley Centre. Prior to that time, I had never heard of the Brazley Centre.

It proved to be ideal premises for the type of projects we operated and as the premises were to be free of charge and available two afternoons a week the prospect was even more interesting. There was a large meeting room with a kitchen adjacent to it. Generally, our main problems were the cost of venues and each project had to be

The opening of Horwich WRVS Office by the Mayor of Horwich, 1982

entirely self-financing. There had to be a charge for whatever the project was and the charges varied between 50p for a club and £1 for a Luncheon Club. When there was a need for extra money, we had raffles that paid for parties at Christmas and Easter. The following week I took Lillian Rawlinson to see what she thought could be done with these premises. Lillian was equally as interested as I had been.

'I could open an Over-Sixties club on a Thursday and a Mother and Toddler group on a Friday', she suggested.

I suggested that particularly as her new centre for the disabled and partially sighted was in the pipeline she might schedule these clubs for later in the year, but Lillian had the bit between her teeth and she was off recruiting new members. By the end of October at the Brazley Centre she had opened a Mother and Baby club with Jill Short as Leader and approximately 25 children and an Over-Sixties Club with Leila Jenkins as their Leader and 25 members, all making very good use of the facilities.

Lillian had been interested in opening an office in Horwich from first going to work there. Her constant cry was 'We need somewhere to work from and interview new members – I cannot keep going to visit them individually – it is taking all my time.' I understood this very well; she had recruited around 40 members, which was no mean feat. Headquarters were not happy to pay rent for premises only to have them opened for part of the day and often there was not a full day's work in a Local Office, so it was a dilemma. Eventually, with gentle persuasion from Lillian, the Council officers at Horwich agreed to find us a place within their premises at a very low rent. In November, Lillian officially opened her Horwich office with a small reception. Margaret Spriggs and I , with some of the Horwich staff, were there and there was a write-up and picture in the *Bolton Evening News*.

1983

In January 1983, May Fielding received a call from The Woodlands, a residential home for the elderly and mentally disturbed. The matron wanted us to go and visit her with a view to us starting a facility at the home whereby her patients could shop for themselves. She said she felt they would benefit and enjoy choosing their own goods. Unfortunately, there was no money for us to start with so it had to be a simple operation. It was interesting to visit the home and chat to some of the patients. We decided that a trolley shop would be a simple option, open once a week, the day when patients received their spending money.

A trolley was ordered, a cupboard made available and a wholesaler chosen and in no time at all we were up and running. Shortly afterwards we received a call from Springfields, a home for the elderly similar to The Woodlands on the opposite corner of Green Lane, asking if we would be interested in opening a trolley shop for them.

During the course of 1983, May Fielding and Freda Clunie went on to open trolley shops in Thicketford House and Lever Edge House and, would you believe, at Watermillock, which was still a home for the elderly (unfortunately I didn't know until I was researching for this book that Watermillock was the first WVS centre during the war years).

Great Lever Over-Sixties Club met in the library at Bradford Road. The club had been in existence for some time but due to retirement of the Leader and no one available to lead the club it was in jeopardy of closing. The WRVS were asked to take it over. I was not sure that it was our sort of work but Mrs. Fielding was interested, so together with Freda Clunie her deputy they took it on and made quite a success of it. Eventually the club was able to provide a Leader from existing members so May returned it back to the members.

One morning I was in the office and received a call from a Playgroup Leader from a Church in Eden Street, Bolton. The caller wanted to know if we were interested in some toys as the church had run a playgroup, but as the church was now being demolished to make way for a new church, they had to clear everything out. The call should have been for the Bolton Local Office but as I was the only one in the office except for Kathleen that morning I went to collect them, thinking they would be useful for our playgroups or if they were in very good condition, we may use them for children's presents at Christmas. The members who helped me put the toys in my car explained they hoped to open a new Mother and Toddler group eventually in their new premises.

Mrs. Shaw left the WRVS halfway through this year and Dorothy, her deputy, took over. Phyllis Greenhalgh, the Leader of the Blind and Partially Sighted Club, was invited to be Dorothy's deputy and accepted. Later in the year 50 children from the Mother and Toddler Group along with their mothers were taken to Chester Zoo for a day out – it had to be an exhausting day but Dorothy said they had a great time.

Farnworth now had a trained Emergency Team who helped the local Scouts with their 'Escapade' weekend for deprived and disabled children. This was an excellent way for us to help in the community, and at the same time we were creating work for the Emergency Team. John and Hilda Oxford transported the children to Crompton Park on Saturday morning where they spent the whole weekend under canvas. The scouts had charge of the children during the day but Hilda and John stayed to help for a great deal of the weekend then transported them home on Sunday evening.

The Wheelers and Wobblers' Christmas Fair was as usual a great success, raising money to help with rent and to subsidise trips out during the year

Lillian Rawlinson was extremely busy rushing from one project to another, constantly taking a great interest in each of her clubs. Between her and the club's Organisers they organised trips out to a variety of places. Emily Lomax and her team took their day club members from Hilton Centre on five coach trips during the year.

Horwich opened another mini Luncheon Club, making it the fifth in the two years since WRVS had started in Horwich. To keep all the projects working with the use of volunteers can be a feat in itself. In almost all the places where we worked there was a terrific team of members covering for each other, especially when the holiday season arrived. Jane Whitehead had left the WRVS for a time after a very sad bereavement but now came back to work as Deputy Organiser for Horwich at the invitation of Lillian, for now we had opened an office it needed to be manned and Lillian, being heavily involved in the general running of the clubs in Horwich, needed help.

Having wanted to open a Clothing Store in Horwich, her opportunity came in May. From the beginning she had designated part of the office to operate as a Clothing Store, intending to open it every morn-

ing. It worked well as the members working in clothing could also
staff the office.

1984

Opening Blackrod Luncheon Club, 1984 (top)
Easter Bonnet Parade, Wheelers and Wobblers Club, 1984 (bottom)

Lillian Rawlinson informed me one Monday morning early in January 1984 that two of her members working in at the Hilton Centre were interested in opening a Luncheon Club at the community centre in Blackrod.

I was happy to see us expanding but was also fully occupied. 'If you could set it up and support it in the early days, that would be fine', was my reply.

'I intended to do that anyway, and the two members are prepared to lead it', assured Lillian.

Carol Kay and Ethel Warburton had worked at Hilton Centre since the beginning so they were experienced in setting up and running a club. They opened the club with a visit from Cllr. Bob Radcliffe, who served the first meal, and it became very successful and remained open almost to the end of the century.

This year our publicity was good and we had photographs in the *Bolton Evening News* for the Blind Club, as two of their members had a Golden Wedding celebration, also a club trip to Morecambe. The Farnworth Disabled Club had two trips out and an Easter Bonnet party, all with write-ups and pictures. We received publicity for appeals for volunteers from Farnworth, Horwich and Westhoughton, and Long Service medals were presented to members by Margaret Spriggs.

Our National Conference was held this year in Bloomsbury, London, in January and the highlight was Margaret Thatcher who addressed us in her usual dynamic way. The party from Greater Manchester all stayed at the Russell Hotel in Russell Square, which was a wonderful treat.

The WRVS Conference was usually held in September, the venue being one of the universities. Each Organiser had her own room and shared a bathroom and small kitchenette for late night drinks. We left Bolton usually on a weekday afternoon to arrive at the venue for dinner. Our first meeting was after dinner on the first evening. We were split into groups for a lecture, then a group discussion. These were always interesting and we all agreed that being together with members from other areas enabled us to exchange ideas and agree or disagree as the case may be. It was rather like being at college, sharing facilities, but we never shared rooms. Each day was split into two sessions with coffee after the first one then lunch and two more sessions in the afternoon. Dinner was always a pleasant affair, sitting with our own group. After dinner there was a talk then discussion was held on a particular subject after that we could relax with a drink for the remainder of the evening. The following morning we had group discussions, lunch, then drove home. Arriving home rather tired, we still felt the conferences were worth all the planning and expense that was undertaken by Headquarters staff, as everyone gained something.

By March of that year, Baroness Pike having retired, our new Chairman was Barbara Shenfield, a lady with an accounts background who in the course of her Chairmanship was to bring about great changes in our financial structure, helping to put the organisation on a sound footing.

The level of volunteers required to keep up such a velocity of work would have been difficult without publicity from the *Bolton Evening News* who when approached always helped, but the need was so great at this time we needed to do something ourselves. The need to show people exactly what kind of work we did and where, became apparent. We were being asked to open new projects on a regular basis but the lack of a constant flow of volunteers was a great worry. At one of our monthly meetings early in the year we decided to have major publicity drives planned throughout the year, not one but several.

One comment that was reiterated often when this subject was brought up was we do not have the workforce to plan the extensive publicity we need. The sort of operation we were talking about would take the one thing we were short of – manpower. I could see this as a valid point but could not see a way round it, for there was no one who would do it for us. The only way forward was to increase our profile. Rather than plan a whole year's publicity, which was a daunting thought, we decided to hold two Open Days in the Bolton Office in March. Kathleen, Betty and I set about the task. It was intended that all three Local Offices become involved, as they all needed volunteers. We set out a plan, using all the space in the Bolton Office, intending to use each room for a specific purpose. From our slides taken the previous year we could put together pictures of various projects, along with written explanations and members on hand to help with inquires. The offices were cleaned from top to bottom to give a pristine feel to the place.

Invitations were sent out to all the agencies we worked with. The first day was to be for agencies, the Local Authority and the Health Authority. The second day would be for our own members and people interested in joining. In the Local Office on the ground floor, the exhibits were to represent the work done in hospitals and for children's holidays. The Clothing Store was completely reorganised and looked spruce and smart. Edna was on hand to talk about the job her that her team did there. There was always great interest shown in the

WRVS exhibition at Rotary Show, The Last Drop

clothing and we were able to reveal that the Clothing Store had distributed 6561 garments to 1391 people, plus clothing for 60 children going on holiday.

In the cellar, Betty arranged all our emergency equipment. She built a trench cooker placing pots and pans on top for effect and set up the Soya boiler, which was used for mass feeding in time of crisis. However, before we could even think of using the cellar we had to improve its appearance, it was such a mess, but with help from the Probation Department using youths on Community Service we got the cellar painted, which was a big improvement. The wall going up the staircase to the first floor was covered with cartoons drawn by Frank, the husband of Lillian Punchaby, copying from a tea towel that had been prepared by WRVS previously showing the work we did. They were funny and well copied by Frank. The upstairs offices were used for displays about the Disabled and Luncheon Clubs, and the large front office for refreshments. The walls were covered with a variety of photos, many of them poster size, showing all the work we did throughout the borough, providing lots of interest and conversation.

At the end of two days we felt a certain satisfaction that we had achieved our objective. Everyone had worked very hard to make it the success it turned out to be. The following morning as we put the offices back together we realised we now had all the material we would ever need for publicity throughout the coming year.

Two further full days were planned, staffing a WRVS publicity stand at the Last Drop for a Rotary Fun Day run by the Bolton-le-

Moors Rotary Club on a lovely day in May.

The members who were on duty were able to visit all the events taking place as well as manning our own display. We had no problem filling the 3-hour slots we had planned for that period.

In July, we negotiated with the management of the Arndale Centre, Bolton to hold a recruitment drive in August. We borrowed stands, consisting of metal poles on which display boards were hung. This type of event was ideal except for the fact we had to staff the exhibition the whole time for six hours a day continuously for four days. We decided to staff it in 3-hour sessions. Every morning the stands photos and leaflets had to be taken from the office to the Arndale centre, fortunately, the Arndale Centre was very close to our offices. However to set it up and take it down needed about two or three people. The morning set up was not a problem as there were people around in the office but the evening was difficult. I remember when closing the exhibition for the last day, the person helping me had to leave early so I was on my own. Everything could not be carried at one go, so to make as few journeys as possible, I tried carrying as many of the poles that I could. Then for speed I decided to put a bag with leaflets underneath my arm, and then I tried to negotiate the stairs. As I descended the stairs to the street the poles started to slip from my grip – I never knew such a few poles could make so much noise as they clanged and clattered down the stone staircase. As I managed to pick one up another one, fell. I started to laugh as I looked around to find leaflets and poles everywhere, eventually some kind person helped me.

The Arndale exhibition despite all the work was successful with lots of names being taken for contact later. We looked back, pleased with our efforts.

During the summer months, we had unmanned exhibitions in five libraries throughout the Borough and during the winter I did seven talks to women's organisations in the town. We finished the year with an exhibition in Tesco supermarket for three days in October.

We were pleased to find that by the end of the year we had enrolled 76 new members. These exhibitions were aimed at the needs of all three of our offices and each gained some volunteers.

1985

I arrived home from holiday in January to find Kathleen quite subdued which was most unusual. During the morning the reason for it came out: she had had a job offer. It was no use pretending I was not devastated – I was, and would be so sorry to see her go.

Kathleen had come to work with the WRVS five years previously when her children were smaller the youngest having just started school. The hours had suited her, also being able to bring the children with her during the school holidays when the need arose. Fortunately, her mother lived a few doors away and would often step into the breach if needed. The down side of the job was the pay was poor and Kathleen could earn much more working in industry. One of our members had been into the office whilst I had been on holiday, commenting that her son needed a secretary. Kathleen's job with the WRVS was never going to make her a wealthy woman and this was too good an opportunity to miss. The Company was good and so was the pay, so after being offered the position she took it. Inevitably, we were all going to miss her a lot.

I discussed the prospect of her replacement with her one day and she suggested that Doreen Pilling, the Hospital Organiser, might be interested. Kathleen and Doreen had become friends over the years so Doreen had confided to Kathleen that her family might be moving south in the near future and gaining some experience in the office may help her get a job after their move.

That was all very well but who would replace her as Hospital Organiser? Apparently Doreen had thought her deputy, Doreen Reynolds, might be interested and she had experience and had worked in the hospitals for some years.

Kathleen was due to finish in a month so had time to train Doreen who in turn had time to train Doreen Reynolds. Doreen Reynolds had worked on the trolley at Hulton Lane with Dorothy Dunkerly. It all sounded too good to be true. I thought they had it all planned, not really needing any input from me, but that was fine, I did not mind: 'It's the job that counts'. Kathleen left at the end of the month, Doreen took over from her and handed her reins to Doreen Reynolds who I advised to find herself a deputy. A couple of days after Kathleen first told me, Joan, the member whose son Kathleen was going to work for, came into the office, throwing her hat through the door shouting 'Here is my hat, will I be welcome too?' We all laughed and Joan said she had felt bad about Kathleen leaving but was sure she would be happy with her new job.

February brought another resignation: May Fielding, who had been the Local Organiser since the time we created a Local Office, was leaving us after about three years. May's deputy was Freda Clunie who was invited to take her place and did so. In May's time as Local Organiser she had created the Local Office and been responsible for several projects opening.

Lillian Rawlinson arrived in the Bolton Office one Monday morning in mid-March. She was not her usual chirpy self which was surprising, but after she told me what was on her mind I did not feel too
chirpy either. Having contemplated retirement because of health
problems she thought now might be a good time. For me there would
never be a good time for Lillian to retire. 'We shall all miss you terri-
bly, particularly the people of Horwich – have you mentioned this to
anyone?' I asked.

'No I haven't, I wanted to see you first. I feel sad about it, but
feeling as I do, I do not want to be a bad Organiser.' She looked
downhearted about her decision.

'Have you anyone in mind to replace yourself in Horwich?'

'Yes, I am sure Jane Whitehead would be a good Organiser.' Jane
was of course Lillian's deputy. 'I will still be around and maybe visit
the clubs occasionally, or maybe I can do something else with not so
much responsibility', she offered.

Lillian had a strong personality with a great sense of fun and had
the need to do the right thing. Her organising ability, I felt sure, came
from her service during the war. She once showed us a photo of her
in her Wrens' uniform and she had continued to show the same military bearing long after the war had finished; she would be a hard act
to follow for anyone.

'Have you asked Jane about becoming Organiser?' I asked.

'Not yet, but I will now I have told you', she replied.

Lillian finished as Organiser for Horwich at the end of April and
Jane Whitehead took over.

I was wondering just what had hit me as two of our three Local
Organisers were to leave within a year, however I had to remember
we had been solid for over five years and in a voluntary organisation
I supposed that wasn't bad; we had so many good volunteers and I
was sure we would survive.

By the end of August, Lillian had returned to the Bolton Office
asking if she could start a group for the WVS/WRVS Association.
The WVS/WRVS Association was a group meant mainly for members, who, for whatever reason had given up their work with WRVS
but wished to stay in touch. Generally the groups met several times
a year and should they wish could go to a meeting of all the clubs in
the UK held by Headquarters. This was an ideal task for Lillian. A
list of recently retired members was collated and given to her for
contact. She added some of her own contacts, including several who
had not retired but with whom she had worked. The first meeting

held at Age Concern in September was a success.

Members' Week

Once a month Organisers from the ten Metropolitans in Greater Manchester met at the WRVS Area Office situated at Wilbraham Road, Manchester. Margaret Spriggs, the Area Organiser who always chaired the meeting, had told us at one of the meetings of the Directive she had received from Headquarters. Headquarters had indicated that each County and Metropolitan should hold a special Members' Week later in the year. The idea was for us to show appreciation to the members in our Metropolitans. She asked for our input on this subject. We discussed at length the ways in which we might put it into operation. This meeting had taken place earlier in the year, so now it was as good a time as ever to start. In Bolton the staff made a valiant effort to get around and visit each project. Back at our own Organisers meeting we had long discussions as to how we would go about organising Members' week. Eventually we decided on a lunch at the Pack Horse and a display of the work we did. The following Sunday a service would be held in Bolton Parish Church. One of the Organisers asked whether there would be any funding available, but of course there would not.

We had 200 members accepting the lunch invites and around 150' came to the church service.

Headquarters celebrated Members' Week by making a presentation to our President, the Queen Mother, of a Book of Signatures. They hoped to have as many members as could be contacted to sign it however it could only be in each area for a very short time. 'The Book' was to spend one day each in as many of the Metropolitans as possible. As it did its huge trip around the country it had to be protected at all costs, as sending it around to all the offices anything could go wrong. We were each given 24 hours in which to collect as many signatures from members working in projects as we could. This was no mean feat. One member had to visit as many projects as she could in the day, handing it during the course of the day to a member from an office close by. We did our best, getting as many as we could in the time allotted and duly sent the book off, being glad it was out of our possession.

I received a call later in the year asking if I could recommend a member with a view to her going to Buckingham Palace to present this famous book to the Queen Mother. The member's name would go into a hat with several other names chosen from different towns.

Eventually there would be four names drawn out of the hat. The member had to be in uniform but she was not to be an Organiser. We decided on one member called Joan Wallen. She was to go down on the train with two other chosen members and the Chairman. We were given directions as to the type of person to choose. The main requirement was that we should choose a member who would feel comfortable and able to handle such an occasion – what an honour that would be. After much deliberation, we gave the name, not expecting to hear anything else and of course, we did not inform the member at that time, not wishing to invite disappointment.

Much to everyone's surprise a few days later we received a call to say 'Had the member we'd recommended for the presentation actually signed the book?' I could not remember and Kathleen was out. On her return to the office, she assured me she had. It was one of my greatest pleasures to ring Joan Wallen and give her the good news.

To delay the moment I asked Joan if she was doing anything special that day, to which she replied 'Oh yes, I'm going out in the evening with my sister-in-law.'

'Oh that's a shame,' I said, 'I wanted you to do something which might take you most of the day.'

To which she replied, Oh, I'm really sorry about it but I have promised.'

'Well Joan, wherever it is you are going, I am pretty sure I can better it', was my reply.

'Go on, surprise me then.'

After I had related my story, she was more than surprised – she was astounded. Everyone offered to lend her bits of uniform and she went on to have a wonderful day, a day I knew she would never forget, and as it turned out there were just the three members and the Chairman and Queen Mother. They were with her almost two hours, having tea with her into the bargain.

I had arrived one morning at the office hoping to park my car in one of the spaces to find a large green car taking up more room than it should on our parking space. I came into the office through the kitchen where the clothing ladies were having a cup of tea, asking 'Does that huge car on our parking place belong to anyone in our office?', my eyes alighting on a member I hadn't seen before. 'It's mine', she said and I introduced myself, asking her how long she had been with the WRVS. We chatted for a while then before I went upstairs I called into the Local Office. Freda was in the midst of a discussion, saying she needed someone to help with the trolley shops, mainly collecting goods from the Cash and Carry and delivering them to the homes. As I listened to this, my thoughts went to the person in Clothing Store with the green car. 'Okay, we might have such a person – there is a new member in Clothing with a car large enough to hold anything – go and ask her if she would like to help you.' 'By the way what is her name?' asked Freda. It was Pat Bentley and I was not going to forget that name in a hurry. The great thing was Pat agreed to help. After completing three weeks in the Clothing Store, she took on the collection and distribution of goods, firstly for the hospitals then the trolley shops. All the members working on the trolleys rang their orders each week to be delivered to the home where they were working. Pat called in the office to collect the lists and the individual chequebooks. After she had done the shopping, she delivered them to each of the homes. She must have impressed many of our members for some months later after being approached by Doreen Reynolds to be her deputy, Pat agreed to try.

During October 1985, over 600 members of the WRVS, mainly Organisers and officials, attended a rally in Bloomsbury. In the morning, the rally was welcomed by The Rt. Hon. the Mayor of London, Dame Mary Donaldson GBE, who gave a splendid talk on the differences of a woman being The Lord Mayor. It was the first time a woman had ever been elected. She was a very relaxed speaker and had everyone laughing in no time at all. After Lunch the Rt. Hon. Leon Brittain QC, MP spoke; he was very good but not half as good as London's first woman Mayor. Everyone there enjoyed the day.

I had another shock to come before the year ended as Dorothy Ellison was to hand in her resignation; that was a huge blow. Dorothy was liked and replacing her would not be easy. However, we were at the end of the year, so I decided I would deal with that problem in the New Year.

1986

Before we were well into January, my first job had to be the replacement of Dorothy Ellison, Local Organiser for Farnworth, and for once I had no idea who would take it on. Farnworth had a great set of members working very hard, but I knew no one was interested in the responsibility a Local Organiser carried. I needed someone with strong organisational abilities. The WRVS was not short of members who were capable of doing the job, however for a variety of reasons they chose not to. For many the barrier was family commitments, or occasionally they wanted some occupation without any responsibility. There were also members who might be waiting to be asked, and could not just come forward to volunteer. I understood all the reasons; however, I had to come up with someone very soon.

I asked Pat Bentley out to lunch one day in early February. By now Pat knew me well, so she was aware something was afoot. Eventually I explained I needed an Organiser for Farnworth as Dorothy by now had left. I concluded my appeal to her by saying 'I know I'm asking a lot but I have to solve the problem somehow, even if you could do it as a temporary measure it would give me time to find someone.' I could have kissed her when she offered to try it. Pat Bentley had joined WRVS and started working in the Clothing Store at the end of 1984. Since then she had worked in clothing, delivered goods for the homes for the elderly, been Deputy Hospital Organiser and now she was to be Local Organiser for Farnworth. All in such a short time, as it was still only 1986. She was among the many good hardworking members of the WRVS who were not afraid of a challenge.

At the start of the year and following discussions with the Minister of State, Mr Giles Shaw, on crime, five WRVS projects were about to be launched in Wellingborough, Long Benton, Swansea, Croydon and Bolton, to support the Local Authority in their fight against crime. The WRVS have regular contact with individuals vulnerable to crimes such as domestic burglary; the elderly, disabled and single mothers. We were informed of this initiative from Area Office. We made contact with the Crime Prevention Office in Bolton, resulting in several meetings being set up. One area where we might be able to help was to inform the relevant authorities if we suspected a vulnerable person might need help. In the past, we had come across some elderly who carried what appeared to be life savings in their handbags. However, apart from the times we set up speakers from Crime Prevention to speak to members of our clubs for the elderly, nothing much happened.

The work of the WRVS had expanded tremendously, leaving a gap in the office for someone to keep a watchful eye on the finances. Just prior to Kathleen leaving in 1984 there had been a new initiative given by Headquarters to have each project run its accounts more efficiently. Each Project Leader had to prepare a set of account papers with a different coloured form for each area of work; blue for Hospitals, gold for Luncheon Clubs and so on. I needed someone to get the information from all the Project Leaders and collate them, looking for any mistakes or problems to be dealt with before they were sent to Area. Between our hospital projects, trolley shops and Luncheon Clubs we now had the new vehicles for disabled. We

Presentation of garden furniture to a home for the elderly, with Freda and Ron Clunie

needed someone to take overall control of them, to be responsible for collecting the forms, collating them, working on any mistakes then creating duplicates for Area Office and Headquarters. I asked Lillian Punchaby, the Leader of the Farnworth Disabled Club, who had always enjoyed account work if she would be interested in doing this job. Lillian said it appealed to her and would try, resulting in

The start of a Mother and Baby Group, Eirlys Gabbot and her team

the WRVS finding a Finance Organiser.

Freda Clunie had made great headways with the trolley shops in Bolton and her husband, having recovered from a serious illness, chose to come and help her with the shopping for these projects, which because of Freda's vigilant accounting methods were making excellent profits. Everyone involved in these projects were aware that profit was not the priority; the service was the reason the trolleys operated. Therefore, it was nice to see photos of Freda in the *Bolton Evening News* with her staff at each unit throughout the summer presenting various gifts. Silk plants were bought to help brighten up communal rooms at Watermillock and Thicketford House and garden seats helping to bring pleasanter afternoons in the sunshine to recipients at Lever Edge Lane and Woodlands homes for the elderly.

Pat Bentley and her team at a recruitment drive in Farnworth

The staff at Deane Children's clinic approached Freda Clunie with a view to her opening a Mothers' Group at their Children's Health Clinic on Mondays. It would help to bring together mothers new to the area. This was also a problem for new mothers, who having had busy careers had not had time to make friends. Mothers attending could sit and chat whilst toddlers play and new babies slept.

Pat Bentley eventually became Local Organiser for Farnworth but realised if she was to expand work in Farnworth, which I knew was her intention, she needed to recruit more volunteers. Pat suggested we might hold an exhibition of the type of work WRVS did in Farnworth. An ideal place to hold the exhibition would be at one of the community rooms at Trinity church on Market Street. Pat and her staff prepared a collection of photos of work done in Farnworth then produced display stands. She advertised the exhibition in the *Bolton Evening News,* providing coffee and biscuits to people on arrival. One never picked up many volunteers at these events but there is always the hope that the exhibition would be remembered by visitors attending who may want to do some voluntary work later. Pat went on to open an afternoon club for the residents of Crompton Court, a Part Three accommodation unit with a warden in Little Lever which was a very happy comfortable club, opening once a week.

In May, Pat told me she had been approached by the manager of Alderbank, a home for the elderly in Farnworth, to open a trolley shop, and she had it up and running quickly, appointing Eileen Tasiker as their Leader.

Jane Whitehead decided to resign as Horwich Organiser, recommending that one of her members, Marjorie Hale, take her place. She was an enthusiastic member living in Horwich and having worked with Horwich members for several years she seemed an ideal person to take the job on.

Betty gave up her job as Emergency Organiser part way through the year, to concentrate on being Deputy Metropolitan Organiser and handed over the reins to Jane Whitehead who had recently left the Horwich office. In her time with the WRVS Jane had tried her hand at most jobs and was a very popular person. Betty was equally as popular and there were many members who were sorry to see Betty go as Emergency Organiser but we all had no doubt that she would support Jane in the future. Norma Gibbons with her newly achieved Instructor's badge became our Leader for training, as well as organising children's holidays. This was going to be another year of expansion so I was glad Betty would have more time to help me.

Since the time we had our first vehicle, the WRVS car, and particularly after the appeal for the ambulances the WRVS had men working with the women members. They had proved invaluable and helped in many areas. Mainly driving our three vehicles, but when furniture had to be moved and for any general heavy work on the premises the men in WRVS proved their worth many times. In October 1986 a hurricane in the south of the country created the biggest disaster in many years, uprooting many large trees including the famous ones at Sevenoaks in Kent. Bolton had its share of stormy weather that year with flooding at the office in Bolton where water came gushing down the stairs, and the roof being almost blown off at the office in Farnworth. Members in Farnworth commented they were ringing in the rain not singing in the rain as they frantically tried to get help by telephone from roofers and plumbers! With the alterations in Horwich and problems at the other two offices, we were in a mess, but adversity certainly brings out the best in people. Everyone rallied and we were back to working normally eventually with much of the repainting being done by the WRVS men and the cleaning by our members.

1987

We spent much of 1987 preparing for the coming year when we were to celebrate our Golden Jubilee. It was a main topic at the Organiser's monthly meetings at Area, the concern being how we might celebrate it yet at the same time, share the occasion with members.

The Organisers were asked at one Area Meeting if there were facilities in our towns whereby a large celebration could be held and enjoyed by several hundred members in comparative comfort. As it happened, Bolton's Albert Hall had just undergone a complete refurbishment due to a horrendous fire that had happened several years previously. Renovations had taken several years to complete. I had been invited to a special concert for the opening of the new Halls and they were certainly spectacular. I reported this fact at the meeting, and as a result, Bolton was chosen as the venue for the Metropolitan celebrations to take place the following year.

There was plenty of time to prepare for the celebration so after the Halls had been booked, preparations were put on hold until later in the year. There was no shortage of work to keep us going for the time being. As the end of the year approached, I was well aware of the promises I had made for the following year. We talked a lot about the coming celebrations at our Area monthly meetings, and to what extent our office in Bolton were responsible, and what responsibility Area Office would have. Eventually a decision was made: Bolton was to prepare an exhibition in the Festival Hall of all the different types of work done in Greater Manchester. Each area of work was to have its own stand: hospitals, food, welfare for the elderly etc. Material for the stands was supposedly coming from each Metropolitan branch as well as Headquarters. It would be a huge undertaking. Not only had Bolton to prepare the exhibition, but to ensure that all the members who came from Area and the surrounding towns, including HQ staff (who would be taken care of and given lunch) we were looking at feeding approximately 800 people at the best price possible of about £1 per head. We planned that the food should be in boxes, one for each person. One question asked was whether we were

The Jubilee Exhibition team, 1988

going to ask a firm to fill boxes or were we going to buy the food and fill the boxes ourselves? We were to send each Metropolitan Office enough invitations for their members and maps showing how they should get there. Considering that between 700–800 people would all be arriving at about the same time, it was going to be a busy day.

I needed a committee for the exhibition and another person responsible for the display stands. Everyone else had a job in WRVS besides preparing the exhibition so it had to be someone without an existing job. Whilst at a social function earlier in the year I had met an old friend I had not seen in several years. After quite a long conversation concerning the coming exhibition, I realised she might be able to help us. She was organised and paid great attention to detail and had the talent and creativity we needed. Eventually, after a lot of thought, I asked Val Wallace to help with creating the displays and setting up the exhibition the following year. She would of course be helped by many of our members involved with the different projects. No one person could do it alone in the short time we had, but Val would be in charge, first planning, then visualising how it would all look as a whole, making sure with help from everyone we managed to create the effect she wanted, with material supposedly coming from each Metropolitan as well as Headquarters.

In November, we saw a change in venue for our Headquarters; the building we had occupied at Old Park Lane we were leaving for better offices, so it was said, with more room, but would you believe it, our new address was to be Southwell Road, Brixton. I am sure it caused shockwaves throughout the service. The new Brixton offices, whilst having more room, certainly were not Old Park Lane. However, I felt sure, there were other reasons for the move, like the expiry of the lease or costs getting too high, as the nicer part of central London had to be very expensive. Whatever the reason was, we were moving.

Later in the year we were without a secretary yet again, and I had been aware for some time that Marian Hilton would make a most efficient secretary. She had been working with Stanley doing the accounts for Transport so she knew most of the people who came into the office and was popular with them all. It was important to keep relations comfortable in the office considering the number of members we dealt with, so feeling very bad I had to tell Stanley, our Transport Organiser, I was about to poach one of his best drivers. Marian came to work in the office and was a great secretary for the WRVS.

1988

Margaret Spriggs was due to retire during 1988 but intended to stay and orchestrate the celebrations for the Golden Jubilee in her Area. Lennie Holmes was to replace Margaret as Area Organiser in 1989 but would work with Margaret during 1988. This was a rare happening as most newly appointed Organisers were thrown in at the deep end and never had a learning period. Lennie appreciated this. Lennie

Pat Cox, Pat Bentley, Marian Hilton and Norma Gibbons
at the Westminster Abbey Garden Party, 1988

The Queen Mother and the Chairman at the Westminster Abbey Garden Party, 1988

had been the Metropolitan Organiser for Oldham; she was ideal for the job of Area Organiser, displaying great attention to detail and the necessary organising ability to carry the job through.

We had received notification of a special Thanksgiving Service which was going to be held in Westminster Abbey on 26 May 1988 to commemorate the Golden Jubilee of the service. Every Metropolitan Organiser automatically had a ticket for the Abbey and was to take tea in the grounds of the Abbey after the service in the presence of the Queen Mother, President of WRVS. We received three extra tickets for staff members, to been drawn out of a hat containing names of all the staff. We had a large staff but did exactly as we were told; every member of staff had her name put into a hat and the ones drawn out were Norma Gibbons, Marian Hilton and Pat Bentley. We could however send for tickets for anyone willing to come and pay for their train fares. However, for the sake of catering purposes, admittance to the Abbey Gardens was not permitted for these ticketholders. There were, as I remember, two members who travelled with us; Jane Whitehead and Mary Kelly, while Doreen Gwyther arrived the day previously and met us at the Abbey. We were advised not to take a camera with us, as the taking of photographs would not be permitted. I was mortified as my camera travelled everywhere with me but nevertheless I went along without it. However, on arrival into the Gardens many did not receive the information regarding cameras, or completely ignored it. I was fortunate enough to borrow a camera from Jean Rigby, a member at Bury, along with a film. The result was some of the happiest photos I have ever taken and a great memento of such an auspicious occasion. I had copies made for us all. The day had dawned very early for all of us who had tickets, leaving on the 6.00 a.m. train from Manchester. The weather so early in the morning had threatened rain but held off and as we left the Abbey to go into the Gardens, the sun shone for the rest of the day and we had a fantastic day.

With the thoughts of October and the exhibition looming, some interesting ideas were being formed, particularly as to how it should be organised. As we were preparing stands for each area of work, Margaret Spriggs suggested we pay a visit to Headquarters, with a view to obtaining relevant material. I particularly wanted us to have a corner of the exhibition explaining why it was necessary for WVS/WRVS to have started in 1938.

Margaret and I caught a train one morning for our journey to HQ. She wanted us to cover the details of the exhibition day from the start to finish, wanting to know exactly what we were doing concerning the lunch and the organising of the stands, then the registration of members coming from out of town. By the time we reached Euston Station the journey had been an enlightening one. We had covered the items we needed and catalogued the event in total. Each Metropolitan would be offered 50 tickets although not all would need so many, but of course Bolton would need more as it was on home ground for their members. Questions we had raised included: What design were the stands going to be and what material would we need for the stands? How were we going to cope with lunch for so many and what would we be preparing to eat? What we would do

Setting up the Jubilee Exhibition

with the debris left behind? How we could register everyone who arrived? Nothing had been completely finalised yet, however, we were on schedule for most things. I made copious notes from the meeting with Margaret on my return to the office.

Headquarters did not have all the things I expected, but we managed to obtain some of the original WVS uniforms for our early WVS display. The men's Army and Navy uniforms we needed were hired from the Army store in Bolton. We also obtained from Headquarters paper strips in various colours depicting the work we did. For instance, purple strips with Disabled Clubs written on them, blue strips saying Hospital Tea Bars, Trolley Shops, etc. We were given some posters, but they were the only pictures they had. Large coloured photographs were what I had in mind, however before we left I had decided how these items could be obtained. We had enlarged some of the slides I had taken several years previously for our own Open Day so out came the slides and we enlarged more of them, which we backed on to strong card. I had great communications with the secretary for events at the Town Hall who really went out of her way and was a terrific help.

Val Wallace came into the office twice a week for three months. She worked very hard preparing plans for the stands we were exhibiting at the Festival Hall; a stand for each area of our work, gathering exactly what materials she needed for the particular services, with great detail. After creating a template for each stand she cut it out of newspaper; we were on a real shoestring budget and any money we had was saved to spend on the result. When she knew exactly what she needed to create the differing exhibition stands, she planned her requests for the Organisers.

In due time, Val presented us with a long list of items she needed. Some of the items were large round tables approximately 18 inches from the ground, one for each area of work. Each table was to be covered with a cloth of dark red, touching the floor, and on the tables would be items for the areas of work. Considering Val had never worked with the WRVS she caught on to the type of work we did very quickly. As she amassed the items, she stored them in the back office until all was complete. For the stand depicting the office, she went to Whitaker's department store asking if she could borrow a shop dummy which she intended to dress up representing the secretary in WRVS uniform. They were kind to consider this request but they did, making the stipulation that we could not collect it until the morning we were to use it and were to return it the same day. The morning of the exhibition saw two members dressed in WRVS uniform carrying a naked dummy across the Town Hall Square.

The evening before the exhibition day, most of the staff took all the boxes containing hundreds of items to the Festival Hall to begin the set up. Arriving at 6 p.m. we all worked until 10 p.m. but the results were worth it; it looked wonderful and Val's plans had worked well. The exhibition in the foyer was so interesting; we had some of the WRVS men dressed in Secod World War uniforms in settings that depicted our early days, with enlarged newspaper cuttings displayed relating the deeds that were carried out in Bolton during the war. Jane Whitehead and Norma Gibbons were instrumental in setting up the preparations for the lunch. Our first idea was to prepare the boxes ourselves, until we realised how many we were preparing for and all the other jobs there were would be to do on the morning of the exhibition. Jane went to ask Molly Bentham, Bolton's local caterer, if she could collate it all. There were many suggestions made, and the costs had to be kept to a minimum. However, Molly delivered approximately 700 lunchboxes to the Town Hall on the morning of the exhibition at a cost of £1 each and each one contained enough food to keep us going all day and a drink to wash it down. Her generosity and cooperation that day were amazing particularly given the budget we were working to, and we really did appreciate her kindness. It was arranged that members, after they had been around the exhibition in the Festival Hall, would make their way upstairs to the Albert Hall were lunch was served. A boxed lunch was passed to everyone as they sat in their seats in the Albert Hall waiting for the afternoon show, then all the debris collected by the team that had given out the boxes. It was a massive operation for us to undertake but it worked like clockwork.

A Fashion Show was given by Area of clothing that could be handmade from a variety of larger items into fashionable everyday clothing. Such items came into our Clothing Stores on a regular basis and often we had no use for them.

Registration was one thing we had problems with; we had overlooked the time it would take to process so many people, but eventually it was done and around 700 people saw the exhibition that day. Included in the dignitaries were the Mayor of Bolton, Cllr. Allenson and Mrs. Allenson; the Chairman of the WRVS, Barbara Shenfield; and Vice-Chairman Mary Corsair, who was due to take over the Chairmanship at the end of the year.

When everyone had gone home the Bolton members started to dissemble it all for transportation back to the office where we then had to pack it all away, and we arrived home around 8 p.m. that evening completely exhausted. It had been a marvellous experience to organise the exhibition and although we had no doubt we would change a few things if we were to do everything the following week, overall it had gone well. We had the help of everyone in the Bolton Metropolitan and the Local Organisers from all three offices worked particularly hard.

At the end of 1988 Mary Corsair became our new Chairman and was first introduced to Bolton during the Jubilee Exhibition. She was to oversee many changes in her occupancy as Chairman in the coming years.

I had informed the Parks Department earlier in the year of our coming celebrations, asking if they would plant out a garden in our colours. They could not promise but if we sent them some information, they would do their best, they said. In August, we found the WRVS badge planted out in flowers in Queens Park, looking very smart.

A service in Manchester Cathedral was held, similar to the one in London, with rehearsals the day before. Each of the Metropolitan Organisers carried a mark of the service: I carried a dark red satin cushion with ivy, which was displayed on the WRVS badge. On the day of the service we took a coach full of members. It had been a very nice warm sunny day and after the service there was tea and sandwiches for the members who had taken part in the service but everyone else was expected to sit outside in the sunshine and wait. With the result that one of our members was so fed up she caught the bus home without anyone knowing, leaving us all waiting around for her for another half an hour. We were all a bit put out at having to wait, but then who could blame her – at least a cup of tea should have been given to everyone who attended.

Bolton Office organised a service in the Bolton Parish Church during August, following the same format as the one in Manchester.

We had a celebratory dinner at the Pack Horse Hotel for all WRVS members with Ald. Allenson, the Mayor of Bolton, and his wife Mrs. Mavis Allenson. The Mayor cut the large WRVS celebration cake with a ceremonial sword and several speeches were made and everyone enjoyed the evening.

The Rotary Club of Bolton presented me with a Paul Harris Fellowship, awarded for services to the community, at one of their Rotary meetings on a beautiful sunny day in June. It was indeed a prestigious award as very few women at that time had received it.

Betty Taylor had been the deputy Metropolitan Organiser for as long as I had been Organiser, but this last year had expressed a desire to retire in the coming months. She had enjoyed the year, which had been a wonderful one for both of us, but she had some health problems that needed to be addressed. Betty's job was an important one and I needed her level of support. Therefore, to be in place for the coming year I approached Dorothy Todd who agreed to take her place. Dorothy had been Deputy Local Organiser with Freda Clunie. We both agreed Sheila Leyland would be a good choice for Dorothy's replacement.

Betty Taylor was one of the nicest people I ever met, and one of the most willing. She was well thought of by everyone and had a great sense of humour. There was no doubt she would be greatly missed.

Apparently, in the period just before 1987, there had been growing concern amongst some of the more experienced Area Organisers concerning the future of the service. One of the main was whether the WRVS could comply with the demands of the Charities Commission, following changes in Charity Legislation introduced about that time. Barbara Shenfield the Chairman was due to retire in 1988 and had apparently not properly grasped the whole problem, which, make no mistake, was a huge problem. Other factors were also looming: the Government grant WRVS received was now in excess of £6 million but the Organisers questioned whether the grant would be allowed to continue rising. The turnover of money from the hospital projects was considerable as was the involvement with Meals on Wheels, Luncheon Clubs, prisons and courts canteens etc. The cost of administration for much of that work landed at the door of WRVS. It all needed addressing.

Barbara Shenfield retired at the end of 1998 and Mary Corsar became Chair; these problems Mary would have to deal with in the coming decade. One of the many things that needed consideration at that time was a decision to approach the Government requesting a survey of the whole of the work done by WRVS. Eventually Sir Phillip Woodfield was appointed. Sir Phillip, a senior civil servant, had a wide-ranging brief: he was to look at activities in all areas of WRVS work in England Wales and Scotland and talk to Social Services departments, hospitals, Health Authorities, prison governors etc. He also discussed with various government departments the work WRVS did in relation to the needs of the country. His report on these finding was to be delivered to WRVS Organisers at a future conference.

1989

Dorothy Todd started as deputy Metropolitan Organiser in the New Year, and her expertise was in food and Luncheon Clubs. Wherever you started work in WRVS was usually the place you remained, be it a Luncheon Club or the hospital. Dorothy had lots of experience, which would prove invaluable in the coming years.

In the past, we were always conscious that many volunteers coming to join were introduced into jobs because we were desperate in that particular area. This was often corrected as members became familiar with the service but I never thought it was the right way to go. We were at risk of losing these valuable members with the potential to take responsibility. I always felt I should find the time to interview every new recruit. In an ideal world, that was fine, but I was as committed as everyone else was. Earlier in the year, we decided that Freda Clunie would take the first interview of a new recruit. When she had enough people ready for the next stage, another meeting for new recruits was arranged, which gave me the opportunity to meet everyone. At these meetings, I explained what work our service did and our expectations from a volunteer. It was an excellent opportunity for me to meet new members as well as look for what potential they might have. Freda eventually enjoyed this work and felt she could expand it, given more time to concentrate on it. She had been Local Organiser for a number of years and done a good job. She had increased the work and the volunteers, putting the Lo-

Pat Cox at the Garden Party at Buckingham Palance, 1990

cal Office on a sound footing and now she was happy to take a lesser responsibility. During the course of 1989, she passed the reins of Bolton Local Organiser on to Sheila Leyland and then took up a new position as Training Organiser. Freda had been at the cutting edge of recruiting volunteers; she had done lots of interviewing and had a good feel for where a person might fit, knowing what an Organiser would be looking for in a volunteer and able to spot potential. By 1990, Freda was giving talks to 60 new members.

During the summer I received an invitation to go the Royal Garden Party at Buckingham Palace and I was so thrilled. In the past, members who went were allowed to wear whatever they liked, but now the rules had been changed and we had to wear uniform. I was

Pat Cox leaving the Bolton Office, pictured with Marian and Dorothy

not too disappointed by this decision, as it saved a lot of expense and worry. I did have one big worry however, in so much that as the time came nearer, British Rail were having one-day strikes on a Wednesday, the day of the Garden Party. I checked out hotels, thinking that maybe I would go the day before. Only the most expensive, costing over £200 for a room for one night, were available. I would need two nights, so I flew down and took the bus from the airport. There were about 15 members of WRVS from various areas throughout the country attending and we were meant to meet at Headquarters, and all go to the Palace together. However because of my difficulty in travelling I made my own way there and met up with everyone in the gardens. How did I know who were our members, amongst all the people attending? By their uniform of course! The day was sunny and very warm and we were a bit warm in uniform, but it did not deter from the wonder of it all.

Early in September I went to Area Office at the request of Lennie Holmes. At the start of the year, Lennie had taken over Margaret Spriggs's position as Area Organiser. It was always a big job, requiring a full staff. As Margaret left, some of her staff had retired and some moved on, so there was a place for a Deputy Area Organiser and Lennie asked me to consider it. I was very sad at the thought of leaving Bolton but if no one ever moved positions, nothing could grow, so I decided to try it. I asked Marian and Dorothy if they would consider taking over as joint Metropolitan Organisers at the start of 1990, which they eventually agreed to do.

It was a sad time for me, leaving the Bolton office, but I felt a great satisfaction knowing how much hard work had been done. Between us all we had created so much for the town of Bolton. Our members had increased from just over one hundred, to over six hundred. We had three offices with work in several areas. Members working in the hospitals had created many upgrades in the projects and earned thousands of pounds, all going back to the hospitals in refurbishment or gifts, benefitting local people staying in our hospitals.

The work in Luncheon Clubs had been phenomenal: from five clubs, where the meal came from Social Services kitchens to eighteen, where the majority of meals were cooked by volunteers on the premises. Meals on Wheels were again operating in Bolton along with six afternoon clubs for the Over-Sixties. Our three vehicles worked hard, with several of our clubs, including the three clubs for the disabled, bringing much pleasure to many. We now had a *News Talk* team and Mother and Baby clubs, a Contact centre and seven trolleys going into homes for the elderly around the district. The members managed all this as well as the existing work we inherited and Clothing had been expanded from opening just three mornings a week to five. In addition, there were Blood Donor sessions, visits to several war widows, plus the running of the Court Tea Bar. We had trained a very active Emergency Team, which now with our own trainers fulfilled our obligation to be ready for any incident when needed. This was indeed a record for anyone to take a pride in.

7

→ *Marian Hilton and Dorothy Todd* ←
Joint Metropolitan Organisers, 1990–92

1990

To take on an a job the size of Bolton area with its many projects had to be a great learning curve for Marian and Dorothy and they would undoubtedly take a while to become familiar with everything. For me, expansion had arrived comparatively slowly and as the increase in projects developed so did my expertise. It all happened as I grew with the job. However, the only way to become knowledgeable was to work at it constantly and I was confident that, given the right amount of time, they would do the job well.

After Marian and Dorothy took over the position of Joint Metropolitan Organisers, they set about putting their own individual mark on it. Marian asked Mavis Stubbs to join their team, becoming the Metropolitan secretary. The bonus for Mavis was the fact that Marian had been secretary for a couple of years, so was very able to give Mavis much help. Mavis had previously worked in Clothing, undertaken several other jobs, and had experience in office procedures before joining WRVS. Mickey Hale, our Organiser in Horwich, was leaving the area at the same time, so Pat Bentley moved from Farnworth Office to become Organiser at Horwich. Farnworth replaced Pat Bentley with Joyce Armitage. Joyce had previously worked at the Disabled Club in Farnworth and at Topholme Court Luncheon Club and had local knowledge of the area.

In a very short time there was a complete new team working in the Bolton Metropolitan Office. To announce their arrival, Marian and Dorothy planned an Open Day to mark the Queen Mother's 90th birthday celebrations in August. Rather that just have an Open Day they bravely did an Emergency Team mock-up in the yard behind the offices. Invitations went out to all the local organisations in the town, and the Mayor of Bolton, all the political Leaders and statutory bodies were invited, and they received a superb response. The lunch consisted of a wartime stew made in an original Soyer Boiler (the Soyer Boiler was used as an outdoor cooker during the Blitz.) The recipe was to be the same one used during the war, oldfashioned potato hash with onions, potatoes, meat and carrots although a bit of cheating was allowed, using Bisto for thickening. Wood was collected for the fire, and I'm sure there was a great deal of worry. Val remembers going into the office very early on the morning in question to a kitchen full of weeping women: the onions were of a very strong variety! Fortunately, worry was mixed with excitement – not only had they to concern themselves with the weather, but also would the fire stay alight long enough to cook the stew? The weather was not a problem and the wartime stew cooked well, creating a lot of interest with both the public and our members. It was a memorable day.

The Mayor of Bolton at the Open Day, with Lennie Holmes, Tom Sackville MP and Marian and Dorothy

Norma Gibbons had been with WRVS in Bolton since the early 1980s. She had worked on many different projects, from Luncheon Clubs, children's holidays, the Farnworth disabled club, and helped with many other projects over the years. However, for several years she had been Deputy Emergency Organiser to Betty Taylor and had now gained her Headquarters Instructors badge, recently moving to Area Office as Area Emergency Organiser. In the years to come, she proved to be a great strength to Lennie. The Area Organiser for Greater Manchester, Norma, eventually became the Division

Instructor for Emergency for the whole of the north west and really made her mark in WRVS.

1991

Farnworth Outreach Centre

Meetings had started for the Outreach Centre in Farnworth in early 1989 and after many meetings, lasting what seemed to me to be forever (the project had started initially when I was Organiser in Bolton) it was about to come to fruition. Alice Crompton, soon to become Chair of the group of organisations involved with the centre, had worked tirelessly to put together the five voluntary organisations in the refurbished Farnworth Clinic building. There was St John's Ambulance, Farnworth Mencap, the British Red Cross, Age Concern and the WRVS. Most of the organisations needed premises for administration and space for their particular activities. The WRVS needed a small administrational office with some space for clothing distribution. To accommodate so many differing organisations, each with their own ideas, all required more space than there was. Alice Crompton worked very hard trying to please each organisation – not an easy task.

Farnworth WRVS finally moved into their new premises in September. The clinic, as it had been known up till then, was situated on Albert Road and it was a nice clean modern building, more convenient for volunteers.

The Mayor of Bolton, Cllr. Geoffrey Smith, officially opened the Centre; the council had purchased the building in 1989 for £65,000 and they then looked to the Urban Aid Programme for help with conversion costs, which would be in the region of £150,000. Government grants totalling £75,000 had been pledged to keep the centre operational until 1993. It was considered a very important venture for Farnworth, providing a range of vital services for the people in the town.

Horwich WRVS had worked in the office behind the Council Offices since 1982. These premises were less than ideal, but had worked quite well and were inexpensive. The premises had served the needs of the volunteers quite adequately originally. However, when Horwich Council was looking to open an Outreach Centre similar to the one in Farnworth, the WRVS was interested in becoming part of it. In 1991, the WRVS moved their offices to the Resource Centre, Beaumont Road, Horwich. Horwich Council, in conjunction with Bolton Council, had funded the renovation of the Army Barracks on

Longworth Road. Considering the length of time the Farnworth Outreach Centre had taken, the speed with which the new Horwich Centre became available surprised everyone. The centre would provide a home for the WRVS, Archway and several other charities. Services to be available included the Community Psychiatric Nurses, Old People's Welfare Committee, Welfare Rights Advice and a crèche. Young people's groups included the Scouts and St Johns Ambulance which would operate in the evenings. The price charged for the use of the centre would be based on the time each group would spend at the centre and the space required.

The National Conference

The National Conference in 1991 was held in Nottingham and the great thrill was that the Princess Royal was to be the guest of honour. In her speech she praised the work done by the WRVS for families. The theme for the conference was 'Focus on Families: Highlighting and Addressing the Needs of Families in the Nineties'. Contact Centres and their work were explained in detail. Seminars were arranged for a number of subjects, and each member could chose two they wished to attend. There was an exhibition of work and firms were showing a range of goods used by the WRVS in shops and Luncheon Clubs. Nottingham Constabulary and the County Council displayed two special projects, one on domestic violence and one on a mobile crèche and a development project allowing women take part in forums connected with these.

Marian and Dorothy meeting Princess Anne at the conference, 1991

A new uniform was also introduced, the first since the mid–1970s. This was the conference that initiated the most dramatic changes to the WRVS. I am sure many members attending the conference would not have been aware of the degree of change that was to come from the conference of 1991.

Sir Phillip Woodhead gave his findings from a survey that had been taken the previous year.

The result of the survey on the WRVS was a report with a list of his recommendations. Devolving management to a more local level was one of the recommendations with the idea of creating Divisions in place of Areas. The appointment of a Chief Executive was another. Sir Phillip believed that the post of Chairman/Chief Executive was too much for one person considering how the service had grown. The WRVS also needed Trustees for governance of the Service; volunteer representatives would support the new Council that would emerge. The North West had four company members appointed and the Divisional Director was Lennie Holmes. In the Headquarters Annual Report for 1991, the Chairman recognised that changes need to be made and that some of the changes would be radical.

There were a great many members present at the conference, which was a wonderful experience and a great way of meeting like-minded people. Both Marian and Dorothy enjoyed their first conference immensely. They came back, as one did from a conference, full of ideas for the future of the Service, and also wearing the new uniform, soon to be available to everyone. However, the highlight for Marian and Dorothy had to be meeting the Princess Royal.

In her WRVS report for 1991, Marian commented on the slight drop in the numbers of people volunteering their services this year. In the past, we had enrolled approximately 70 new members each year but this year it was lower and we seemed to be losing more members than we had done in previous years. The climate of change was upon us as more and more women were going out to work. The opening of privately run children's nurseries had to have had some input over the past year, but unknown to many of us this was to be the start of many changes.

1992–93

In 1992 Pat Bentley left her job as Horwich Local Organiser and handed over to Sheila Johnson. By the end of 1992, Dorothy Todd resigned and Marian Hilton prepared to take on the full role of

Metropolitan Organiser. However Marian was only able to serve for about three months before her husband was diagnosed with a debilitating illness and she felt she had to lighten her load with WRVS and resigned from her position as Metropolitan Organiser in March 1993.

After working at Area Office during 1990–91, I took 1992 off from WRVS and returned at the beginning of 1993 as one of the temporary Liaison Officers, by which time the WRVS had changed its structure to Divisions. My job was to support the offices of North Manchester, Salford, Rochdale, Tameside, Wigan and Bolton so now I had to find an Organiser for Bolton. In the meantime, I would keep the office going. It was difficult as much of my time was taken up with my existing job, which involved quite a bit of travelling. However, with the little time I had to spare and much help from Shirley Woods, the Metropolitan secretary, and most of the other staff, we managed it. Sheila Leyland was asked if she would be interested in taking the position and agreed, however, it would be October of that year before she could start.

8

When Sheila accepted the position of Metropolitan Organiser in 1994, none of us had any idea of the upheaval there would be and the difficulties Sheila would encounter, nor how her job as Metropolitan Organiser would be such a different undertaking than any of the Organisers before her.

By April 1994 the changes in the Bolton staff began, with Doreen Gwyther having to resign her position as Food Organiser. Doreen hadn't enjoyed the best of health and had been hospitalised several times during the time I knew her. However, her health problems required another hospital stay and this time there would be a long recovery period. The Food Organiser's position had always had been a hard gap to fill, so now Sheila Leyland had to take on the Luncheon Clubs and keep them staffed until she was able to find another willing volunteer, as well as maintaining her role as Organiser.

As the hospital work expanded, we needed more and more recruits for new projects so volunteers for Luncheon Clubs became even harder to find. After a recent advert in the *Bolton Evening News*, we had over one hundred volunteers apply for work at the Ophthalmology Tea Bar. About the same time, we placed a similar advert for volunteers for a Luncheon Club, which was completely ineffective. I remember in 1993, when we were having problems staffing Rushey Fold Luncheon Club, having the good fortune to have a half-page advert in the *Bolton Evening News* for new recruits in Luncheon Clubs. It was an excellent article but still only brought us two new members. We now found ourselves in this sad demise yet again. Advertising did bring volunteers – there was never any doubt of that – but if people did not want to work in certain places, they did not volunteer.

Many of our existing members were not getting any younger and we were soon to be short of volunteers in many of the clubs. Not only was it volunteers we were short of, but in some clubs, also recipients for the meals we provided. This had never happened in the past, and was another sign of changes. However despite their staffing problems, most of the clubs kept their cookers cooking and their doors open.

By the time Sheila was making her first Annual Report, Joyce, the Organiser for Farnworth, had resigned and this was going to be another difficult role to fill. The Community Café that had opened only the previous year in Farnworth was struggling for customers, and in danger of closing. Prior to my retiring at the end of 1993 I attended a meeting with Sheila concerning the Café. As luck would have it, the Local Authority had opened a job club through the Youth Training Initiative in the same building and the young people using the club might use the facility which perhaps would solve our problems. Many of the volunteers involved with the café were pleased as they did not want to see the Café close. However, it did eventually close when it was still found to be unprofitable.

The Care in the Community policy altered the type of residents in many of the Local Authority homes for the elderly and closed some others. Also altered was the nature of some of the other homes, for instance the Lillian Hamer Home which changed to respite care and included an Asian Elders Day Centre. Thicketford House also became a day care centre – at one time we had trolleys in both these homes which were not now needed. There were changes in many areas of Social Services work that helped to change the nature of the work done by the WRVS.

However, with the passing of time, many of the residents were now frailer on admittance to their home for the elderly. Often they were not capable nor indeed needed the traditional trolley service. We became to realise that over a period of several years these changes had taken place slowly but surely. Trolley Shops because of loss of sales became uneconomic and could not recoup their running costs so eventually they closed.

Earlier in the year, an inspection took place at the Bolton Office and as the wiring was not up to the standard required, it needed replacing completely. The work started at the beginning of 1994 and by April was finished. When the offices had been redecorated and cleaned up, the working conditions were better, resulting in a nicer environment and a happy staff safe in the knowledge that the Health and Safety would not serve a closure order on their WRVS office.

Our previously long awaited new office premises in the Horwich Outreach Centre and were to close when the lease was up at the end of April to save costs. Another new initiative from Headquarters was that all Local Offices were to close and the staff would work from home with administration done though their Metropolitan Office. This was to apply to Sheila Johnson, Local Organiser for Horwich and Deputy Emergency Organiser for Bolton. Sheila would now work at home, coming into the office as and when she needed.

In 1995 Wigan Office had merged with Bolton, creating one large Metropolitan for the WRVS. The merger happened just after Sheila took over as Metropolitan Organiser. Her job became Metropolitan Organiser for Bolton and Wigan, as well as trying to cope with the vacant role of Food Organiser. She took on a seven-day Meals on Wheels in Leigh, and a few Luncheon Clubs and social clubs in Wigan. However later in the year she found a new Food Organiser to whom she was more than glad to delegate Luncheon Clubs and Meals on Wheels in Bolton and Wigan. Margaret Spriggs had recruited Barbara Harvey for us as she sailed around Australia on a cruise. Margaret had started talking to a person she met on the ship at a social gathering and was amazed to find that she lived in Bolton. Despite the fact that Margaret had almost retired from the WRVS she began to recruit her for Bolton. By the end of the trip, Margaret had extracted a promise from her that on her return she would contact the Bolton Organiser and she went into the office and got the job as Food Organiser.

The Wind of Change

Lennie Holmes, our previous Area Organiser for Greater Manchester, became a Divisional Director for the North West in 1993.

After the Woodhead Report in 1991 had been digested and the engaging of the new Chief Executive, Gerry Burton, whose brief it was to restructure the WRVS, making us accountable and bring us in line with Government policy, many changes were made. Just a few of them are outlined here.

A four-core plan was introduced at Headquarters consisting of Food Services, Hospitals Services, Emergency Services, and Community Services. At Headquarters, a Director of Operations whom the Core managers reported to was appointed, and in turn, he reported directly to the Chief Executive, Gerry Burton.

Primarily, we were to reduce our expenses in whatever way we could. WRVS had always received a Government grant, which covered office premises and expenses, also any personnel grants, and the general cost of running the WRVS. The size of the grant was becoming prohibitive and so cutbacks to make us more efficient had to be made.

The wind of change about to blow through the WRVS had started with the Woodhead Report and the Charities Commission. Following the Charities Act 1993, the WRVS took its new Registered Charity status. Prior to that, theWRVS was registered or at least the WRVS Trust was. When the Charitable Status of the WVS was established by Lady Reading many years before, the entry in the Charities Register consisted of literally a couple of sentences outlining the general purpose of the organisation. When VAT accounting was introduced, all transactions were paid through the WRVS Trust as that was the only part of the Service able to handle it.

Before the Charities Act 1993 came into force there was a long run-up period to give the various charities the time and space to improve their accounting methods and deal with issues like centralised accounting which would be necessary for audit purposes.' The WRVS was a huge organisation, with many projects, holding in some cases very large funds. A major change in the way we were to bank was another initiative coming from Headquarters.

Central banking was introduced partly to enable WRVS to produce satisfactory accounts for the Charities Commission, also having all project accounts with one major bank meant a deal could be struck in that all the small funds could be treated as one major fund so there was a higher rate of interest paid on the money – the bigger the pot the better the rate. Each project retained its own account and chequebook and still produced reports and accounts for the WRVS. Central banking also solved the problem that had occasionally occurred when the sudden disability or death of the authorised signatories on a club account meant that banks had to be persuaded to accept other signatories without the authorisation of the previous ones. In addition, many projects held bank accounts in a variety of banks and not all were handled as well as they might have been. Many were very small and perhaps seemed hardly worth the bother. However, in a few places large accounts also gave problems. I have to say these were not the norm; in general everyone was most careful but there are always a few exceptions to the rule. From now on, that time was going to be over. These were difficult changes to make; removing people's power caused much aggravation and some saw control of finances as power. However, over the years to come many changes in the WRVS over the length and breadth of the country were made.

For many the changes were seen as catastrophic, but we have to remember that change is often not popular and very few people like it. If we think of the length of time the WVS/WRVS had been operating and the many changes we had seen in Britain as a whole during this period it makes us realise the needs of society now were completely different to the needs of its earlier years.

Costcutting exercises were being implemented everywhere. For the training of its Emergency Teams and the training of trainers, the WRVS used the Police Training Centre at Easingwold, quite an expensive operation, causing the Chief Executive to think that maybe we should own our own Training Centre with accommodation that would include premises for Headquarters on the same site. When the centre was not needed by the WRVS, it could be rented out for a profit.

Milton Hill in Oxfordshire opened as a Training Centre with WRVS Head Office in the Garden House in 1997. There was a lot of activity before the opening due to the bedroom block being upgraded, and Head Office used the first floor of the main house for their work. The London property in Brixton was eventually disposed of with some difficulty because of a complex lease agreement. The Training Centre was purchased with appropriate Trust monies and in partnership with a Company of Conferencing and Training experts, who were bought out soon after by Initial. The Training Centre was proving to be successful and already had secured contracts for training from one of the largest IT companies. The Training Centre was eventually turned over to the company Initial to manage on a long lease. In return, WRVS retained 200 nights' accommodation free every year and a percentage of the turnover of the business. On many occasions the management committee had to be moved to other premises because the centre was fully booked, such was its popularity. The Centre was thus run at a profit and provided a return on the Trust monies.

Five years after the introduction of the new management, The Home Office undertook another scrutiny of the WRVS, which became known as the Compass Report as it was undertaken by a company called the Compass Partnership, a management consultancy specialising in not-for-profit organisations. The intention was to look at the Service and make recommendations as to how WRVS could self-fund in the future, as Government funding was expected to reduce over a 10-year period, to approximately £1 million a year, a loss of approximately £5 million. Formal fundraising was introduced at that time; the aim was to become self-funding in part, rather than as a whole. This was a difficult decision and one that many of the membership were unhappy with.

A Director of Fundraising and PR was appointed, with fundraisers appointed in the Divisions. They were employed on the basis that they would meet a target which consisted of their salary in addition to a figure of net fundraising. This was apparently normal practice in similar organisations. This appointment was still in place in 1998.

After the Compass Report, Cranfield Business School became involved with WRVS at Headquarters in the setting up of a future business planning strategy. Each Core of the service, e.g. Hospital Services, Food Services, Family Welfare and Emergency was to create a business plan for the future and to cost it. At the same time, the Divisional Directors were preparing a business plan for Volunteering, working with all the Cores to slot into their needs for volunteers. With the loss of Local Offices, the cost of recruiting was a major issue. The Divisional Directors had to work out how many volunteers WRVS needed to service the projects and how they would be managed and how much it would all cost. Recruiting and training volunteers has many hidden costs and they were asked to extract all costs and prepare and cost a business plan on that basis.

Much of Bolton's recruiting was easy and done by word of mouth or editorial advertising in the *Bolton Evening News*. This did not always bring results for every office as some offices did not have a rapport with their local newspaper like Bolton, so some actual advertising costs had to be dealt with. Without an office, one had to find a room in which to hold interviews and meetings, at minimum cost to the service. If this was not possible, some allowance had to be made for hire charges.

Food hygiene and handling and kitchen safety is often compulsory in outlets handling unsealed food. If there is no suitable venue or trainer then these costs might be borne through the Food Services or Hospital Services who might pick up the bill. The cost of registering volunteers and taking up references also had to be borne, as did the cost of providing badges and membership. In the view of several of the Directors, it was too theoretical, as the figures being talked about were too high to be practical, also the cost of recruiting, supporting and training volunteers was not being properly addressed. The only Core in with a fighting chance was Hospitals as there was a known value base before development. Everyone was aware of the profits made in hospitals. All this debating occupied the service up to 1998.

This process of reorganisation eventually led to the closure of the Bolton Office. The new structure went from Head Office to Division.

Eventually most Local and Metropolitan and County Offices closed.
Bolton was part of the North West Division, which stretched from
Cumbria to Staffordshire and Shropshire and also included
Derbyshire. However, boundaries for the Hospitals were smaller, as
there were so many hospitals, and a great deal of volunteers. Ann
Wood, Bolton's Hospital Organiser, amalgamated WRVS projects at
two hospitals in the Wigan area with several other projects and all
the projects in Bolton hospitals. With the reorganisation of the WRVS
Ann Wood became a Manager for Hospitals and Sheila Leyland a
Manager for Food Services at Division, which took effect in January
1997, hospitals first and Food following later.

In the early 1990s, the cost of running offices was realised. For the
Service as a whole, the offices were costing over half of the government grant. It was felt that the money should be used supporting the
work of the Service rather than tied up in bricks and mortar, also
many of the premises were substandard, and below HASAW standards, so that keeping open offices which needed staffing was not
the ideal. The North West had 120 of the 600 offices in the WRVS
portfolio. Lennie had to reduce this number to 40 over the first three
years. This was well before the Bolton Office closed. The Offices
funded by Local Authorities were unaffected.

After reorganisation took place, the Bolton Office remained open
until the last possible minute. Had they been involved with large
Meals on Wheels schemes as some other offices were, things might
have been different. A few Metropolitan Offices received funding
from the Local Authority, when their Meals on Wheels had large
rounds with several vans delivering meals. This saved the Local
Authority office space for administration and the running costs of
the service in general. This is what was required to upkeep an office.
Hospitals had always been our largest employer of volunteers but
that did not count.

It was a sad day when the WRVS office in Bolton closed, although
Headquarters benefitted from the eventual sale when it realised over
six times what the WRVS had paid for it in 1980.

Part Three

The work: 'It's the job that counts'

9

→ *Food Services* ←

Having made our mark throughout the 1960s by delivering Meals on Wheels, the WRVS eventually lost them but retained the Luncheon Clubs, with the meals provided by the Local Authority. The numbers of people coming to these clubs had dropped considerably however. At the start of Luncheon Clubs in the mid-1960s there were between 50 and 60 people every session, but now we were down to about 15 per session. However, the people using them still enjoyed the company. Although Luncheon Clubs were a relatively minor part of the WRVS's work in Bolton, for many of the Metropolitans Food was the major part of their service, with some running Meals on Wheels seven days a week and also operating several Luncheon Clubs.

The Start of Luncheon Clubs for Anchor Housing

St Luke's Luncheon Club

Margaret Spriggs rang one day to ask if I knew Anchor Housing had invited the WRVS to be involved with a Luncheon Club at St Luke's church on Chorley Old Road. St Luke's had been an old stone church that like many of its kind was too big for the needs of the community. The Anchor Housing Association had the church demolished and in its place they built the local community a smaller more comfortable church. At the side of the new church they built a retirement home for the community. I had not heard about this scheme, but when I said to Margaret that I would be happy to look at the project she went on to say, 'David Smith, an officer of Anchor

Housing, wants a meeting between himself, me, Olga Churchill, the Food Organiser at Area and yourself'.

At the meeting he explained he wanted a Luncheon Club for two days every week for some of the people living in the complex and some elderly people living close by. It was Anchor's intention not to have the Luncheon Club solely for the residents but to invite people from the locality also. He expected there would be many applications for this service. It was Anchor's policy to invite people from the surrounding area with the intention of spreading good-will. We were expected to cook a lunch and be self-financing, with the cost being comparable to Meals on Wheels in the district. The kitchen in the unit had not been completed so we were allowed to have some input, which was helpful. We were able to find room for a freezer, which in time proved essential. The potential for a very nice club was evident, the lounge area being well furnished and comfortable.

It was a particularly interesting project to me, as the Luncheon Clubs we had operated had worked very well over the years, but homecooked food had to be better. The people coming in for lunch could stay if they wished, and spend the afternoon in the comfort-able, warm and pleasant surroundings. I was completely unaware at that time how, in the not too distant future, our involvement with Anchor Housing would increase throughout the Bolton area. There-fore, it was at St Luke's we started to prepare for our first two-day Luncheon Club, cooking fresh food on the premises.

Staff at St Luke's Luncheon Club in the early nineties

I had regular meetings subsequently with David Smith, and visited another similar project looking for ideas to bring to the club. I talked to the volunteers at these projects, getting their input. As opening day drew closer, we recruited the right number of volunteers; five members per day were needed and the intention was to cook for a maximum of 25 people on each day. The same 25 did not come every week, although a few did, but for many it was once a week and for a few it might be once every two weeks. We managed to get the services of Pearl Hanson, a new member prepared to take on responsibility as Leader, with an excellent team of people to help her. Her particular forte was menu planning and the ability to manage a tight budget, having to purchase food and make a decent well-balanced meal costing just £1 to the recipient and cover all costs at the same time. There was no charge for fuel, just the food but it was still tight. Pearl did this and made a profit as well, ensuring extra funds for a special meal and a small gift when Christmas and Easter came along. The menus were done for a six-week period, making sure that if a person only came once a month she wouldn't get the same meal every time.

Pearl was able to cope in emergencies too, arriving as she did one day to find that the freezer had been accidentally switched off. Immediately she switched to ready-cooked food without anyone realising what had happened. After about two months, we opened on the second day Tuesday, with an equally good team. It was to this club in the 1980s that Mavis Gammidge of evacuation experience eventually came to work and stayed several years. Towards the end of her time at St Luke's she celebrated her eightieth birthday. As the years rolled by, we used St Luke's Luncheon Club as a role model for several other clubs. We were fortunate in finding members possessing equal talents in most of the fields we needed, and their ability to cope and levels of caring were second to none, and by now we had recruited a Food Organiser, Joan Walsh.

St Luke's mission statement was to include the needy in the local community alongside the needy in the facility. The warden sometimes had entertainment, and encouraged anyone to stay after the meal should he or she want to.

A review by the officers and staff of Anchor Housing Ltd done in 1995 told of how the use of social housing worked well for the community. To be working in partnership with other caring organisations had worked for tenants and for the elderly in the local communities, bringing a better understanding of their needs.

All Saints Church Luncheon Club

All Saints Church where I had collected toys in a previous year now had a new church, much smaller and more modern, which could be used as a community centre as well as their place of worship. The members did get their playgroup back, with new toys. The new Anchor Housing Association home now occupied the site where the church had stood, providing accommodation for the elderly of the district. Anchor made a suggestion to the churchwardens that the WRVS might be interested in opening a Luncheon Club in their new premises. This was not an Anchor Housing Luncheon Club they were proposing, but a Luncheon Club for the parishioners of All Saints church. Therefore, in November 1984 we opened yet another Luncheon Club in a cosy comfortable room, a big improvement to their original premises. The first Leader was Liz Collinson replaced a year later with Edna Shields, the wife of Stanley Shields our Transport Organiser. Edna told me that as Stanley was so busy she thought she would join too – if you can't beat 'em join 'em! Edna Shields worked in several Luncheon Clubs, eventually going to work at St Luke's.

Topholme Court Luncheon Club

I was invited to a meeting at a new facility to be called Topholme Court situated on Longcauseway, Farnworth, with a view to opening a two-day club similar to the ones we had opened previously.

Topholme Court Luncheon Club was to be available mainly for the residents but also to people from the local community. The intention was for the WRVS to collect some local people using our transport. The Local Authority requested we have a Leader who would work both days and be prepared to organise entertainment and activities. For this position, they required we employ one person.

An initiative had been approved recently whereby we could apply for a grant to the Charity Options Scheme, enabling us to fund a paid worker to help run the club for a year. Social Services told us of this scheme in the hope that we would apply. The WRVS applied for the grant and were successful. The person we were looking for had to be sympathetic and of course enjoy the company of the elderly. Her brief was to look after the people the WRVS brought in the ambulance, providing them with a cup of tea on arrival and some kind of entertainment after they had eaten lunch. It took most of the morning with two vehicles to collect the people who came to the club. As they arrived, they were able to enjoy the company of other members until lunchtime. With a Leader in place it meant that on arrival people coming to the club would be looked after while the WRVS cooked the meal.

After the news came through that we had obtained the grant, I advertised and had just one reply; Betty Roberts started working with us as the club opened. The WRVS employed her until the year's grant was up, then the Social Services Department took over her employment from us, putting her permanently on their payroll. We still needed more drivers and realised a grant could also be available for a driver for the ambulance on the Charity Options Scheme. That was a boom as we were able to have him drive at other venues whenever he was available. He did not start as the club opened, but a few months later.

Topholme Luncheon Club opened in April for one day a week to start with, extending to two days within the first month.

We were working on recruiting enough people to organize into two teams with a Leader for each day and hopefully an overall Leader. Certain projects lent themselves to volunteering but we were beginning to realise Luncheon Clubs were not amongst them. Many of our members had families at home and to work in the hospitals, Blood Donors, Clothing or in the office was a change of scenery, but to work in a kitchen was not. Although we had some stalwart members who did this job willingly, this was one of the times we wished we had many more. Doreen Gwyther, Mal Symons Daphne Kershaw and Joan Phillips were Leaders during the course of the club's life. Doreen Gwyther had joined the WRVS and had obvious potential as Leader. She had previously lived in London and was a professional singer. At her first Luncheon Club, she met Daphne Kershaw and later Joan Phillips. These three members made a sound team. Joan had come to work with the WRVS after losing her husband. I remember taking her to visit various projects and encouraging her to join the WRVS. At that time, she was not particularly interested in Luncheon Clubs saying she preferred to work at a hospital. One day we were desperate for volunteers at Eden Street Luncheon Club and I asked Joan if she would try it for a month as we had one member on holiday for two weeks and another member for the following two weeks. Joan ended up working permanently at a variety of Luncheon Clubs but in later years she did work at the hospital.

Ryelands Court and Rushey Fold

Ryelands Court Luncheon Club and Rushey Fold Luncheon Club were the last two clubs we would open for Anchor Housing Association. Ryelands Court was in Westhoughton and was started in 1986, and the venue was so warm and comfortable that during that year the disabled Luncheon Club that had opened in Westhoughton a couple of years previously was now incorporated into Ryelands Court. Those coming to the club all agreed the venue was an improvement. This club was operated in the same manner as Topholme Court Luncheon Club in Farnworth, using the ambulances to bring the elderly from the area for their meal to sit alongside residents of the home. Members from Westhoughton ran this club very successfully until the mid-nineties. However Ryelands never had a paid leader as did Topholme. It was a very pleasant venue and a lively and enjoyable club. Entertainment was in the main dependant on the season and time of year. In the year of the Royal Wedding of the Prince of Wales to Diana several of the clubs hired large TVs enabling them to all watch the wedding together and two couples at different clubs dressed in pearly king and queen's outfits. The schools were a great source of entertainment with children coming to sing. Trips out to a variety of places, including local shows during the evening, were especially enjoyed. At these clubs we had many characters working with us, who no doubt enjoyed the work they did. To entertain the elderly they went out of their way to make sure a good time was had by all, including themselves.

By the time we were opening Rushey Fold Luncheon Club we had to advertise yet again for volunteers. We needed cooks, one for each day. A lady came to join the WRVS from the same street in which Rushey Fold Club was situated, and was interviewed by Doreen. She had apparently said she would be prepared to do anything. The following day I visited her and accepted her offer to cook on both of the days we were to open. This was against everything I had ever wanted to do but it did turn out well in the end. Rushey Fold was another nice unit and it was suggested we might all put our names down at one of these homes for the future should we ever have need of it. After the opening of Ryelands Club and Rushey Fold Luncheon Club Doreen passed on the running of it to Pat Bentley and her original team in Westhoughton, then when Topholme Court Club opened the reins were passed to Joan Phillips and Mall Simmons.

Luncheon Clubs for the Local Authority in Bolton

Another unit similar to Campbell House, the afternoon club we ran in Farnworth, was being set up at Eldon Street, Tonge Moor, Bolton. The Officer for Day and Domiciliary Care, Mr Warren, said to the

Bolton Evening News that his department had inherited the building from the Housing Department and he was reported to have said that he hoped the WRVS could provide the staff to run a Luncheon Club at the premises in the near future.

There would be approximately 90 residents in Eldon Street when they had settled in, and a staff of seven Care Officers were to help residents who had difficulty preparing a meal. However, the residents could have as much or as little independence as they liked. After being contacted by Social Services, I went along with Dorothy Todd, the Deputy Organiser for Bolton Local Office to meet the staff who would to be looking after the unit when it opened. It was hoped that Dorothy would find the staff needed for the Luncheon Club and take responsibility for it when it started. We were to provide a meal for any of the residents who chose to come, including people from the surrounding area. Dorothy found a Leader and the volunteers needed. The club had a visit from the Mayor of Bolton, Cllr. Allan Briggs, along with Cllr. Mrs. Betty Hamer on its opening day. Some entertainment was provided by one of the club members, a 92-year old lady, Mrs. Livesey, on the piano. Mrs. Livesey had paid a visit to the club and had apparently been playing the piano for approximately 80 years, she told the newspaper reporter. This club was to expand its operations in the coming year by adding another day to its openings.

In most Luncheon Clubs, menus were prepared on a monthly basis. The meals were nutritious and good for the elderly and although likes and dislikes were taken into consideration, everyone did have to have the same meal on a club day. Imagine the confusion if we had to prepare separate meals. Often there were minor grumbles concerning the meals, but liver and onions on the menu created the loudest moans. We found it quite amazing as not only was liver nutritious but also it was a real Lancashire dish.

We had many good volunteers working in the Luncheon Clubs but Joan Walsh was our first Food Organiser and she was a great help in the setting up of St Luke's. Joan stayed with us for about two years but in that two years in addition to Luncheon Clubs she helped with many other projects including one of the Disabled Clubs and Emergency.

The Food Organiser following Joan was Doreen Gwyther who stayed with us until the mid–1990s helped by Daphne Kershaw and Joan Phillips.

Doreen was to help set up several clubs, including Eldon Street, Ryelands Court, Topholme Court, St Augustine's and Rushey Fold, with help from many volunteers over the years. Reliving some of her memories, Doreen talked of Alice who worked at Topholme Court who was wonderful in the kitchen, thinking of it as her own kitchen. She had recipes with her own names for them: mince beef cooked without onion was 'Mince', mince with onion was 'Savoury Mince'. One ingredient could change the name of a dish, however there was no doubt who the cook was on her day at Topholme – she was a treasure.

Doreen also worked at Eldon Street and recalls on one occasion cooking the lunch at home because of staff shortages. She had made a cottage pie for about 25 people. She woke up on the day of the Luncheon Club at 7.30 a.m. to a blanket of snow on the ground, which was not a problem until she found her car would not start. Not being able to reach anyone who might be able to help her, she set off to walk to the bus stop, waited quite a while but the bus never came, so she set off to walk to the next bus spot and then the bus passed her. That happened all the way from Bromley Cross to halfway down Tonge Moor Road. Eventually, carrying the pie for 25 people, the milk, and a few other bits like a jar of pickles and napkins, trudging through the snow, she arrived at her destination rather tired. However, she perked up until lunch was over, telling her tale to anyone who might listen. Then she asked one lady who was rather deaf and hadn't said much that morning 'How did you enjoy the pie, dear?'. She replied, 'It were all right but pickles were better'. Doreen sighed and thought 'All in a day's work'.

On a similar occasion after a particularly nice lunch at another club, Doreen asked a similar question to be told 'Aye dinner were all right, love, but misel' I cum fert custard and Bingo'.

Doreen and Daphne went every week to the cash and carry as many Leaders of clubs did, buying huge bags of custard powder, cake mixes and pastry mixes but always they used fresh vegetables and meat.

As people became aware of our vehicle, we were getting more and more requests for WRVS to provide transport. During 1995, in addition to our existing work we were asked to transport some of the less able members of a Luncheon Club that had been started in Moss Bank Park. We did not work for that Luncheon Club in any other way than transporting its members. We were invited to one of their special evening concerts where a troupe of dancers, all children, performed. It was a good night and the children were wonderful.

The church of the Sacred Heart in Westhoughton also asked us to provide transport for their Luncheon Club. This of course increased the need for more drivers so by the end of the year we were again advertising for more drivers.

Another Luncheon Club was opened at St Augustine's Court off Tonge Moor Road in 1987 bringing the total in the district to 14 and including the Disabled Clubs it jumped to 19 clubs. From first opening St. Augustine's Luncheon Club, we had a good group of members working there and one member I heard a lot about was Eileen, another good cook who worked with Doreen Gwyther as Leader for a number of years. However during the late 1980s when forms had to be filled in Lillian Punchaby helped out, which she did willingly, taking care of the forms to be filled in half-yearly. She really went beyond the call of duty by arranging the Luncheon Club's trips to a variety of places.

Such was the work in the Luncheon Clubs now that Doreen Gwyther, having started most Anchor clubs, looked after them and. Dorothy Todd, Deputy Leader for the Bolton Office, looked after the remainder of clubs in Bolton. Horwich Office took care of theirs and Farnworth their own afternoon clubs. As each Anchor Housing Club opened, eventually Doreen passed over the Leadership to the group running the club and moved on to the next one.

Meals on Wheels in Bolton for a Second Time

I received a call from Ian Hilton from Farnworth Social Services towards the end of 1987, explaining that Meals on Wheels in Farnworth had been organised for many years by Farnworth Old People's Welfare Group. They had operated successfully but now, due to lack of new volunteers coming forward and the increasing age of some of the existing members, they were giving up the following year. He asked if the WRVS would be interested in running the service. We were planning a very busy year for 1988 but this was something I was not going to turn down. We had not done Meals on Wheels in the Bolton area since 1974. I explained I was interested, but after speaking to Margaret Spriggs, our Area Organiser, I would get back to him, knowing she would be as interested as I was.

At the end of that year, I had given a membership talk to new volunteers who had been working with us for about three months. If the new member was happy to continue it was at that point that her WRVS badge was sent for. It also gave me the opportunity to meet the new members. I was always on the lookout for members

Meals on Wheels being delivered, 1988

with the potential or those willing to take some kind of responsibility, however small. With the thoughts of an Organiser for Meals
on Wheel in my mind, amongst the new members one day was
Sandra Badland. Her background included working alongside her
late husband in his business and she was well qualified for what
was required in a Leader. I asked her to remain after the meeting
broke up and put the proposition to her. She was sufficiently interested to come into the office the following week to discuss it further.

Sandra Badland accepted the position of Organiser for Meals on
Wheels, which was due to start on 1 February 1988. There was a lot
of preparation to replace the old People's Welfare Group who had
run the service for many years, along with several Luncheon Clubs,
very successfully. They had an Austin Metro van, bought specially
for the Meals on Wheels, for which they had raised the money. They
gave the van to us along with £1,200, which we invested for use when
a new vehicle was needed. Lillian Worthington was the Organiser
for the Meals Service and Sandra met her on several occasions during January. Sandra spoke highly of her, commenting on how much
help Lillian had given her. Sandra also visited the WRVS office in
Bury who had successfully operated a meals service seven days a
week for many years. It was from the members at the Bury WRVS
Office that Sandra gained the knowledge to prepare the books and
accounts needed for Social Services. Betty Taylor had had experience with Meals on Wheels in the 1960s so was a great help. Betty
and Sandra went out with the drivers from old Peoples Welfare on
their rounds, learning the routes. This was by far the most difficult
of tasks as many of the streets were not on a map and had to be
learned by heart, before passing on the information to new drivers.

Apart from the speed they drove, which was apparently quite fast the Old People's Welfare drivers did a great job and were very helpful to our members. The WRVS were to take meals out three days in every week, with Social Services taking them on the other two days. Fifty-three meals each day were delivered, which was almost too many in the one-and-a-half hour period over lunchtime. No one wants to eat lunch before 11.30 a.m. or much later than 1.30 p.m., so it was no wonder the drivers had to be quick off the mark. Sandra came up with a good idea. She suggested we deliver the meals slightly differently; if 40 meals were to be delivered from the van, and 13 by private car, it would cut the timescale down and there would be time to have a word with the people we delivered to instead of rushing in, placing the meal on the table and running out. The cost for the meal was 70p and any future vehicles were to be provided by the WRVS. However, maintenance, tax, and fuel for the van, and driver's expenses plus administration costs were paid by the Local Authority.

Administration for the service was done in the WRVS office and many messages were given and taken and lists were altered daily. Drivers collected the lists of people needing meals from the office, delivered the meals, collected the money then paid it into the office on their return and the admin assistant in the WRVS office banked it.

One of our admin assistants had joined the WRVS towards the end of the previous year. Freda interviewed the new lady but could find nothing that attracted her. The new Meals on Wheels were mentioned but she wasn't keen on that either. Freda then suggested the admin work for the Meals on Wheels, a job she was willing to try.

Dorothy Kelly was a kind lady with a good sense of humour and her stories were very funny as she later related them in the office.

'We had a lady on the phone this morning as I arrived [she arrived at 10 a.m.] saying "Where's me dinner, it's not come yet"'

To which Dorothy replied 'No it won't have, it's not due till about twelve, don't worry, you won't be forgotten.'

'But I'm hungry now, I've bin up since five-thirty.'

'Well love, I can't do anything for you, wait a bit, have a sleep, then you will feel better.'

'Aye okay, I'll try, ta-ra.'

This conversation took place every Monday morning without fail. After a few years, our rounds were changed from the Farnworth area to an area of Bromley Cross. The change over took place quite successfully and all was well until the following Monday morning when, the same lady rang, saying 'Me dinner's not come again'. Dorothy proceeded to tell her of the change of plans and that she would have to ring Social Services, they would sort her out.

'Why, are they doin' the dinners now?'

'Well, yes they are,' Dorothy said, not wanting to confuse the lady any more that necessary.

Therefore, for a few weeks the calls stopped. One Monday she rang again and said 'Them meals they send now, they're not as good as what you sent, and can I change back?' By now, the lady and Dorothy had become firm friends. The meals were the same so Dorothy could only presume it was not the meals but the drivers and mates she enjoyed seeing and the Monday morning chats on the phone.

An elderly man would ring, saying 'Eh, I'm sick of 'avin mince, can you send me a pork chop?' To which Dorothy answered 'Certainly, I will order it for you today'. (Aware he would forget, but trying to humour him, as we had no control with menus of course.) 'However, it will be next week now before I can do that.'

'Well, that's okay, thanks very much love.'

That conversation also went on for a few weeks, changing his order as his fancy for a variety of food changed.

Another man threatened one week to cancel his meals forever if they brought him rice pudding again, and you can guess what happened next – as the driver took the lid of the container this particular day it was rice pudding again. She eventually convinced him not to cancel, as he had no one else to cook for him. The ladies were the ones who were the most grateful, probably having a meal made for them was appreciated as more of a treat.

In essence, our Meals on Wheels service was not as large an operation as it had been in the early 1960s. However, every year we took 7,600 meals to the housebound elderly. The constant problem of new volunteers reared its head regularly but we kept going. The one day we did not deliver meals was Christmas Day, a day when the family normally stepped in. However, a lovely story was related to me this year of one of our helpers who, realising two of our recipients would not be having a Christmas dinner as they had no family living close by, cooked extra food for her own Christmas dinner, and delivered it herself to the elderly couple on Christmas morning: what a great gesture.

The Demise of our Luncheon Clubs throughout the 1990s

Most of the clubs at which we were cooking on the premises were in sheltered housing they had opened as the first residents moved in, but over the years the residents in the homes became older and frailer, gradually becoming housebound and in some cases moving to nursing homes. The new people moving in were often active and mobile and could get out in the community. For instance, the residents at St Luke's had to be able to look after themselves to be accepted as tenants. Rushey Fold Home was the only home that employed carers. It was suggested that on the whole older people had become fitter and healthier and were able to retain their independence longer, and many more were mobile and self-sufficient to a greater age and no longer were in need of the type of Luncheon Clubs we were providing. This had happened once before: when we had first started Luncheon Clubs in the 1960s the numbers were around 60 per session although at that time they met in church halls not half as comfortable as the ones we opened in the 1980s. In the late 1970s people wanted higher standards and better facilities and numbers fell. Maybe it was happening again – facilities were good but people needed some sort of change. On the other end of the scale, the ones that needed care were older and needed care to a greater level. Several of our clubs did provide transport, but not all of them, so we were not able to cater for the people who could only leave home with help. In addition, with the advent of Care in the Community, services such as Meals on Wheels and day centres had expanded, which had to be good for the people in need of care.

At the height of the 1980s, in the Bolton, Farnworth and Horwich area the WRVS were serving thousands of meals each year. Volunteers had always done the cooking and often they were older than the recipients were, however in spite of many appeals for help, replacements were getting fewer. Luncheon Clubs had been struggling for volunteers for some time; often a team that worked together for years would lose a couple of volunteers, putting the harmony of the team at risk. When a new volunteer stepped in to help, very often it 'Was not the same' and the new volunteer often had a hard time settling and the existing team missed their friends who had left. This was not the case in all clubs but it had happened in certain places. Recruitment of a volunteer who would fit in with the existing team was not an easy task. On several occasions, the retirement of one volunteer led to the loss of the whole team.

The Clubs that had opened in 1964 by now were on the brink of closure. I suppose we should have been glad they had lasted so long, as some of the premises left a lot to be desired. They were mainly church halls, mostly warm places but without the comforts required today In the early 1990s Trinity Methodists and Tonge Fold had closed along with Avondale, Chorley Old Road, and Sutton Trust at Over Hulton.

Eldon Street was one of the first Luncheon Clubs to close. Apparently, at about that time the kitchen was found not to be up to the required levels and meals had to be delivered to the club from the central kitchens. The result was that the club turned into a 'pair of hands' club, where the food was served by WRVS members but prepared elsewhere. Soon after this happened, a decision was made by the Council to change the usage of the premises, resulting in the services of the WRVS being no longer required. Unfortunately, the Luncheon Club at Eden Street finished in the same year. In the earlier years when we first started opening new Luncheon Clubs there was often a waiting list for places as they were so popular. However, in recent years attendances had been in decline so where we operated a two-day club it became more practical to have just one session a week with a good attendance and merge our decreasing teams of volunteers.

The circumstances of many people who had volunteered in times past had also changed, more and more people were working, particularly younger women. Nursery care was more easily available so mothers of school-age children were able and often needed to work. Early retirees were still volunteering but many were not attracted to the weekly commitment needed in many of the Luncheon Clubs. Many people, having retired early, had the yen to travel more, and for many grandparents, their grandchildren commitments lessened their ability to volunteer on a regular basis. It looked as though times had changed.

Aspinall Luncheon Club in Horwich closed in 1992, followed by the Hilton Centre Luncheon Club in April 1993. However, Blackrod Luncheon Club, even when their numbers were in decline continued to work for many years and in the end found it was the rent increases as well as falling membership that helped to hasten their closure, nevertheless the team worked for 15 years before eventually closing its doors in February 1999.

By the end of 1996, the level of volunteers at Topholme Court was so low that ready cooked food was served to the recipients at the home in the absence of members to cook. Sheila was asked to start cooking again, but considering the absence of volunteers, thought it unwise.

At the end of 1997 Sheila Leyland had changed her job as Metropolitan Organiser, becoming the Food Manager at Division, increasing her patch tremendously. She became responsible for Food for the WRVS in Greater Manchester with the exception of Tameside which had already lost its Food projects.

As the position of Metropolitan Organiser in Bolton had been abolished for the time being Sheila was taking responsibility for both the WRVS office with all its problems and Divisional Food Organiser. Eventually she enrolled Barbara Harvey as the Food Organiser for Bolton. Sheila reports that after 1998 several clubs remained open and Wheels on Wheels continued until March 1999.

10

→ *Family Welfare* ←

Work with the disabled from 1980

News Talk

Bolton *News Talk* started in 1982 at a request from Social Services and consisted of cassette tapes of talking newspapers for the blind. The *News Talk* team at this time wanted to increase their numbers and asked the WRVS if we could help. We agreed to help and provided eight members for two teams. I went along to watch some recording. May Fielding and Freda Clunie were most effective. I thought it looked quite technical and was most impressed with the work they did. Each member required training. The master tape contained news items mainly from the *Bolton Evening News*, for partially sighted and blind people and was recorded by volunteers every Sunday in a studio in Castle Street, Bolton. The operation involved many different skills by several people: editors, producers, technicians and narrators, and at the end of a session a master tape was produced from which two copies were made for other teams to copy the number required. Each Monday evening, the copying of the tapes was done in Castle Street Centre by different teams of volunteers from a variety of voluntary organisations, everyone working on a rota. The volunteers made around 350 tapes in total, which were checked then posted to residents of Bolton needing these tapes. It was a worthwhile programme, given freely to the people of Bolton by the voluntary organisations of Bolton.

Wheelers and Wobblers Club for the disabled

At a meeting at Age Concern in 1979 Ian Hilton, one of the development officers for Social Services for Farnworth, had said he would like to see a club in Farnworth for the disabled. He said there had been such a club previously, operating from Holland School, Market Street, but it had disbanded a few years previously. We agreed to make a start, contacting as many of the old members of that club as we could find. Ian had given me the name of a person involved with the last club as he thought she may be interested to help with a new one.

Prior to any thoughts of starting a club for the disabled, I had attended a conference at the Area Office dealing particularly with the needs of the disabled, so with this in mind, Farnworth and its needs appeared to come together. We had discussed at the conference not only the benefits these clubs brought to the disabled person, but also to the carer of that person the benefits were immeasurable.

I took along a good friend, Lillian Punchaby, who had just joined the WRVS working in the Courts Tea Bar. We met the person in question in her own home; she suggested we visit her on one of her days at the Jubilee Centre, Bolton's Local Authority Centre for the Disabled in Darley Street, Bolton. That was a real revelation and she introduced us to several people who she thought might be interested in the re-opening of a club in Farnworth. After discussing transport, we realised this would be the greatest difficulty. Several of the people interested in coming were in wheelchairs, including some whose legs did not bend at all, so sitting in a car was not possible. We realised we had at least three people with those difficulties, making the problem seem insurmountable. However the husband of one on these ladies offered his services, saying he was very familiar with his wife's difficulties and would be prepared to bring not only her to the club, but anyone else needing this type of transport and would instruct us in how to manage patients with these difficulties. He informed us we had to open both back doors (so it had to be a four-door car), we then should sit the person on the seat going round to the other back door and gently sliding him or her in so that they could sit comfortably without bending their knees. His name was Albert Murtha and he stayed with the club long after his wife died, until the time the club closed, some 20 years later. The members of this club were so brave to put themselves into our inexperienced hands. We had taken possession of a WRVS-owned car the previous year and garaged it at St George's church, and in the months to come this proved a great help.

On one day in June we managed to get all our people there, with lunch being prepared in the kitchen. Sixty-four people sat down to lunch on the first day. We had a great feeling of satisfaction then Lillian said 'What are we going to do with them for entertainment this afternoon?' and staring at each other we both said simultaneously 'I've no idea!' Having got all the new members to the club, then served lunch, we had forgotten to organise any entertainment.

Lillian dashed across to Salter's sports shop on Market Street and bought a boxed game of Bingo, which we all played after lunch. The next club day we were more prepared, having discussed at length a programme for the coming year. On a cold day in October 1980 Lillian Punchaby took over as Club Leader and Pat Edmondson as Deputy Area Organiser.

The Club eventually took the name of 'The Wheelers and Wobblers'. Lillian had arranged a competition for the most appropriate name and The Wheelers and Wobblers won easily. The person who suggested it said, as she watched members arrive at the club she realised they were either wheeled in or they wobbled in. Lillian organised a Christmas Fair at which we all helped, the funds going towards a trip the following year. There were parties for everything: Christmas, Easter and special birthdays.

Norma Gibbons and Lillian remember particularly well the day trips out, and making sure they had been to the toilet before lunch, which was quite an operation. These days, there are toilets for disabled in most places but not in the early 1980s. After lunch, the club members were taken out in wheelchairs for a trip to the shops and to many of our

The Wheelers and Wobblers setting off for a trip to Southport .

members this was their biggest thrill. In some cases, they went to the nearest pub, only to find several others had arrived there first.On one memorable trip to Blackpool we had lunch at the Norbreck Castle Hotel and a walk along the cliffs at Bispham afterwards with a convoy of 28 wheelchairs. It was the first club we had opened in Farnworth, and the first under my tenure and it was to last until the end of the century some 20 years later.

In 1981, the club for the blind and partially sighted was opened and although clubs for the disabled were a lot of fun they were a nightmare when trying to sort out the necessary transport as we had to make sure there were enough members with cars who were willing to help. At the Bolton Office one day in 1983, imagine our surprise when Lillian Punchaby rang to say she had been offered an ambulance for use in Farnworth at no cost.

'Can I accept it?' she asked

I was astounded, saying 'Who on earth has offered you an ambulance and why would they give it to us?'

'It's the Multiple Sclerosis Society; they have bought a new vehicle and this one is twenty years old and really quite worthless. They will not get anything for it if they sell it, and they know how we struggle at times. They assured me it is in good working order and plenty of life left in it. Pat, it will help a lot with collecting members. It will also help the Blind Club', she said in her usual positive way.

Members of Farnworth Blind Club with the old ambulance

'I know it will,' I said, trying hard to think on my feet and sound equally as positive at the same time 'Nevertheless I will have to ring Area Office. I'm sure we will be expected to pay for any repairs it might need, Headquarters couldn't take on the running of a 20-year-old vehicle' I said, thinking out loud. 'I will ring you back as soon as I have spoken to Margaret Spriggs.'

Margaret's comment was 'As long as you think it is in good working order and it will not cost Headquarters anything, I would go for it. However I might suggest you get it looked over before you take it.'

We took it on and never regretted it once. It certainly made life a lot easier for the Wheelers and Wobblers and for the club Farnworth WRVS were soon to be opening for the blind and partially sighted.

The ambulance gave us several years of service and did many trips to the seaside and days out, as well as bringing in members for the club days. However, during the course of 1984, the ambulance was beginning to give us problems. It was threatening to cost us a lot of money for repairs or be deemed unsafe to use. We were at a crossroads; having begun to rely heavily on having a vehicle the thought now was would we have to abandon it? If we did, what would we do for transportation to these clubs? When the clubs had first started, we had members who were prepared to use their cars to transport the people to the club. However, now that was not an option as the workload had grown tremendously and the volunteers who had used their cars at the start, were doing other work. Yet there was no doubt the clubs had to continue. The pleasure derived from them by the people using them was obvious. Whenever anyone visited the clubs they always came away feeling better, as the members we had were some of the nicest people, most of them with such good attitudes to life despite some of the most devastating physical conditions. They did appreciate everything done for them; a club day, a day out or even a holiday.

Ambulance Appeal

Lillian Punchaby announced one day that the Wheelers and Wobblers were starting an appeal to raise money for a new vehicle. I could not believe what I was hearing – we needed this vehicle badly but it was such a huge undertaking and I wondered if we would manage it. I realised very soon if we did try and raise the money it had to be an appeal by all our members, not just the members from Farnworth. At that time, I could only think of all the work it would create, and we were already very busy. However, we were fortunate to have lots of enthusiasm from members like Lillian so maybe it was a possibility. I called a meeting of the staff to discuss it.

I spoke at length to various members who had never worked in any of these clubs, explaining the work we did for the disabled and elderly and that if we intended to continue, we had to do something. Fortunately everyone agreed, promising help where they could.

The thoughts of fundraising for something as expensive as an ambulance with our existing workload seemed quite forbidding. Before the meeting, I enquired from our Area Office which way we should go about it. I explored the possibility of asking permission from the Health Authority to use money made in the hospital projects, but was told we could not do that. The WRVS was funded by a Government grant and because of this funding were not allowed to fundraise directly under the WRVS name. Margaret Spriggs suggested I try to form a committee to do it on our behalf.

'There is nothing to stop you helping in the raising of the money, but you can't fundraise in our name', she said.

A committee to act as a front for us had to be the only way forward.

I went to see the Director of Finance for the Health Authority, Richard Sutherland. to get his help and ideas. We talked the whole thing through and he suggested people who might help us. He rang John Bradley from the firm of architects Bradley, Cuthbert and Towel, explaining our problem, with a view to him and others forming a committee for us. Richard arranged for me to see John Bradley the following week. John was interested in the work we did, and how we should go about raising the money required. At the end of that first meeting, suggestions had been made as to whom we were going to ask to join us. For the next meeting we had the basis of a committee of five: John Bradley, Richard Hurst, Muriel Arkwright, Betty Taylor and I. In the years to come, I could not believe how kind they were in giving their time to come every month and listen to how we had done during the previous weeks. They did it with great enthusiasm right up to the end of the appeal.

The next time I met Lillian she greeted me with 'I have been given our first donation from a 12-year-old boy, Michael Kay, the young son of Carol Kay the Joint Organiser of the Blackrod Luncheon Club. He raised £50 by running in a six mile marathon.' Our aim was £15,000 so we only had another £14,950 to go. At that time, it appeared to be a mountain.

Monthly meetings of the committee took place at John Bradley's offices. Present at most meetings were John, Richard Hurst and Muriel Arkwright, along with Betty and myself. We discussed the various ideas we all had, what donations we had received and what our proposed fundraising activities were, and a meeting at the WRVS office followed on from this to keep everyone there up to date and informed. Several times, the nature of the appeal had to be changed.

Kathleen from the Bolton Office was our Committee Secretary and Alan Summerfield, Manager of the Farnworth branch of The Royal Bank of Scotland, agreed to be our Treasurer.

The Appeal was launched in style with a lunch at Smithills Coaching House, inviting people from local business, town officials and anyone we felt might help. Members of the committee spoke on our behalf explaining why we needed these vehicles, and what they would be used for and Angela Kelly, the Women's Editor for the *Bolton Evening News* promised us good coverage on our fundraising events.

Several large events were planned for the coming year. Horwich wanted to try their hand at an auction to take place later that year, with all our members helping. Lillian Rawlinson talked to Angela from the *Bolton Evening News* aware that advertising for goods would give us the publicity we needed. Through the efforts of the *Bolton Evening News*, we acquired many items to be sold on the night. The event was held at Horwich Leisure Centre and raised over £1,000.

A fundraising party at my home also raised £1,000; a coffee morning and crockery sale at the Town Hall raised £500; Farnworth Office organised a raffle with a computer as first prize, given to us by Patrick, the husband of Norma Gibbons. After selling thousands of books of raffle tickets, most of them sold by the members from Farnworth Office they raised yet another £1000 for the fund.

Many of the clubs had their own fundraising ideas and events, from wheelchair pushes done by the Wheeler and Wobblers to variety concerts. The wheelchair push attracted quite a crowd of members wishing to take part. It was decided that Lillian should borrow enough chairs from the Jubilee Centre. A chair was borrowed for everyone that needed one, and a WRVS member or friend of a member found to push it. However, on the day of the push, the police came to check what was going on and who was in charge of this somewhat large and rather unruly group of folk in wheelchairs.

To the request from a constable 'Who is in charge here?' we all passed the buck to Lillian. Unbeknown to her we should have informed the police of the gathering that was taking place. On hearing of our intentions they were very cooperative, telling us next time we decided to do anything remotely similar, remember to get their permission.

Local schools supported us, as did local businesses. Many members raised amounts through their own initiative, often in their own homes. By the time the Christmas holidays arrived, we were well on our way to achieving our goal. Our next problem was going to be, who would look after the vehicle? We needed a person who would take control of the cleaning of the van, sort out petrol and paperwork for Headquarters, plus repairs when needed. Kathleen put an advert in the *Bolton Evening News* and Stanley Shields answered it. He very quickly became a great asset to WRVS, working several days a week, and always with a smile.

During the first quarter of the year fundraising for the ambulance continued and I was able to place an order for a vehicle. When we first started with the appeal, I visited various garages to familiarise myself with the type of vehicle we would need. I think, looking back now, I imagined a vehicle would be sitting on the proverbial shelf, waiting for me. Of course, I soon found out it was not like that. I had to decide on a van that was large enough then plan the fitting out of the vehicle with help from the garage fitters.

As the months went by, Betty Taylor and I continued to meet with the members of our official committee, and we discussed the type of vehicle we needed and the maintenance issues. The idea was becoming a fact – we were going to make it. We were getting quite excited.

During this period, Stanley Shields offered to take on the full responsibility for the vehicle when we eventually got it. He had some experience with vehicles and helped us decide on the type we needed.

The fund was doing better than our wildest dreams. Support came from everyone and we were very thrilled. We began to look at the work the van had to do when it did arrive. Horwich were working hard for the fund, looking forward to being able to use it on Wednesdays for their Club for the Disabled, as up to now they had used members' cars just as Farnworth had done. Farnworth were working just as hard for the fund with fewer members and were looking forward to using it for their Club for the Blind getting rid of the old vehicle which was by now causing some trouble and letting them down, and if it broke down members could not be brought into the club. Both these clubs were operated on Wednesdays. The club for the disabled, the Wheelers and Wobblers in Farnworth was also expanding and we were beginning to think one vehicle might not be enough. It crossed my mind more than once whether we could raise enough money to buy two vehicles – it had to be worth some discussion at the next meeting.

When the first vehicle was due, we were all excited and wondering how we should publicise its arrival. We had talked about it but could not decide in the light of a possible second vehicle. I thought we should back off, and let the fund run on until October when it was scheduled to finish anyway. We should wait and see what we could achieve by October rather than have an early finish to the appeal, a regret we might have later. The demand for our services was looking as though there could be work for two vehicles. It was a pleasing moment when Stanley collected the first vehicle in March and delivered it to my drive at Albert Road, where it was kept, no WRVS premises being available.

During the spring and summer, we received many donations, all worthy of a mention but these were just a few of them.

- £5000 from Joint Funding recommended by the Health Authority, and £5000 from the Urban Aid Fund
- Horwich Inner Wheel presented us with the proceeds of a Fashion show given by Miss Kenyon raising £350
- A presentation to us from Bolton-le-Moors Inner Wheel charity fund of £72
- There were several anonymous donations including one of £500 and despite the fact we were unaware where they came from, we were so grateful.
- We had a splendid offer from Warburton's Brass Band to perform a concert for the appeal held in the Jubilee Centre
- Bolton Barbershop did a show at a dance held at Horwich Golf Club who also kindly gave their premises for our use.
- Lillian Punchaby, Organiser of the Wheelers and Wobblers Club, organised an Autumn Starlight Show at The Jubilee Centre. Lillian took a coach full of people from her club the Wheelers and Wobblers and sold tickets to everyone she met in the weeks before the show. It was an excellent show given by Bolton Barber Shop Choir and the Chantelles.
- Lindsey Banks School of Dancing Show did a show and donated the proceeds.
- Help the Aged donated their charity fund to us, which was a surprising £2000.

We continued the appeal until October and hoped we would have enough for the extra vehicle, which by now we needed. During the early summer, Stanley was able to place an order for the second one. It was a great achievement by so many people. We heard at the end

*Pat Cox, Muriel Arkwright, John Bradley, Richard Hurst and Betty Taylor
at the handover of the new ambulances*

of August that the second vehicle was ready for collection and it was
to be garaged at John Oxford's home. Stanley went to collect it and
took responsibility now for both vehicles. We prepared a handover
of the vehicles and a celebration with our committee and the members who had worked so hard.

The handover happened in October. Again, we had long discussions on how and where we would make the official handover. We

A donation to the ambulance appeal from St James's School, New Bury, Farnworth

*Mr. Geoffrey Redgate accepting a donation for the ambulance appeal
from Bolton Round Table*

decided to invite everyone we knew had made significant contributions. The final decision for the venue was Bolton School Tennis Pavilion. It was a memorable day and everyone felt delighted with the final achievement.

We had started the appeal with the hope of raising £15,000 to buy one adapted vehicle, and ended with enough to buy two and have enough left over to maintain them both for the foreseeable future.

One of the last donations we received for the ambulance appeal was from Bolton Round Table. It was to be presented at their AGM by their retiring Chairman, Alex Henshaw and Mr Geoffrey Redgate was to receive it on behalf of the WRVS as he was a Patron of the appeal and had received cheques on our behalf many times. Little did we know that night it would be one of the last presentations he would make, if not the last. Just two days later, the *Bolton Evening News* reported the death of Mr Geoffrey Redgate. It was a big shock to the whole of Bolton as Mr Redgate had always looked a picture of health. He had been Chairman of Bolton Health Authority since 1975. Many tributes were made to his exemplary service to education for the deaf and continuing service and support to Bolton.

Towards the end of 1985, Freda Clunie came into the Met office with a smile on her face, saying that Social Services had rung to ask if we would be interested in opening a Tea Dance at Cobden Community Centre in Halliwell.

'Well Freda, that's a new one, do you know where is it?'

'Yes, the centre is behind Charlotte Street at All Saints church. I think it is an experiment, but Social Services think it will go down well. If I can get the volunteers, we'll have a go.'

In what seemed no time all it was up and running and about to open once a week from 2 p.m. until 4.15 p.m., with Florence Ball and her husband Arthur to lead the couples around the floor. I was able to be there at the opening, and Freda had a lively group of volunteers and Edna Eckersley and Alice Sandiford were the Leaders.

On the first day, 24 people became members which was a good start. I felt from that start they should do well as their numbers were sure to increase, but they did not rise as quickly as we had imagined so to the rescue again came the *Bolton Evening News* with a comment and a picture. Sure enough, it worked again and the following week the helpers were sending out for bread for extra sandwiches and extra cakes for the afternoon tea. From 24 people the previous week, that day 84 were dancing around the room, the numbers eventually settled at around 60 but the experiment had been a great success.

Due to a heavy fall of snow in December, the Disabled Club in Farnworth had their Christmas Party this year postponed until the following spring. We had decided when the transporting of people began that transporting anyone in the snow was not an option. The organisation was covered for public liability and the vehicle had its own insurance but in walking a person from their own doorstep to the vehicle, no one could assure us as to any cover we might or might not have. It was too risky.

During the course of 1986, this club moved its premises from Holland School to a newly refurbished ambulance station where it continued to flourish. In 1989 through difficulties in recruiting volunteers for cooking Social Services began to bring meals in. Our numbers of recipients began to diminish although it was still a good club, remaining open until 2000. Lillian gave up as Organiser in 1992 and was replaced by an existing member, Joan Preston who was Organiser until the club closed.

Over the years I was Organiser, I had given talks each year on the work of the WRVS several times during the course of the winter. On one occasion, I was asked to give a talk to Farnworth Rotary Club and at about the time I gave a talk, the ambulance appeal was just ending. That day I spoke of the work done in Disabled Clubs and our many helpers. Several weeks later, I received a letter from the Rotary Club explaining that Farnworth Rotary had considered giving an award to one person in the voluntary sector who had worked hard and gone above and beyond the call of duty. They asked if I would recommend someone I felt deserved the award. It was discussed in the office and the decision was unanimous. We recommended Albert Murtha from Farnworth. He had looked after his wife who suffered greatly with arthritis and was in a wheelchair. He also helped at Age Concern and took several people to the Jubilee Centre. Albert was one of our most willing drivers. I had the pleasure a few weeks later of going back to Farnworth Rotary Club to see him receive his award.

Children's Holiday's

I went to a meeting at Area Office in the earlier part of 1981 organised by Rita Waite, the Children's Holiday Organiser at Area. I was very impressed with Rita and her enthusiasm for children's holidays. I returned to our office feeling we should be preparing to send as many children in need as we could possibly afford. A meeting of members who I thought might be interested in being involved was organised at our office to explain what children's holidays WRVS-style was all about. Joyce Scully attended that meeting and came forward at the end and offered to organise this operation and form a team to help from members at the meeting that day. We were expected to contribute to the cost of sending children on holiday, but Rita had made us aware that a fund was available for charity schemes such as this, called the Urban Aid Fund available from the Local Authority. A Metropolitan wishing to be involved in the holiday scheme had to first try to obtain any funding that might be available. This was not to say that if we had no funding we could not apply to send a child on holiday. However, Area Office had only so much funding available. Finding our own was a better option. Kathleen our secretary sent off for the necessary application forms and we eventually received £500. The money was sent to Area Office and helped to send twenty boys to an adventure camp on the Wirral. The Adventure camp was a boy's only camp in 1981 but the people running the camp gave the boys going a great time, introducing pursuits many boys were never likely to come across. To send the children to the camp we had to arrange helpers to accompany them. Usually Rita managed this for us, particularly as we were new to the whole operation. However, this year we were short of one helper, a boy of about 18 years old. The requirement was for one boy to accompany five children and an overall leader, the leader had to be older, usually a boy who had left university before he started his career. We were sending 20 boys and had only 3 helpers. My third son Christopher was the right age and was about to start at the University of Wales the following September. I thought he might be interested in filling the place.

On returning from the office one day I asked him if he was interested in a free holiday. By the time he'd heard all about it he replied 'It doesn't seem much like a holiday but I will do it'.

Chris Cox with children at Heswall Camp for boys, 1981

Ten boys and girls had a week at Pontin's holiday camp at Morecambe. All the children went on the same Saturday, returning the following Saturday, making for two very hectic Saturdays for Joyce and her team. The hostess holidays that had started just after the war ended were still going strong in Bolton: in 1981 we sent 20 children who had to be escorted all through the summer to various parts of the country making a total of 50 children who enjoyed a holiday that year. The work of sending children away on holiday always started very early in the year, with a team of members making at least one visit and sometimes more to each child who had been recommended, to ensure the suitability of the child for the right type of holiday. The recommendation for a child to have a holiday came mainly from Social Services and schools with a few coming from churches.

In 1982 we were planning our largest children's holiday programme to present. Joyce unfortunately found she had to resign at this time, which was a great blow, particularly as we had been asked to host a special children's holiday meeting at our office for several of the Metropolitan offices. It was to be a mini conference and we, the host, did not have an Organiser. There promised to be a large turn out for the meeting so on the morning of the meeting I

Children on WRVS holidays

asked Norma Gibbons would she please take the position of Holiday Organiser just for the conference day. It was my intention to have her pass on the information gained that day to whoever might become Organiser later. Thankfully I never needed to do this as Norma accepted the challenge and did a superb job for several years. She shared some interesting thoughts with me for this book

Making visits to some of the homes was an education in itself. One did not always receive the reception imagined; often we were in competition with a TV switched on at a pitch that made it difficult to hold a conversation. Norma remembers going into the home of a couple whose child had been recommended only to find a CB radio in the corner which all through the interview continued to talk away to its elf quite loudly 'Over and out –over and out.' The member accompanying Norma was not as young as some of our members were and could not take her eyes off this talking object in the corner, finding it very difficult to concentrate on the meeting in hand. In my limited experience of interviewing for children's holidays the mother always did the talking, and the father never contributed except in the case of the father being the child's only parent. Norma said she had experienced this also.

When it came time to arrange children's holidays for 1983 Norma and her team did a fantastic job. They prepared 62 children to go on holiday. The team visited each child in its home on average twice, with another visit where he/she came to the office for clothing for the holiday. Fourteen boys went to the adventure camp on the Wirral, looked after by the camp staff. In July, 13 more children went to Pontin's Holiday Camp where we provided several members to look after 5 children each. In addition, a family of 5 people; mother, father and 3 children were taken to Pontin's. We were thrilled to receive confirmation that 9 children from Bolton would be going on a Sun Tours holiday to Spain in October.

Sun Tours were kind enough to offer the WRVS approximately 30 reduced holidays for the benefit of children in need. Norma asked all 9 of the children going to Spain to come to the Bolton Office one Saturday afternoon to have their passport photographs taken. Marching them two by two to Woolworth's, she sat one child on a stool in the booth for two pictures, with another child crouched down at the foot of the stool ready to hop on the stool when the first child jumped off. The photos came in a strip of four so that halved the cost of each child being photographed separately.

Twenty-one children from Bolton Farnworth and Horwich spent a week with individual families, being taken throughout the summer to their hosts by WRVS members. Norma talked to me of some of her sad memories concerning some of the children that passed

Children on a WRVS holiday in Spain

through her hands in those years. One child in particular was his parent's eyes as they were both blind, another child talked of his many uncles, nevertheless they were always fun and the children were worth all the effort she and her team put in. Four girls went to a girl's camp at Boley and this was the first time we had had holidays for girls at a camp.

Two families asked the children they had hosted in the summer back for Christmas, which was rather nice.

The following year was just as busy, going to similar place – except for the Spanish holiday – sadly that was never repeated.

The first holiday arranged for 1985 was for a family going into selfcatering accommodation at Pontin's Prestatyn Holiday Camp. We were pleased about this; a family holiday had been suggested and talked about often. The member who went to interview the mother In 1986, the Family Support team spread their net further afield by making contact with headmasters from several local primary schools, introducing them to our Children's Holiday Scheme. Very often, the headteacher of the school knew which children might benefit. We had a great response and 38 children had a holiday during the summer. Many of them went on a hostess holiday for a week. The hostess holiday was very suitable for younger children, some of whom had never had a holiday and they benefitted from any extra care and attention the hostess gave them. The hostess would often devote much time to that one child for his or her one-week visit.

A group of boys stayed on a farm for a week in Wales, which was very successful, making us realise that is the type of holiday we should be planning in future years. The benefit some children got from working with animals was phenomenal, many making one animal his friend and pet for the week and being sorry to leave it behind on his return home.

Five children went to Kendal on an Outward Bound-type holiday, for the older more adventurous child this was very enjoyable, but was expensive, however the following year we intended to put a bid in for funds from the Children in Need appeal, hoping to be able to afford send more children next year on this type of holiday.

Our trip with a group of children in September to Pontins almost had to be cancelled for lack of volunteers to accompany them. We had to have one volunteer to approximately four children and two of the members who had been with the children for several years were unable to go. We were desperate not to lose this holiday so made a request to members, asking if they would like a free holiday. 'To where?' they asked. 'To Pontins Holiday Camp, of course.' It was a joke of course, one thing it would *not* be was a holiday, just hard work. However, two of our members did volunteer for 'The free holiday'.

Every year Norma would make visits to see some of the children whilst they were away and I would go with her on occasions. On one of the trips this year, we went to Pontin's Holiday Camp. The day we went it was overcast and tried to rain, this did not however spoil the day. It was quite an experience; they had one child who no matter what they did or said to him, however much they created, tried to cajole him, the members in charge were unable to keep him out of the water. His clothes were changed at least five times a day and bearing in mind these children did not go away with that much attire, this was difficult. He was full of fun but a very exasperating child. One little girl, much smaller than the others, always had to hold a grown-up's hand and played very little but was very content to be there. Mealtimes were a hoot to watch, they had self-service and for many of the children just being allowed to go to the counter with an empty plate and fill it up was a wonder in itself.

I used to take photographs whilst I was there and one photo I would never forget was a very handsome 9-year-old with blonde hair to die for and the sunniest smile tucking into a plate full of salad, masses of beetroot, cucumber and tomatoes – I could see why he looked so healthy. Another little boy had the largest ice cream – he had filled his sundae glass until it was overflowing and escaping down the side of the glass. They did have a great time.

Fifty-three children went on holiday in 1987, 14 going on a new type of holiday in the Peak District. For these holidays we received funding from Children in Need without which this type of holiday would have been too expensive.

Our Family Organiser at Area Office was always on the lookout for any type of holiday she thought might be suitable and a change from the normal holidays. Her idea was to give a child as many experiences as we could. She had scored a hit this time. The place was Hope, a beautiful village surrounded by countryside and hills. Each group of children were organised by a team of well-trained volunteers from the Endeavour group. Their Leaders each had specialist training in a particular pursuit from abseiling to canoeing, archery and many more activities. Most of the children had never done anything like this before so thoroughly enjoyed it. The week also included a midnight hike and a trip to a nearby iceskating rink.

Norma and I visited one of the groups and were most impressed with the organisation. We saw the huts were they lived, six boys to a hut, not salubrious but adequate. With the donation from Children in Need that year were able to provide the children with the waterproof clothing they needed as well for their holiday.

Several children were due to go to Wales for a holiday but unfortunately it was cancelled at the last minute. WRVS members from that area of Wales however stepped in at the last minute and took the children to a Guide Camp (with huts not tents), saving the day, or the week in their case. On returning home, we found they had a great time, but heard later that the Welsh members were worn out after the week. However, they had shown great hospitality to the Bolton children.

The move to take a family away, discussed previously, came off again this year and we had two families go to Prestatyn for a week in self-catering accommodation, which worked well.

The bulk of the children again went to hostesses, travelling to many parts of the country.

Norma remembers going on several long train journeys down to Banbury, taking children from all over Greater Manchester to a centre where they were collected and taken to their hostess for their holiday. It struck me on reading Norma's account that it was not unlike the evacuation days, but only for a week. We even had a hostess this year from Westhoughton who took a girl from Salford; it must have been enjoyed by the hostess and the child as she returned later in the year for another week.

Before 1988, we had many organisations applying for children's holidays, however this year we saw a decline and by the end of the year we had managed only 19 children for a holiday and three family holidays. However one child who had been on a hostess holiday to High Wycombe was collected by the family for an extra weekend at their home including visiting the pantomime – they obviously enjoyed having the child.

In 1989 much more emphasis was placed on holidays for the family instead of for individual child Letter s were sent out to the various Social Service departments, Probation, Welfare and Health Visitors, explaining this. We asked that they would take these considerations on board when recommending holidays. Holidays for children who would benefit going alone were however still on offer if required.

There was some good reaction to the new policy although the response was less than we expected but by the end of summer, 10 families had been allocated a holiday, comprising of 15 adults and 31 children. Nine families went in a caravan for a week to Fleetwood with transport and a box of groceries. The remaining family had a week's break with a hostess in Llandudno. Several children were asked back by a previous hostess for their week's break in different parts of the country.

The WRVS had a long and successful career in dealing with deprived children and providing holidays for them. However, during the course of the year the Children Act 1989 was introduced by the Government to protect children against any form of abuse. The main points that were to affect WRVS were: children could not travel in a car with a single adult, there had to be two present, and all personnel had to be vetted to assure everyone that he or she was a suitable person to be dealing with children. Nevertheless, the main problem was that a child had the right to accuse, and if there was any doubt at all that there might be some truth in a statement an investigation was done. That threw a great problem on to the shoulders of the volunteer, as true or not, the stigma to a perfectly innocent person would be horrific. Also the children going into the home of a hostess, as successful as it had been over all these years, now had to cease. It was a great shame but the problem of child abuse had to be dealt with. We never had a problem that I knew or even heard of. It appeared that sometimes unfortunately the baby has to go out with the bathwater.

The Contact Centre

In 1988 Probation Welfare Services made contact with me with a view to the WRVS running an Access Centre (the original name for a Contact Centre). Their representative, Miss Jenny Holditch, came to see me in July and we got on famously. I listened to what she had to say and I thought was a most worthwhile cause and was very interested in the WRVS being involved. She explained that the law states a child should have the right to see not only the custodial parent but both parents. After a difficult divorce, often where another person was involved, the situation was made worse. There were occasions where money was tight and the partner, having gained access, had to try to occupy a child for a whole day with little money and sometimes that proved difficult and often impossible. A centre where children could meet their non-custodial parent was greatly needed, one that had toys and games etc. and where no charge was made. Could we help? I was very sympathetic, however I felt right now in 1988 (it was the year of the WRVS's Golden Jubilee) I had as much as I could cope with, but assured her should she wish to come back to me in the early part of next year I would look more closely at her plans. After ringing Margaret Spriggs to explain what it was all about she was as interested as I was, and commented that Stockport had also been asked to start a similar Centre.

Jenny Holditch from Probation Welfare rang early in the New Year of 1989 asking if we could now start working on the proposed Access Centre for Probation Welfare. She came to our offices and we discussed the project at length and it seemed as good an idea then as it had done when I first heard of it. It was worthwhile and fitted the WRVS objectives perfectly. Jenny explained how she saw the centre. I had never been in such a centre but agreed with what she said. It was decided that each team of four or five members would be needed to staff each Saturday afternoon. Each team would work one Saturday in four or five, depending how recruiting went. With that timescale, members could not get emotionally involved. Neutrality had to be observed at all times as we would not be looking after the children, just providing support and understanding and never being judgemental.

The new recruits would require training, which we would do at our office. Included in the training were the WRVS guidelines, and the role the WRVS were to play in the Centre. A training session with Jenny for instruction in court procedures would also be necessary. As well as recruiting staff for the Centre, I was on the lookout for a good Leader. This person needed to have the right characteristics and to be sympathetic, non-judgemental, strong, but fair and have some training in basic office procedure. Records had to be kept of all the visits, when the custodial parent arrived and when they didn't, and these rules applied also to the non-custodial parent; permanent latecoming, not turning up for visits, or bringing friends along were all frowned upon. Any incident that occurred on the premises by parents or relatives, including alcohol, drug abuse or bad behaviour was reported in our daily log. The log was kept at the WRVS Office and not on court premises. The reasons the log was taken at all was, should the need arise, we had a record of everything to back up our case. To my knowledge it was never needed. All this sounded scary but we would cope. The majority of people just wanted to see their children in a place that was warm, comfortable and cheap.

Premises in the town centre would be preferable but proved hard to find. Eventually we were offered rooms at the Thomason Memorial School for the Deaf, just out of town: that was fine for a start.

However, as the client base grew we were offered ideal premises at The Salvation Army Citadel. It had a large room for play, a kitchen and a small quiet room for supervised access and the Citadel became our home until after the year 2000.

We were recruiting volunteers from new recruits and existing members, however, I still had no Leader for this project. I was not too worried and with a project like this, I felt sure we would find one Leader. Within a matter of weeks, a new member came to join the WRVS and the interviewer came into my office saying 'I think you might want to see this lady today'. Freda knew the type of person I. needed. In the normal course of events all members came back after they had been working for several weeks for a membership talk before their badge was sent for. I agreed to see this new member right away and much to my surprise into the office walked my new Centre Organiser – straight away I knew we had found the right person. We chatted for a while and I explained what this job entailed, the training needed and the people she would be working with, and then I asked her to go away and think about it, then ring me when she came to a decision.

Norma Hanscombe had organising ability, sensitivity, a sense of humour and the ability to defuse an incident, peppered with an air of authority. She appointed a Deputy in Audrey Juliff and between them they pulled together a great caring team of volunteers.

For several months we had been training members interested in working in the Centre but I realised how much better it would be if we could experience a working centre in operation. We needed to talk to members who had been at the sharp end. Therefore, in the late summer a group of us travelled to Nottingham, which was the nearest Contact Centre to Bolton. It proved a worthwhile day, enabling us to speak to members who had experience of what we could only imagine at that moment.

They told us stories of uplifting experiences and how couples had their lives put together again, and sometimes their marriages. They also told more stories of the worse situations they had encountered, going on to say that they were rare and we were not to be put off. However, those were the only scenarios we talked about on the journey home, probably increasing the anxiety we all felt.

It took some time to get everyone through the training but eventually we did and we opened our doors in September, starting with one family but often reaching 50-plus people as many of the families had several children. They did not all come every week but as often as the judge conducting their court hearing decreed. Nevertheless,

*The opening of the Contact Centre, with the Mayor, Cllr. Geoffrey Smith,
Cedric Fulwood, Chief Probatin Oficer for Manchester, Miss Jennie Holditch,
Norma Hanscombe and Pat Cox*

we never knew how many families or children would come on a
given day.

The name Access changed to Contact so we became the Contact
Centre and The Mayor Cllr. Geoffrey Smith officially opened the
Centre early in 1990 in the Salvation Army Citadel. Present at the
opening were Cedric Fulwood the Chief Probation Officer for
Manchester and myself and Norma Hanscombe.

The Centre prospered, if that is the right word. We had a very
competent team of about 20 members, most of whom stayed for all
the years we were open, well into the new century. This project was
a different type of project to any we had ever done, and we felt it was
necessary that members learned from each other. At each session of
a Contact Centre, new scenarios would arise. It was important that
all members gained from these experiences and passed on their experience to other members. Meetings every month were organised
for the members. We met at my home, each team gave a short talk on
any problems that her team had encountered, and how that particular team had dealt with them. This was a learning process for us all
and worked well. As our experience developed, the meetings changed
from every month to every three months and by then they were a
very competent team. Jenny Holditch was there at almost every meet-

ing and answered any queries we had concerning court procedure and any other issues. She kept us up to date on new court procedures.

Transport

During 1985, the clubs made good use of the new ambulances, bringing people into the clubs and for many trips out. Towards the end of the year, Stanley, our new Transport Organiser, went to see a Sister from the psychiatric hospital at Bolton General who had written to ask if we could help with some transport for a relatives group they were trying to start for patients suffering from Alzheimer's Disease. The idea came from members of staff at the hospital, recognizing the need for the relatives to meet each other and share their difficulties in being a carer for sick family members. We eventually started this service and it became very worthwhile. During the period I had helped at the Farnworth Disabled Club Lillian, the Organiser, had a member who suffered with Alzheimer's and over the years he went to the club gradually became worse with each passing week. His wife was involved in this carers' group from the beginning and after he died she eventually became the Leader, having had so much experience with Alzheimer's, she did a wonderful job for many years, and helped many families.

Transport was one of our busiest areas of work again in 1986. We had day trips out to many interesting places and our volunteer drivers drove some 13,265 miles. Visits included trips to Stoke Garden Festival, several visits to the Last Drop and day trips to Morecambe and Southport. The clubs now using the WRVS vehicles were the Disabled Club in Farnworth, the club for the partially sighted at Farnworth, Moss Bank Luncheon Club, Eldon Street Luncheon Club, Horwich Disabled Club, St Vincent's Afternoon Club, the Relative Support Group meeting at the hospital, Ryelands Luncheon Club, Lever Gardens Afternoon Club and Daisy Hill Luncheon Club.

During the year, between all the clubs, they did 35 trips, all organised by Stanley Shields and his team of volunteers, plus three holidays for the elderly. One amusing incident occurred on returning from a day out, when Stanley was helping an elderly lady across the road she suddenly stopped and told him her knickers had fallen down and looking down he realised they had and were sitting around her ankles. 'Can you pull them up?' he asked. I must say it was obvious when Stanley was embarrassed as he blushed profusely. 'No, I can't bend down' was her reply, an answer which he had dreaded, and still feeling embarrassed he shuffled her gently to the nearest side street where he hoisted her pants up to their proper place. When he straightened up, still embarrassed, he was to find a bus full of very amused passengers watching him. Fortunately our elderly lady was completely unaware of all this.

The transport helped children's holidays, taking groups to the station to catch a train and in some cases to their destinations. The members of various clubs were able to visit parties, shows, Christmas fairs and social evenings. At the end of 1986, we realised what a contribution these vehicles were making to many lives, enriching them immeasurably. In 1987 14,666 miles were covered, with 32 trips to the seaside and to a variety of shows for members of the clubs for the elderly.

In 1988, at Christmas members distributed toys to the needy, also needing help with transport. The Parkinson's Society were using the vehicle once a month taking members to a monthly carers' meeting. The Multiple Sclerosis Group asked us to help in taking two of their members down to Leamington Spa for a week's holiday. They were taken to Helen Lay House, the first purpose-built house of its kind catering especially for Multiple Sclerosis victims. The home was set in beautiful grounds and the patients enjoyed a week of friendly calm rest. After the success of the first trip Marian and Stanley did an annual trip with two ladies from Bolton, accompanied by a Red Cross nurse and a representative from the Multiple Sclerosis Society.

Welfare for the Elderly

During July, we took a call from Area Office telling of a new Government initiative whereby the EEC's excess butter 'The Butter Mountain' as it was being called, was to be distributed by volunteers to the elderly and young. To have it disposed of this way meant little or no cost to the government. The WRVS were to be the sole distributors for Bolton. We had to collect the boxes of butter from Area Office, being told to expect cheese for distribution later. However, the first batch was collected by Stanley Shields and contained some cheese as well as butter. Our instructions were to deliver the goods to all the clubs and any clubs we had for children. We had only two clubs catering for the needs of children at that time but the clubs for the elderly were going to be provided for.

Many of the organisers took cheese and butter to their various clubs, including myself, with some interesting experiences. After collecting my batch for delivery, my first call was at a Club for the Disabled where the meals were provided by Social Services. We did

Setting off for a trip to Helen Lea House, The Multiple Sclerosis Society home

not have a say in menu choices. The Organiser smiled when I explained why I was there.

'I will be interested to see who takes the cheese, we get more complaints when we serve cheese pie than anything else – one member walks about muttering constantly saying "It's not right, cheese pie twice in two months, I don't like it, gives me wind it does." We always send out for a sandwich for her but still she niggles, if there is lettuce on the sandwich, she gets heartburn.'

We both laughed and I said, 'We will soon see'.

I introduced myself and explained to the members of the club what it was all about, however most people had seen it in the press so were already aware what was happening. I explained that if anyone did not want either product, it was not a problem as it was not compulsory. The interesting thing was, everyone took both the butter and the cheese regardless of any heartburn or wind.

Dorothy Todd had her picture in the *Bolton Evening News* delivering butter to Delph Hill in March with a caption saying 'Buttering up the old Folk'.

In addition, during March I received a call from Area Office asking if we would deliver that afternoon to our Mother and Toddler Group. Margaret Spriggs explained that the TV cameras would be there to film us giving out the butter and we were quite excited, realising we might be appearing on TV. I met the presenter as we arrived and was disappointed when he wanted any adverse comments I might have on the Government's decision in making this gesture. I tried hard to keep the conversation light, refusing to make any comment on behalf of the WRVS. Causing, in my opinion, the TV interviewer to degrade the action by encouraging the children to open packs of butter and play with it as they would with play dough. This was disappointing as it was meant to be a generous gesture and I think that overall it was appreciated by the majority. The programme on television that night showed a club for the elderly in a different part of the country where one man did exactly what the presenter wanted him to. When asked what he thought of the gesture he said, 'What good is half a pound of butter to a pensioner?'

Clothing

Clothing was one of our most used and useful services and had been in operation since the Service started. We took clothing from people volunteering their used goods. Mrs. Kay had said in the early days that one person's cast-offs were another person's needs. Goods with at least six months' wear in them were the only stipulation we made. Our main customers were men and families with children. However, men's clothes were the hardest to obtain, particularly shoes.

Children needed clothing all the year round but in summer the need was greater. Many of our clients had also applied for a holiday for their children. Having got a holiday they needed help with extra clothing, so Edna Foweracker and her team were on hand to help with this. On one occasion we had a little boy requiring clothes for his holiday; he was duly given what clothing we had for him and told he must not wear it, but pack it up ready for the holiday at the weekend. The morning of the holiday arrived and upon checking his bag the clothes were missing. 'What has happened to your new clothes, Jimmy?' the Organiser said.

'Ah well, mi Mam said as I had got the holiday it was only fair that mi brother got the clothes.'

Logical I suppose, but we then had to rummage around the store to find more clothes for him for the holiday.

The Clothing Store was always busy so during 1981 it was decided that we extend the opening hours from three half days to three full WRVS working days, 9.30 a.m. to 3.30 p.m. Clothing for men and children were our most needed goods, along with blankets in the winter but I think highest on the wanted list was men's shoes. I had the surprise of my life one Monday morning when Jane, our Hospital Organiser, brought around to my house a large bag containing 38 pairs of men's shoes in excellent condition.

'Where on earth have these come from?' I exclaimed, to which she replied, 'We were having a party at the weekend and asked each couple to bring pair of men's shoes, used but in good condition, instead of a bottle of wine. It created a wonderful talking point, and I thought you would enjoy the gesture.'

I most certainly did, and Jane looked just as thrilled, what a wonderful idea! My husband said later I was more thrilled with the bag of old shoes that Jane brought, than my birthday present. Not true, but I was pleased.

We were asked to provide what we could in the way of clothing for the boat people, as they were called, in 1981. They were people fleeing from their country, Vietnam, in fear of their lives. They came in large numbers to many parts of Britain including Bolton.

Underwear for men and children had always been a problem, I suppose because they wore out so we never received any. However, we coped by selling unusable goods to the salvage man and with the money we received we bought new underwear. The Clothing Store provided 4883 garments during the course of that year.

In 1982 the opening hours of the Clothing Store were increased again. The members working in Clothing could have as many as five people waiting in what was quite a small hallway. In 1979, our opening hours were six hours a week, which by now increased to a total of 15 hours. Many times we had advertised for clothing highlighting

The Clothing Store

the particular need of the moment, be it men's clothing, blankets or children's clothing at the onset of winter. However, during the course of 1982 we received a steady but constant flow. We had certain members in the Service who after a phone call would collect clothing for us given a few days' notice. On one particular day Kathleen took a call from an estate agent, asking if we would be interested in picking up some clothing, but then saying he thought it might be mainly bedding and general linen from a house he was getting ready to sell. He had someone else organised to collect the furniture but he thought we might be interested in the other items. We said of course we were, but when did it have to be collected?

'Well,' he said 'that's the problem – if you want it you will have to come right now.'

'Is there a lot?' Kathleen asked, thinking one of us might go quickly.

'Yes there is, mountains of it.'

Kathleen put her hand over the phone, and explained. 'Okay, we will both go now', I said.

We walked up the path and into the house, and on entering the hall we could hardly move for all the items that were in boxes and piled high on both sides. The householder had collected anything and everything for approximately 30 years. The hallway leading into the kitchen was head-high with newspapers, boxes of goods and ornaments, as were the living rooms. The kitchen was filled with every possible utensil imaginable, some old, some ancient and some quite new. All the way upstairs there were boxes but the bedrooms were something to behold; everywhere was stacked high with blankets, sheets, bedspreads, table linen and towels. Some of the items were old, but most of them still in their original packaging. There were boxes piled on the beds, bedding boxes full to the brim. We had a two-foot space to walk into each bedroom. Kathleen and I were mesmerised: it was an Aladdin's cave.

'This is wonderful, how long have we got?' I asked.

'About a couple of hours at the most', he said.

We had to decide quickly what we could take in two journeys as we proceeded to fill my estate car. I was never so torn in all my life: do we take that eiderdown or three blankets or four sheets, I wondered. After the first carload was unpacked we returned and was asked by the agent if we could be as quick as possible, as he wanted to lock up. We worked quicker this time, again filling the car with many of the things we were short of. As we left, we both agreed we had not made a dent in the pile. To have sorted it out and assessed it all would have taken all week, but we were grateful we were able to go and take what we could in the time allowed. The people requesting bedding now certainly would be surprised to get new bedding. We found out some time later the reason why all those goods happened to be into one house. Apparently, the person who had lived there alone was almost a recluse and had never thrown anything away.

We served many of the 'men of the town' throughout out the year and most of them were compliant and didn't give us any problems at all. Odd ones did, but left the premises quickly if we threatened to call the police. On just a few occasions we actually sent for the police, who were aware of our situation and vulnerability and sent an officer round immediately, but by then the offending person would have gone so we were never in any real danger.

We had an unusual story that year concerning a man who came in looking for the free but good tailors on St George's Road, said he had been told 'by a mon at the Social' they would give him a made-to-measure suit. The member on duty tried hard to explain there was no tailor around but we might be able to help him.

'Well I were towd there were a tailor's shop here and I could ger a suit.' He was adamant. Therefore, as the penny began to drop she played him at his game.

'Did you receive a note from the man you saw at Social Services?' she asked him.

'Aye I did, it's here somewhere,' he said as he rummaged in his pockets.

'Well, I think you want our other department, just a minute.' She then asked him for his shoe size and suit and collar size, disappearing into the store and eventually bringing him a good suit, two shirts, socks, underwear, a pair of shoes and an overcoat. On receiving his clothing he said 'Ee, missus, do I not require a fitting either?'

Smiling at him, she shook her head.

'Can I come again?' he asked

'You have to wait a full six months first and don't forget to bring another note.'

'Aye a will, I'll cum back, that's grand, thanks a lot missus. Best tailor I've ever bin to', he said, leaving his dirty and much worn shoe and socks behind.

In 1985, our issue figures were up again and we had some interesting stories related to us by Edna, the Organiser for the Clothing Store. She had received a contact from the police, who had arrested two men in connection with a murder. Their clothing was confiscated so we had a request for everything from underwear through to outer clothes so they could appear in court decently dressed. We did this but nothing was to have a belt or shoelaces. When the media reported that the two men who appeared in court were casually dressed in shirts and trousers, we thought maybe it should have said 'Courtesy of the WRVS'.

Another unusual request was for a dress suit for a father of a bride. The letter was rather crumbled and dirty with a slight bloodstain, causing the Organiser to wonder if the groom was a reluctant one and force had been applied. Not being able to provide a dress suit, he was given a dark suit and a dress shirt and shoes; he was pleased with his outfit, and we hoped the wedding went as well.

The store received quite a lot of new children's clothing and women's clothing, with a request from the donor that some was to go to Fortalice, the home for women and children needing a place to stay, benefitting both charities. Pillowcases were made up from shift-type dresses by one member, helping our bedding supplies.

Prior to Christmas everyone helped to make into parcels the influx of toys given to the WRVS from schools (Bolton School being the largest donor), Church groups and other charity organisations, and it was a busy year all told.

Early in 1986, we had a man who handed his note in one morning saying to the effect 'Please supply this man with trousers before he gets arrested', which we did, smiling as they were handed over to him.

Another man came one day for curtains and when asked the length of his windows he stretched out his arms and said 'So long missus'.

Often we were offered furniture but we could not accept it because of the handling and storage, however one morning we had been offered several items and the donor was prepared to deliver it so we took the man's telephone number, saying if we received a request that day we would get back to him. During the course of that morning, we had a request for bedding and any furniture we might have, and a dark suit. There had been a fire at the home of an elderly couple, the wife had died and the man had lost most of his possessions including his one suit he needed for the funeral. We were able to direct the furniture and supply bedding and one dark suit, a shirt and tie, shoes and socks and underwear, all part of the service. Unfortunately at the end of the year we received a call from Social Services saying in future no notes for clothing would be provided; they would still send people who were in need but without notes, the note had previously always been a prerequisite of someone coming for clothing. However, in spite of this the Clothing service carried on regardless.

The previous winter the Clothing Store had suffered from a lack of blankets and we were only able to give one blanket per person, so low was our stock, but often requests were for several. Many customers needed bedding for the whole family and even one blanket per person could deplete our stocks. This year we decided to make an early appeal to be properly equipped when winter arrived. The appeals made in previous years were a general appeal to the public for items for winter. Every winter in the past goods had trickled in but never did we include any specific requests. This time we tried a change of tactics, and remembering some of the reasons for requests from the previous years, it was decided to highlight some of these stories. For instance, one person had come to us after a fire had wrecked their family home; another had been flooded, and both families had lost most of their possessions, including clothing and bedding. We had had requests from Social Services on behalf of homeless girls, single parents and families out of work. This time when the appeal went out the response was phenomenal. We were never quite sure why it worked so well – was it the strength of the appeal, or that fact that many people had changed over from blankets in the recent past to duvets, so were disposing of their surplus bedding at the same time, to what obviously was a good cause? Whatever the reason, it worked. Stanley Shields and John Oxford were amongst the men who made many journeys collecting donations, mainly of bedding. At one point, I wondered if the floor of the attic, where it was all stored, could carry the weight, and for years to come we were able to provide bedding for anyone in need.

The Clothing Store was one of our major services, along with Emergency Services ensuring us the Government grant. Clothing the underprivileged had always been of great importance before the WVS/WRVS had been thought of, as far back as the Depression years. However, in my time I had witnessed several changes to the service. We had always served the men of the town, and generally, they were full of character, grateful and ready for a laugh and our members enjoyed many of them returning year in, year out. Of late, members realised that a lot of the fun had gone out of the job and they were meeting more and more aggression and dissatisfaction. Since the rescinding of letters from Social Services, we were getting more requests from men we had never seen before, fuelled by tales from some of the men concerning this group of women who gave away free clothing. We had an incident where one man who didn't get what he wanted – he had asked for a pair of jeans and we didn't have any that morning – he was angry. He seriously threatened two elderly members as he was leaving. It had happened before and members were beginning to be nervous. They were all aware that when the Store was open, often there would only be women in the building, so sadly those members resigned. This was such a shame as these members had been working on the same day with the same group of people for ages. It was their day out together. That incident made other members equally nervous, so for the first time ever the door, which had always been open, was closed. A peephole was inserted in the door and a security chain installed.

One day a member brought in a large bag of good clothing which we were pleased to have as we were getting low on men's garments and in the bag were very nice suits. However, six months later they were still on the racks as customers offered this type of clothing refused it, saying 'It's anoraks and jeans we want, not bloody suits, however good they are'. Times really had changed.

There were lighter moments however – after handing out a pair of shoes and two pairs of socks to one man and then seeing what a bad way his socks were in, both feet having great holes, allowing both big toes and heels to peep through, we asked him if he wanted to change into his new socks and shoes. He was so thrilled and he proceeded to take off his shoes, peeling five layers of socks with holes in exactly the same place from his white and very smelly feet. The member serving him picked the socks up with wooden tongs, and as he left the building she promptly placed them in the bin, outside of course.

Another man, after receiving his quota of clothes, proceeded to ask for a football strip. That was an unusual request and we asked him to ring his social worker, who explained to the member serving him that he needed the strip for a five-a-side football team as part of his rehabilitation. He returned the following day and the member had acquired him a strip and a tracksuit – he was delighted.

Sadly, we lost the services of Edna, our Clothing Organiser, this year but we hoped her own Deputy would take over in the New Year

During 1988, we were asked one day to attend a meeting with the Development Officers from Social Services and Angela Kelly from the *Bolton Evening News*, who were preparing an appeal to go in the paper as a series. The name given to it was 'The Old and Cold Campaign' and it was to be a joint effort by the three services. The paper appealed for goods particularly for the elderly. Social Services could direct where specific items were needed and the rest would be directed to our offices where the elderly could obtain items they needed.

This fitted in well with our Clothing Store and we all remarked even though the winter was not as cold as in previous years the scheme worked well.

For the customers at the younger end of the age scale, we were once time asked for a pram, a baby bath and baby clothes for a young mum in desperate need. We also had the usual funerals and weddings to equip. In addition to the rest of goods we handled, we received a large supply of school uniforms, all seconds, but all new. Most of the blazers we acquired were sent to schools where there was a special need. Headquarters asked every store if they would like something to improve the look of the Clothing Store since it was our Jubilee Year, and all three of the stores opted for curtains to cover the clothing racks, making everything look tidier.

In 1989, 7639 garments were issued to 1,000 people and one story I heard made that figure seem quite possible. A lady came into the store one day needing 12 children completely reclothed – she had ten children and two of those had a child of their own, all living together. Their ages ranged from 18 years to two months. Fortunately the store was comparatively quiet that morning, as it took the whole team three hours to equip them all with such a variety of garments in so many sizes. These were the kind of requests our members enjoyed serving. Consequently, appeals went out the following week for women's and children's clothing.

The Bolton Clothing Store continued throughout the 1990s with Eirlys Gabbot in charge. Eirlys had been working with the WRVS for many years and took a great interest in most of her clients.

Clothing Store closures came about gradually. Hygiene regulations meant that secondhand clothing was deemed a health risk and therefore all garments should be washed or cleaned before issue, or at least be in pristine condition when it was brought in. We were not able to deal with this, in general. There was also HASAW risk in sorting clothing; gloves had to be worn and the risks increased with more litigious attitudes on the part of clients.

Charity shops, fleamarkets and car boot sales had developed throughout the late 1980s and 1990s where individuals could purchase for very little cost items of decent quality. There was more dignity in this and thus a lesser need for our Clothing Service. The quietest stores were the first to close, as were those situated in buildings where the lease ended. The rental cost of Clothing Store square footage was enormously high in some instances and Local Authorities were not always willing to contribute even though they derived a benefit from the service. It was a sad day when Clothing closed, we had a farewell party and I was invited to make a thank you speech to our members.

11

✧ *Emergency Services* ✧

The start of the Emergency Team in Bolton

In 1978 we had been recruiting members to join the new Emergency
Team, which was to start its training sessions under the auspices of
Evelyn Barrett, the Area Emergency Organiser. We met in the office
on a weekly basis for several weeks, learning how to cope in the
event of an emergency in the community. We had been told at the
beginning of the first session we would enjoy ourselves and we did;
it was great fun and most of us were sorry when it ended. When we
were called on to go on an incident there were several items we had
to take, one being a pint of milk should tea be needed and one of the
others was a bucket. Funnily enough no one who took the training
ever forgot being told to take those items and said for years they had
a bucket ready and waiting for the time we were called to go on an
emergency.

Evelyn took us through some of the exercises she had experienced
in her time as a member of the team and as the Organiser. She spoke
of a particular exercise held at Manchester Airport when the WRVS
was asked to help with Asian refugees. They were coming to Britain
escaping oppression and bringing with them all their extended families and the WRVS were to meet several groups on arrival. Realising
the language would be a barrier, Evelyn instructed signs to be put
up with pictures rather than words. On the door of the men's room,
she had put a picture of a man with trousers, only to realise as they
approached that all the men wore a kind of skirt, creating some confusion for everyone. She talked of help the WRVS had provided in a
hospital when cleaning staff had been on strike, and she told us many
amusing stories. However, it was an excellent way of showing us

the kind of situation we might find ourselves in one day.

Susan May, who did the hospital projects accounts, had also taken the training course and became the new Emergency Organiser. In the spring after six training sessions, approximately ten of us became the founder members of the new Emergency Team of 1979 for WRVS in Bolton.

Twice that year we held training sessions for the Emergency Team, primarily to increase the size of the team should we ever be needed in a large incident, and to ask other members to join us.

During May of that year, the Emergency Team went to Bury to help at a Scout Jamboree, joining up with Bury WRVS. The teams cooked 300 meals twice on Saturday and twice on Sunday and Alice Williams and Marjorie Taylor peeled a whole sack of potatoes and buttered what felt like a shelf full of Warburton's bread, such was the quantity of food needed. I worked with them for a few hours on the Sunday, washing up endless huge greasy baking tins in an improvised hut with little hot water and between us we ended the day eating the leftovers, cold baked beans. It was indeed a memorable weekend, and had been brilliantly organised by Betty Taylor and remembered for years to come by everyone that took part.

At the end of 1981, Betty Taylor, now the Emergency Organiser, decided to put two of her team and herself in for an Emergency Training course to be held at the Area Office, Wilbraham Road, Manchester. Betty took Norma Gibbons and Dorothy Ellison with her to take part in the course but Dorothy decided after the first day that it wasn't for her so the result was that Betty became Bolton's Emergency Services Organiser and Norma her Deputy. Betty and Norma between them organised all the events described here.

It was the intention that all WRVS members should be trained in

John and Hilda Oxford with the Emergency Team helping at a Scout weekend

emergency procedure. We had received a Government grant since the war ended partly for this purpose, to enable us to help the Local Authority in times of crisis, particularly in clothing and emergency training. The two often went together as at the site of an emergency clothing might be needed. In a town such as Bolton we realised there would not be many emergencies happening on a regular basis. However in remote areas like the coastlines of Britain and the Lake District and the mountainous areas in the country, the need was much greater and could be the main source of WRVS work for that particular office.

Betty came to the office one day enquiring what might happen if an emergency arose and she was not available: we might have a problem on our hands. The Local Authority held a list of contact names and we needed to know how well it would work. Therefore, in 1982 Betty organised a keyholders' exercise to make sure whoever was available they would be able to take charge of the team and get into the building for equipment and supplies. It turned out to be a worthwhile undertaking as she was able to find out and list the people who had keys to the building. However, as Betty did a mock callout, she was quite glad she had, as we found we had more people holding keys than we realised. We weren't supposed to hand out keys ad-lib, which we didn't, but running a busy office with mainly volunteers, who all needed access wasn't easy; it usually worked well but we now knew how many members really did have access.

Some of the call-outs we had were interesting work and took us to some varied places.

Four members made coffee and served it at a conference for the disabled. Eight members helped at a sports day, again for the disabled, held at Rivington Park. Helping out at a small marathon in the summer prepared us for a bigger one later in the year it was a good exercise. The members handed out drinks and wet sponges to runners as they ran past, helping keeping them cool.

At the Bolton Pony Marathon in August 1982 we served refreshments to the officials and gave juice and wet sponges again to the runners on route. Approximately 12 members handled the runners' clothes bags. The runners travelled to the starting point of the race by bus. Each person was given a bag with a number attached in which to deposit his or her clothing, then changed into shorts and tops for the race. The bus dropped the bags at the finishing point and the WRVS were instructed to put the bags into numerical order for the runner to collect at the end of the race. There were 4,000 bags in all, and it took us from 9.30 a.m. to 7 p.m. The weather in the morning was warm but very wet, making quite sure we were completely wet through before allowing the sun to shine, drying us out – quite a day.

During 1981, Christopher, our middle son had been a helper with the group of children going to the Adventure Camp on the Wirral. On his return, I was eager to know how he had found the experience.

'Well it certainly wasn't a holiday,' was his reply to my questions, 'but it did make me realise how lucky I am. Motivating the children to do things, like going out walking, playing games and holding a conversation was the hardest thing to achieve and extremely tiring. There were times I really felt like giving up but did not, and we all worked together hoping the boys would go home having enjoyed it and having had some fun by the end of the week.'

The first thing he did on arrival home was to collapse on his bed and sleep for four solid hours. Later in the evening after he recovered, he then told me of some children who were up at six in the morning and others who continually wanted to play until midnight.

In the early part of 1982, Chris and a friend decided they would make a financial contribution. They intended to help our children to have a holiday by running in the Bolton Marathon, which he did, eventually raising over £400 in sponsorship. He continued to be involved in charity work for years to come.

At the end of that long day I was waiting at the finishing line for Chris to cross, which he did in 4 hours and 10 minutes, excellent for his first attempt. It was a long tiring day for everyone concerned, but for those of us who took part it was a day we would remember for years to come.

The Emergency Team were kept busy with 'Home from Hospital' in 1983, an ideal project for them as the jobs consisted of a maximum of three visits: we were not encouraged to make ongoing visits, typing up members for long periods. Betty had to make sure we were available when another Home from Hospital call came. The type of work the team did was varied. One visit was to help a lady pack the contents of her flat ready for removal. Another was a pregnant mother with three children; two at school and one under school age who had recently broken his leg. The mother needed help to occupy the child with the broken leg while she visited the hospital for checkups. As well as continuing to train extra members for their teams, Betty Taylor organised a day where members from Blackrod, Horwich and Westhoughton spent a day cooking on a trench cooker that they helped build in Betty's garden. The idea behind it was so they would know how to feed people should a disaster cut off all power. We all hoped that that would never happen, but the key was to be prepared. The meal consisted of soup, sausage, mash and beans, finishing with rice pudding – not bad for an outdoor trench cooker.

In September we helped at the Bolton Marathon once again, it was a bitterly cold day this time and we were working from 9.30a.m. to 6.30 p.m., a long day.

During the following years, the team helped many organisations and many individuals. The Local Authority never called us out again for a major problem but we would have been ready had that occurred. The team was constantly on the increase, with new members being found from new volunteers. Betty held several training meetings for the existing teams in both the outlying areas as well as Bolton.

In 1986 Norma Gibbons, a long serving member on the team who had now done her Instructors badge, was helping Betty with training. During the earlier part of that year, the Scouts Group asked us to help with their 'Escapade' for socially deprived and disabled children on the weekend of 7–8 June. The children were brought in by one of our ambulances driven by John Oxford and taken home again on Sunday, also John and his wife Hilda were helping the Scouts most of the weekend.

We were again asked to help with the Marathon, which this year was to be held at the running track on Leverhulme Park, which we did, mainly working in the refreshment tents serving drinks to the runners and the organisers of the event, albeit a smaller team this year. Help from the volunteers was forthcoming for most of the day and they received a medal at the end of the day, 'And without having to run for it', commented Vi Callander; she had been a member since the team started and participated at almost all the events we did, we all felt hers was well deserved.

Betty gave up her job as Emergency Organiser part way through the year, to concentrate her energies as Deputy Metropolitan Organiser and handed over the reins to Jane Whitehead, who had recently left the Horwich Office. There were many members who were sorry to see Betty go as Emergency Organiser but we all had no doubt that she would be on hand to support Jane. Norma Gibbons with her newly achieved Instructors badge became our Leader for training. This was going to be another year of expansion so I was glad Betty would have more time to help.

Jane was enjoying her job as Emergency Organiser, particularly as they were invited to prepare and serve refreshments for 200 people at the Institute for the Blind in May. After a service held at the Parish Church, they all trooped back for afternoon tea. A new Instructor was qualified, with another member going to Easingwold, the Government Civil Defence Training College. Two members of the existing team went for extra training at Area Office.

A weekend was spent feeding 80 Scouts at a Scout Jamboree. We were asked yet again to help with refreshments at the Bolton Marathon. Several of our Emergency Team were called out to help with a mock emergency at Pendleton College involving all the services, named 'Operation Tri-Star'. This was to be an all day affair with most of the voluntary services present and all the statutory bodies. Jane, Norma, Dorothy and Marian went as the Bolton WRVS Emergency Team. The operation consisted of two situations. The first was an air crash at Manchester airport where an incident room, a mortuary and a medical room were available. The statutory bodies dealt with this incident but an explosion in another locality was dealt with by the voluntary sector. The plan was the same as the incident at the airport. Obviously, it would be of great value to assess how both the statutory bodies and the volunteers coped. None of the Emergency Teams knew when it would happen, but had to drop everything when the call came. Our team did just that but were three minutes late. They were rushed to their various stations, Marian's being the Incident and Information room. Everyone coming in to the centre had to be registered. This also happened in the mortuary with the mock dead, and the mock injured were brought to the medical room and registered as injured. Unfortunately, after being registered several got up and walked about, some being registered twice, I suppose as a joke. I think everyone had a great time and I am sure valuable lessons were learned.

We always knew 1988 would be a busy year but didn't expect the blast to be quite so sudden. Our Emergency Team throughout the years had increased and was training new members as well as re-training original members. There was no doubt how well they could work together, having proved that repeatedly with the many exercises they had done with local initiatives throughout the town. However I hadn't expected the phone call I received one day as I lay in bed with a bad dose of flu. Marian said she had had a call from Bolton Housing Department asking for help with bedding for the setting up of a rest centre in Farnworth after a gas explosion had occurred.

Jane was contacted and proceeded to call members out, who set about bundling blankets and sheets in the office, to be delivered to the centre straight away. Later that day Jane was contacted again. The Local Authority wanted us to help set up the rest centre and provide refreshments. Bread was collected from Warburton's bakery and fillings for sandwiches were prepared. The team arrived at The Hollins, the designated site for the centre at 6 p.m. and proceeded to make sandwiches and hot drinks. Because the explosion had occurred during the day most of the people had made their own arrangements for the evacuation, so there were far fewer people at the centre than imagined and the following day we were stood down. It was a great opportunity for us to experience a true call-out proving that should the need arise we could perform.

Norma Gibbons who had been with the WRVS in Bolton since the early 1980s working in so many different places as Deputy to Betty Taylor had now gained her Headquarters Instructor's badge and moved to Area Office to work as Area Emergency Organiser. She was to become a great strength in years to come for Lennie Holmes, the Area Organiser. Norma went on to become the Division Instructor for Emergency when reorganisation came, and eventually Lennie's Deputy.

Val Wallace, after her work on the exhibition, became Emergency Organiser replacing Jane who by now had a full time job outside the Service. Val eventually went to Easingwold, the Home Office Training Centre. She passed the course and became a Training Instructor. She worked hard preparing the Bolton Emergency Team, holding training sessions and then appointing Leaders from each area of the town as Team Leaders responsible for their own teams. That was how Emergency should be planned; equipped to be ready when the

The Emergency Team helping at an emergency call-out at New Bury, Farnworth, 1988

The Emergency Team learning to cook outdoors

call came and everyone knowing whom they were working with. During her time she set up an exercise in a church on St George's Road, the Claremont Church, the idea being that an accident had happened in a busy street and the WRVS organised the information point and rest centre.

During 1993–94 there was continued training and in 1995 the WRVS were asked to do two community assistance projects. However, by now Val had been off sick for a period and was not expected to return. The team carried on with Val's Deputy for a time but continued to recruit for an Emergency Organiser. Headquarters policy on Emergency Services had little changed by 1998, however it was one of the four core services included in the new WRVS business plan.

12

→ *Hospital Services* ←

Work in the hospitals is almost a book in itself, such was the expansion that took place from 1980 until 1998, a period of almost 20 years. In 1980 we were very busy (as we thought) with much work and many volunteers. At Hulton Lane Hospital, we were still running the trolley every week that had been the beginning of WVS work in the hospitals. At Bolton Royal Infirmary, we took a similar trolley around the wards twice a week and a kiosk in Outpatients opened every morning, with a trolley going to the Outpatients Clinics.

At Bolton General Hospital, we had a kiosk in the Outpatients Department and one in the Maternity Department. Each opened five hours a day, with different volunteers covering the mornings and afternoons. The shop on the main corridor opened for some part of every day and was very busy. A trolley went on to the wards every Tuesday and Thursday for the needs of the patients and there was a shop and trolley service on the opposite site to the main hospital known as Townleys side. The projects together took approximately 50 members to staff them.

Work in hospitals, 1980–98

1980

Before Bolton became a Metropolitan, the office staff had managed all the work at the hospitals, and this had to continue. Several thousand pounds of Health Authority money was handled each year on their behalf and had to be protected and spent wisely under their control.

In 1979 the position of Hospital Organiser was created. Previously the Administrator and Treasurer of the Health Authority dealt with

Madeline Wadsworth who would pass on whatever was required to the Leader of the particular project. After 1980, when I became Metropolitan Organiser I dealt with the Health Authority initially then briefed the Hospital Organiser who would manage any changes.

At the end of 1980, Ann Crosbie, Leader of the kiosk at Bolton Royal Infirmary, turned eighty, and decided to retire. I felt I might have a difficult time replacing her. However, to my great surprise an experienced member working on the Monday morning duty at Bolton Royal, after hearing of Miss Crosbie's retirement, came to the office and volunteered to take on the leadership. Lillian Rawlinson had impressed me during the many visits I made to the Infirmary as Hospital Organiser. The truest of sayings is that one volunteer is worth ten pressed men or women. I discussed all aspects of the job with her and some changes she might consider making. Lillian had her own ideas, having worked there for several years and the changes she intended to make were for the good of the patients and members alike.

After becoming Leader she continued her own duty on a Monday morning then came into the Bolton Office during lunchtime to discuss any problems she had. Lillian did a tremendous job and made several important changes. She took charge of the rota and ordering of goods and generally organised the kiosk. After Lillian left to take over Horwich as Local Organiser, the duties were split and Wendy Gill took over the rota at the Infirmary while Margaret Hall did the ordering with help from Alice Williams, and another member brought the takings to the office for counting. In the office, the bookkeeping was done for most of the hospital projects. Appointing members to increased responsibility was always difficult but it was satisfying when the person who had volunteered proved to be right for the job, as Lillian was at that time.

During 1980, the Hospital Authority asked the WRVS to consider a new scheme, 'Home from Hospital'. Betty Taylor and I attended several meetings with various bodies concerned with patients who after leaving hospital were going home to an empty house. If we took on the service, we would visit the person within an hour of his or her return home. The requirement could be as simple as collecting shopping, ringing relatives or making a light meal. What was required depended on the patient's needs.

We considered it long and hard: was this going to be a similar service to the Home Help Service? That was not what the WRVS were about and we explained this. However, we were reassured we were not to do the job of a Home Help and it was decided to try it for an experimental period and see how it went before totally committing our members and the Service. We intended using the Emergency Team for the visits, as it seemed to fall into that category reasonably well. During the coming months, we held training days for members who were interested in becoming a part of this service and got quite excited. We waited for a call-out in vain, but no calls came. Everyone connected with the hospitals thought it was a wonderful idea but the people at the edge of the situation were obviously not getting the message or did not think of us when the need arose. We made what we thought were the right noises to people but still, no one was using the service. It was not to take off until 1981.

When I was Hospital Organiser, I became concerned about the large amounts of money handled by the Leaders of projects at both the General Hospital and the Infirmary. Each day's takings were held in a safe in the hospital, the Leaders collected it at the end of the week, took it home to count and banked it the following day. After giving this a lot of careful thought, I concluded that our safety precautions were not good. Some members actually carried the cash home on the bus. We should not be expecting our members, some of them quite elderly, to be doing this.

After contacting several security firms to see if they could help us, my idea was to have the money counted in the WRVS Office then ask a security firm to collect it. The firm we eventually chose were most cooperative but insisted the money was counted on hospital premises by our members, saying the money should not leave the premises until it was counted and bagged by a member. They would collect the money on a Thursday, calling the same day for the Infirmary takings.

The money was bagged after the count and sealed in special bags that could not be opened except by bank employees. The money bags then went back in the safe for collection later. It all sounded quite simple but we would need members to count the money, and a place to count it in. The hospital staff were extremely cooperative and in the end a place was found, albeit a very small room and a bit cramped but it served us well for several years. We had hitches on numerous occasions with the collection but it was great improvement on expecting our elderly members to carry cash outside the hospital.

The constant need to be vigilant was always with us and our takings and stock did cause us problems from time to time. We noticed one such occasion during the early part 1980 when the takings at the Main Corridor Shop did not seem to be enough for stock we were ordering. Being concerned about this for a number of weeks, we decided to take stock. We counted stock for the annual audit every spring and as it had been done recently, by doing another stock take quickly, it should tell us something. It did: it told us what stock we had at that moment but nothing else. We used that as a starting point and decided from that week on we would do a weekly stock take, which soon confirmed we had a problem. Cigarettes were our biggest concern and we could not afford to have them stolen. We decreased our general stock temporarily and took stock twice weekly, then eventually daily, narrowing it to once every opening. We never found the source of our problem but it stopped and we continued to take stock on a weekly basis for a month to make sure the problem had resolved itself, so whoever was responsible realised we were aware of the situation and quit while they were ahead.

The shop had sold cigarettes from its first opening and the loss of several packets made a difference to our profit. At my next visit to the Health Authority I approached the subject of us discontinuing the sale of cigarettes, but permission was refused as negotiations were taking place about that very subject and when changes could be made I would be notified. It couldn't come soon enough.

The Klix drinks system by now was working well and to compliment this we replaced all the kettles with water heaters, cutting down on the possibility of accidents.

The hospitals have always been by far the largest 'employer' of WRVS members, and this sector was expanding as we hoped it would, but we needed still more volunteers. Our workforce in 1980 at the three hospitals in Bolton needed close on 70 members per week to cover all the duties. Many members did two duties a week but often we were desperate. We tried hard to improve our efficiency and at the same time look after members which eventually paid great dividends. Madeline Wadsworth often said WRVS members had to look forward to going on duty and enjoy the time they were there, for that is the reason we volunteer our services – volunteer work should be all about enjoyment.

1981

Jane Whitehead, the Hospital Organiser, was keen to make the cash more secure so she introduced a cash register into the Main Corridor Shop with the idea that if it went well we would introduce them into the other projects. Everyone had to have the training needed to operate the cash register and Jane spent a lot of time on this. Some of our members accepted the cash register and were excellent. However, other members just left the drawer to the cash register open: as one lady said to Jane one day, 'I don't bother with it, I just leave it open, it's easier than ringing up every sale'. That made it impossible to tell whether the money was right or not. The introduction of cash registers was one idea we did not pursue again for the next few years.

The accounts for the hospital projects were produced in the office monthly then taken to the Health Authority offices at the end of the year for auditors to produce balance sheets. Each project had its own set of books and records of items gifted from projects.

In March 1981, a waterbed was given to the Infirmary from the profits made by the Trolley Shop. In June, cubicle curtains and a TV set were presented to a ward from the General Hospital Kiosk.

In September, the Trolley Shop at Hulton Lane bought a piano for the use of Sunday services, as well as occasions like birthday parties and Christmas parties. In December we bought Blood Pressure Monitors, especially useful for patients suffering with heart complaints. The machine was attached to the patient and set to operate as often as needed. This was a more comfortable way of taking the blood pressure of a very sick patient and the Trolley Shop at the General Hospital funded this equipment. These gifts were presented to the hospital formally and with publicity from the *Bolton Evening News*.

We started a very small tea service in the John Mackay Clinic at the General Hospital in November, which would always be a small operation but as waiting patients could not otherwise get a drink

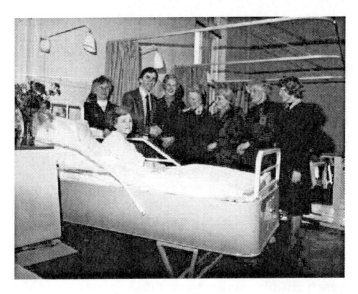

The presentation of a waterbed to BRI, funded from the proceeds of the Trolley Shop, 1982

without walking some distance and perhaps missing their appointment, we thought it was a worthwhile one.

Since the previous year, we had been trying to get our Home from Hospital project going and eventually it took off. The hospital Social Workers, after hearing about it, wondered why they hadn't heard about the service previously, as they thought it was a great idea. These were the people at the cutting edge and very often were the ones left trying to get a patient a lift or a visit after leaving hospital, which was just what we were offering. During the course of that year, we made 61 visits to a variety of people needing assistance and these visits were made by members of the Emergency Team. Betty Taylor met regularly with staff from the hospital to iron out any problems arising with this operation.

1982

In March of this year, Jane Whitehead, our Hospital Organiser, gave up working at the hospital due to a very sad bereavement and handed over her post to her Deputy, Doreen Pilling. Doreen had initially worked on the trolley at Hulton Lane Hospital before Jane asked her to become deputy hospital Organiser. She accepted her new appointment as Hospital Organiser and was very good. She dealt with the problems concerning the constant breakdowns we had with the Klix trolley, eventually going back to the manufacturer for repairs. Doreen coped with several staff changes over the year. When Jane eventually returned to work, it was at the Main Corridor Shop at the General Hospital, working with Doris Simister, the new Organiser of the shop. Townleys Branch Trolley Shop had always worked without a specific Organiser but earlier in the year one of the members involved with it, Mrs. Hunter, had retired. I felt the project would benefit from having its own Leader so persuaded Mrs. Simister to act as Organiser for that project as well. She was going to be one busy person. Another change was Mrs. Mitchell becoming Leader of the Outpatients kiosk.

Our services at Bolton Royal Infirmary ticked along, albeit with problems from the Klix trolley but we had a change of Organiser there this year: Mary Kelly took over the stock ordering from Margaret Hall. Mary had worked for years at Boots the Chemist and was a well known face to most people in Bolton. She had come to join us after early retirement and the death of her husband. Many of our members found it was a great way to keep busy after retiring or suffering bereavement, as volunteering often gave a sense of purpose.

Every year I went to Mr Sutherland, the Hospital Treasurer, to discuss our expected profits. There had been a change in policy from Headquarters as to how we were to distribute profits. In the past, comforts were the only items we could buy for patients, but all that had changed. The profits at hospitals where WRVS had a large input, were often substantial and could be of great benefit towards expensive hospital equipment. Headquarters decided equipment had to be a priority. In addition, requests had to be made by the hospital administration to our office, not from members of staff as had often happened previously. We then requested permission from the Area Office. For items costing £500 to £1000, authority could be given from Area but anything above that amount required permission from Headquarters. This was one year when I was having difficulties getting requests from the hospital for any gifts at all – even though I had passed on to them a copy of the new procedures, these were obviously having a hard time getting through. Apparently, the staff were the people who knew what was needed, but now they had to apply to the management and requests were sometimes lost in the process.

Home from Hospital was continuing to thrive with almost one person a week visited.

1983

Responding to a summons from the Chief Medical Officer, I found myself wondering if it could possibly be for further discussions regarding the No Smoking in Hospitals Policy. I went into his office and, after pleasantries, he informed me of the Authority's decision to limit the sale of cigarettes in the hospital, with the exception of the longstay patients, where he thought we should continue to put them into the comforts packages. It was music to my ears. I suppose selling cigarettes in the hospital was never ideal but from that day we did not have to openly sell them.

'Why has it taken so long?' I asked, only to be told of all the levels of procedure it took to gain everyone's consent on a matter like this. One consideration was that many of the staff smoked and were in the habit of buying their cigarettes from the shop whilst at work. The doctor chatted for about half an hour, making me aware of a disease that in 1983 not many people had heard of, that broke down the immune system, making the carrier susceptible to any other disease that came his or her way, saying it wasn't rampant now, but in years to come could be, and as yet, was incurable. It sounded so strange and bizarre: its name was Acquired Immune Deficiency Syndrome, or Aids for short.

From opening the first Hospital Shop the key to the shop door was kept in the Administrator's office, conveniently situated in the corridor facing the shop, and was used by the member on duty who after completion of her duty returned the key. This worked well, however, the Administrator asked one day if we would remove the key from their office, which was understandable. Leaving the key on virtual display had become unsafe and no one wants responsibilities without control. After much consultation we decided to change the locks and give each member a key of her own. When a volunteer left the WRVS the problem was retrieving her key and it was a difficult situation without a real solution. Often members did not resign, they just stopped coming. Vigilance was going to be the only way we could hope to correct this problem, a problem that was to frustrate us for years to come.

During the course of the year I became aware that the Authority still had not made any request for the money we held in the WRVS Trust Fund. The money held by us for the hospital went in to a special fund along with monies from all the other offices throughout the UK, thus gaining the WRVS a higher level of interest. I had mentioned this again recently to the Treasurer at a meeting and he promised to pass it on to the administrators in the hospital. He would be interested in us funding a special room for relatives of sick and recently deceased patients. Several years earlier, I had lost my father to a sudden coronary with no warning at all. I had followed the ambulance to the hospital in a distraught state. He died within hours of arriving there and there was no place to sit and grieve. Remembering that day, I felt that the facility we could provide would be of great use to others. I applied for permission from Headquarters to spend the amount of money it would take. After their approval was given we waited for the start of the project.

I was aware that when Madeline Wadsworth retired nothing was done in the way of a dedication marking all the service she had given to the hospital on behalf of the WRVS, which had to be at least 30 years, including 21 years as the County Borough Organiser. I always felt there should have been something commemorating this and if an opportunity should arise, I would suggest we dedicate this project to Madeline.

During the course of 1983 the Administrator, Mr Phillip Scully, left the General Hospital to work at Bolton Royal Infirmary and was replaced by Mr Malcolm Price. Mr Scully had been my contact at the

General and had helped with many of the problems concerning the Main Corridor Shop. At the first opportunity, I visited Mr Scully in his new position to discuss WRVS involvement at Bolton Royal Infirmary. He asked if we needed any help from him with anything in the hospital. I said yes, we did. I had always believed the kiosk was closed in the Outpatient's Department at the time it should be open, lunchtime. While it was often a quiet time with not too many patients about, the department could be half full of people waiting for an ambulance and perhaps someone requiring a drink. In addition, we should be using the trolley during the early evening, as apart from a drinks machine a visitor could not obtain a drink when coming straight from work. Therefore, I requested permission to keep the kiosk open from 9 a.m. until 4 p.m., using three shifts of members, and a trolley service going to Accident and Emergency, Plaster Clinic and the X-ray Department between 6 p.m. and 8 p.m. every evening. He agreed and the extra service operated from 1983 until the Bolton Royal Infirmary closed in the late 1990s.

After Mr Sutherland, the Treasurer of the Health Authority, made a request for our donation to the Bolton Royal Infirmary Centenary fund, the WRVS donated £5000 towards the purchase of a laser for eye surgery. The money was presented at a gathering of WRVS members from the Bolton Royal Infirmary. The *Bolton Evening News* had started the Centenary Appeal so Leslie Gent, the Editor of the paper, accepted the cheque from two Organisers, Miss M. Hall and

Les Gent of the Bolton Evening News accepting a cheque for £5000 on behalf of the BRI, from the proceeds of the kiosk in Outpatients and the Trolley Shop

Mrs. Brotherton. The Trolley Shop at Hulton Lane also presented £500 for the Centenary Fund in October of the same year.

Home from Hospital during the year had ticked over very well except for the Bolton Holiday week when we were stretched somewhat. One member visited a man who was dying to talk football to anyone who might listen so next time the member made a visit she took her son and they both chatted to their hearts' content. Another day we visited a man who did not eat much; he was quite sick and had no appetite. It was the start of the strawberry season so when Betty visited him she took him some particularly plump and juicy strawberries, which he thoroughly enjoyed.

1984

About this time Susan May left Bolton to live in the south of the country. Susan had done the weekly accounts for the three hospitals since I became Organiser. She was good at her job and could spot early when anything was amiss, before it became a problem. I often commented, when introducing her to other volunteers, that she sold jewels (she worked at Preston's the Jewellers for her day job and on her day off she did our hospital accounts). I wondered whom I might ask to replace her. I remembered that at the launch of the Ambulance Appeal one of my husband's colleagues had indicated that his wife might help should we ever be short. Margaret Dale, I realise, had worked with accounts in the not too distant past. I was sure she could do the job, providing she had the time. To my delight, she agreed to try it. Every time one changes a job, even if it might be the same type of work, it can appear different. Fortunately, whilst there were many accounts needing attention every week, Margaret soon became familiar with them. As the hospital projects grew in number, she took them on board. Another friend eventually came to work with Margaret, Betty Williams. Betty had done accounts from leaving school until her first child was born. Betty and Margaret worked happily together for several years under the auspice of Lillian who completed the biannual accounts needed for Headquarters.

When Meals on Wheels first began, we were able to interest Betty's husband, Arthur, in driving for us. He gained a reputation as the fastest wheels in town. However along with the other drivers he did a great job. One by one, over the years, I found I was introducing most of my friends who might have a few hours to spare to the WRVS. However, I never remember losing any because of my persuasions. It often surprised me how we had so many members from such a wide variety of occupations: from shop assistants, hairdressers, an

The schoolroom at BGH

opera singer, professional cooks, teachers, Social Workers, nurses and many of our members with office skills.

Work throughout the hospitals continued to be busy that year and from the profits made by the Ward Trolley and Outpatients Department WRVS presented to Mr Geoffrey Redgate, Chairman of Bolton Health Authority, a resuscitation trolley, two hydraulic couches and two blood pressure recorders, amounting to a total of £6,000. A presentation tea was organised in the boardroom for members working on these projects.

During the previous year I received requests from several departments at the hospital, all of which we had been approved by Headquarters. The goods requested were four Kings Fund beds, two net beds, a compressor to be used in conjunction with a neonatal ventilator, two televisions, curtains for around beds, and a tea trolley. That was quite an array of goods for us to consider.

The Sister in charge of the Children's Ward had put in a request for a room to be used as a playroom for children who were well enough and could get out of bed but still needed to be hospitalised. She was concerned for the children's welfare and sad to see children bored as well as sick. If only the children could use it for a short while it would make them happy. The proposed cost of the conversion was £2,000.

Another idea that interested me greatly was the overnight room for relatives of sick patients which was suggested the previous year but had not come to fruition. I would suggest this might be the perfect dedication to Madeline Wadsworth. The WRVS were to provide the fittings and furniture for the room. The area proposed involved two very small rooms no longer used for the purpose they were designated which could be refurbished at a cost of £4,000. The total cost of all these gifts was £14,000

The hospital authorities accepted my suggestion of a plaque dedicating Madeline's 21-year service as WVS/WRVS Organiser and it was placed on the wall in the overnight room. A party in the boardroom was organised. with invitations being sent to Madeline Wadsworth, Evelyn Warr and Margaret Sydall, the idea being that along with myself there would be all the Organisers of WVS/WRVS since 1947. Only Mrs. Kay, the first Organiser, would be missing. On the day of the presentation Margaret Spriggs presented Long Service Awards to four of our members and it was a special day. Mr Redgate, the Chairman of the Health Authority, was there and Mr Sutherland, the Area Health Treasurer. The new Hospital Administrator, Mr V. Peel, and Mr G. Higson who accepted the gifts on behalf of the Authority from myself, representing the WRVS. Invites had gone out to members from all the projects throughout the General and a good number accepted.

However, this year we had still more problems from break-ins. A window in the Outpatients Tea Bar was forced open and goods and money were stolen to the value of £80 and there was also all the inconvenience of dealing with the burglary. We had another sizeable

The Organisers of the WVS/WRVS since 1947 at a presentation of equipment to BGH, 1983

problem but an obscure one, becoming aware that the petty cash (or float for members' expenses) was down every week. The shop carried a change float for the till, which was never quite right although this was the nature of the job. At the end of a duty, members were expected to leave the existing float, if possible all in change, having banked their takings in the overnight safe. The petty cash float had been created a couple of years previously, realising members' expenses should be handled separately. Everyone's travelling expenses were different so the Team Leader left a suitable amount of money as a float. Each member took what they needed then recorded it in a book. At the end of the week the expenses in the book were counted and the money replaced for the following week; the expenses could then be added to our takings, giving a truer picture of our total takings for the end of year. Doreen Reynolds noticed that for several weeks the money had been down by approximately £5. About that time, we received the accounts back from the auditors and we became aware that the profit from the shop was also down. There were as many as 50 people involved in the week's duties. Once before we had had similar problems and had counted stock after each opening but now we were a much bigger operation and did not have the staff time available for this. It was a difficult job to know just what the day's takings should be. Our members were all volunteers and I would have staked my life on them all, but money was disappearing so we had to do something about it. A till recording the day's takings had been installed the year before but had not worked and the total takings for the week often bore no resemblance to the actual takings. These were mistakes not theft, but after discussing our plight with Mr Sutherland, we put a plan of action into place and eventually were able to narrow it down to a few openings and soon we were certain which one it was. I had the unpleasant task of asking the member concerned for her keys and tabard back, requesting that' she did not to come to the shop again.

Through the Hospital Authority, we changed our security system again. A new lock was fitted with as many keys as we needed, but from then on, any further keys had to be ordered and an explanation given as to why they were needed. Keys now could not be cut by anyone else. All the keys were numbered, along with the name of the keyholder. It was a pain for Doreen having to distribute so many new keys at the start of every duty and it was done in a single week but everyone was glad in the end as no one likes a situation where suspicion falls on everyone, it creates discontent and we liked our volunteers to be as content as possible.

Just as the year was ending I received a call from Mr Sutherland, asking would I call and see him concerning a gift he thought we might be interested in providing for the hospital. Deciding to leave early, I asked if I could call that afternoon at his office on Churchgate. On my arrival he explained he had received a call from a consultant at the hospital who was applying for funds to buy a laser for the treatment of cervical cancer. This treatment went a long way to curing this type of cancer providing there was early detection.

'What do you think?' he said, 'My impression is it would be a perfect gift from an organisation like yours.'

I did not have any objection to the idea and there was money available providing we could include the profits from all the hospitals, so I agreed it was an ideal suggestion. I explained to him the intention of using the profit from all the projects, and was certain everyone would agree. 'I will bring it up at our next Organisers meeting which I'm afraid will not be till early in the New Year', I explained.

With that, he rang Mr Hopkins, the Obstetrician, who suggested I went to the hospital right then to discuss it. It was a cold wet miserable day at the end of November and all I wanted was just to go home.

'Okay,' I said, 'I'll be there in about twenty minutes.'

Mr Hopkins was about as enthusiastic a person as I have ever met, where his job was concerned, and was almost excited when I said I did not see a problem with funding the laser but would put it forward at our next meeting and let him know in the New Year.

By the end of the year we had experienced very few changes to staff, but one I was particularly sorry about was that Doreen Pilling and her family were going to live in Bedford, as she had been a good Organiser. Fortunately she was replaced by her Deputy, Doreen Reynolds. Doreen came with much experience gained at Hulton Lane before being Deputy to Doreen Pilling but we would all be sorry to see Doreen Pilling leave us. Doreen Reynolds stepped into the breach wonderfully and you could find her most days at one or other project and she became a very popular Organiser. Mary Ashton took over the running of the Trolley Shop from Edith Bryan who to everyone's surprised left the Service to be married.

1986

Hospitals throughout the Greater Manchester area were at this time changing policies on the outlets within their premises. Large firms, realising the potential of a captive selling point, were making promises of large rents. This had to been seen by many cash-strapped

Authorities as manna from heaven. The WRVS everywhere were losing sites to large businesses. They offered better staffing prospects, longer working hours, enabling the outlet to remain open during the hours we could not. We were hearing this constantly at our Area meetings, not only that it was going to happen to us, but of actual places where it had happened. The WRVS were out and W. H. Smith were in.

About the time that all these rumours were being talked about I visited Mr Sutherland and the topic of income generation in the Bolton hospitals arose. I told him of the discussions we had had at Area Office and what was happening in many other hospitals. He said he was happy to keep the present arrangement as it had worked for many years and this way the hospital received all the profit .However he wanted us to emulate the other hospitals by upgrading our outlets and opening new ones where there was a need. He suggested we open a shop in the Princess Anne Maternity Unit at the General Hospital. In addition, the Main Corridor Shop at the General needed extending. He felt we should have a walk-in shop with a greater variety of goods. Eventually, after completion of work in the porter's lodge at the Infirmary he wanted a shop in the Main Corridor there too. We were going to be busy in the next few months. The Main Corridor Shop extension at the General Hospital would be difficult, as it had to be kept open whilst the changes were made. He then said he would like us to employ a manager for the three shops, to be available for work on most days, and not a volunteer. He or she would be paid from the proceeds of the shops, and have sole charge of ordering and accounting and would liaise with the Hospital Organiser, the Hospital Authority and me.

Doreen Reynolds and I worked on a plan as to how we could achieve all this. At the next meeting, we were able to put our ideas forward. This was something that would not happen overnight. I had what I thought was the perfect person as a manager in Ann Wood, the daughter of Lillian Punchaby, the Organiser of a disabled club in Farnworth. She was a volunteer at the Main Corridor Shop one evening a week and I felt sure she would be interested in a part-time job. However, one big drawback was that her youngest child was two years off school age, but that would not last forever as children do grow up quite quickly! Mr Sutherland was concerned by this, however, I convinced him she was the right person for the job. Together, we looked at the sites for these shops and I reminded him that we would need storage space as well. We went to the General Hospital first to look at a site for the proposed Maternity shop. The

The opening of the Mother and Baby Hospital Shop, 1987 (left), and presentation of the laser, 1986 (right)

only space available was close to the entrance. It was very small and without any storage space so it was decided we would have a small shop with storage elsewhere.

The request, late in 1985, for us to provide a laser for Obstetrics for the treatment of cervical cancer at a cost of £17,000 came to fruition with a presentation in October 1986. The presentation for the laser was organised at the General Hospital with invitations for any member that chose to come. After the presentation, Mr Hopkins the Consultant Gynaecologist, gave a talk on the dangers of cervical cancer, explaining how the laser helped with early treatment. He explained how careful women should be concerning relationships, then realising the average age of members that day he related the dangers to their daughters or even granddaughters. The *Bolton Evening News* was on hand to record the event and I was able to try out the laser on an apple after Mr Hopkins had demonstrated how it worked. It was a great day for all concerned.

That year from the profits made by the Hulton Hospital trolley, presentations were made to that hospital of a net bed, six Contra hand-held hearing aids, bed trays and some wedge pillows. We replaced tools worth £300 stolen from the garden at the Psychiatric Centre. These small, inexpensive items were vital pieces of equipment and cost little considering the pleasure and occupation they gave to the patients. In this unit, many men spent hours working in the gardens, helping with their final recovery. In the summer, there were often beautiful flowers for sale that had been grown in their gardens.

We provided £3,000 for equipment required for a Postoperative Unit at the General Hospital. For the Lady Tonge Clinic, also at the General Hospital, we provided a video, some tapes, a concept keyboard, a printer and a selection of educational disks at a total cost of £700.

The ward trolley at the Infirmary provided over £1,000 for five nebulisers and a television set for the Physiotherapy Clinic.

Earlier in the year at one of our Area meetings, we had been asked to donate £100 from each hospital project for alterations to the Great Ormond Street Hospital in London, so £800 was sent from Bolton. Every WRVS project throughout the country donated £100 to this fund, creating a very worthwhile donation.

1987

I went to see a possible site for the shop at the Infirmary and it proved to be ideal; it was the porter's lodge where I used to collect the key when I first started working at Bolton Royal in 1966. However, there was a lot of work to be done at both places by hospital contractors so we would plan the new shops for the following year.

Plans were discussed for an extension to the Main Corridor Shop but that would not happen either until the following year. It was too early to start recruiting but time enough to inform some of our members as often they were able to find volunteers for us.

I had never opened a shop of the type Mr Sutherland wanted and I needed to talk to someone who had done something similar fairly recently. Most things done previously had a blueprint so there had to be one for opening a shop. We had a member working on the trolley at Bolton General whom I knew quite well. Her husband was the owner of Radcliffe Road Motors and had several garages, each with a shop. I contacted Margaret Smyth to ask if she might take me to look at one closely and have her talk me through what seemed to me at the time to be a minefield. She agreed and we went to their garage at Radcliffe. I knew we would not stock exactly the same products but I was surprised to find what little difference there would be. A garage shop is mainly for people purchasing whilst on the move and I realised our shops would be similar. I made copious notes, taking then back to the office to study, and from then I began to imagine the outcome. I also went to see another friend in Grange, Susan, whose husband had a chemists shop as there was a time we thought we might sell simple over-the-counter medicines, and although that did not happen there were several items that I added to my notes that we eventually sold – it was all part of my learning curve.

During the later part of 1986 and the earlier part of 1987, Doreen Reynolds and I had numerous meetings concerning the development of the new projects in the hospitals. The new shop proposed for the entrance to Bolton Royal Infirmary had its plans drawn up, and after a few alterations and consultation with members and the Authority they looked good, so were passed.

However, before any work could be started on the shop the entrance to the Infirmary had to be altered. Opposite the proposed shop an existing cloakroom and storage place had to be changed into a reception desk for patients who on their arrival at the hospital could be directed to their destination. The work needed would impede the public from using the entrance everyone was familiar with so a temporary entrance was created close by. Now there was a need for someone to greet the patient and give them directions to the wards from the temporary entrance. The Hospital Manager approached the WRVS to organise what was eventually to become a Volunteer Hostess Service. This was a popular service, enjoyed by volunteers, and provided assurance for the patient and visitors alike. Work for the new entrance took approximately ten weeks to complete and by this time the Hostess Service was noticed by the Authority as a possibility for the use at the General Hospital where the distances were greater and the need for patients' reassurance equally as necessary. The Hostess Service went to the General Hospital after it ceased to be needed at the Infirmary, continuing there for many years. It worked with two members arriving at the Bolton Royal Infirmary for morning and afternoon duties each day, working mainly from the temporary main entrance to the hospital.

There was a hope that the work on the shop at BRI would be completed in the same timescale as the reception area but the contractor had met several major problems in the old porter's lodge that had to be corrected before any new work could continue. This delay unfortunately added several weeks to the wait.

With all the work underway at the Infirmary Doreen Reynolds and the Leaders at the kiosk thought that perhaps this was a good time to refurbish the Outpatients kiosk in the department as it had been almost 20 years since it had any work done on it. It needed an upgrade and at the same time enlarging, with more storage space created, along with better security. I took our ideas to the management for their opinions, expressing what we wanted – I knew with all the other work in progress there would be a long wait but we had to start somewhere.

Betty Taylor started a Books on Wheels and Trolley Shop at Newlands Private Nursing Home, operating twice a week, later in the year. The books were chosen from Heaton Library and distributed weekly by Joan Wallen and Vi Callander.

The opening of the newly refurbished Main Corridor Shop, 1987

1988

The beginning of 1988 saw the Main Corridor Shop closed for refurbishment. However, for two months, members filled a trolley with goods from a cupboard. They wheeled the trolley close to where the shop was situated, selling their goods from there. In the short term drinks were suspended and it was not an easy task to keep everything up and running whilst the work was completed, but Doreen Reynolds and her team of members did a superb job. Dorothy Bainbridge, who worked as Doreen's assistant, was a tremendous help and she did the rota duties for the shop. She could find a replacement immediately and knew how many duties each person had completed in any given week. The original shop in the main corridor had been a serving hatch in the wall and to the right of the hatch was the Post Room. Over the years, we worked side by side very well, but as the Post Department grew, so did the shop. There was very little space and the hospital postmen used wire trolleys when delivering the mail. These grew in number as the quantity of the post grew and there were times when we must have been a problem to each other.

One of the reasons the completion of the new shop took so long was the work needed in creating more space for us as well as the Post Department. The next problem was relocating the many pipes running along the wall of the Post Room. Eventually the shop was finished in April and it was much larger and sold far more lines than we had done previously; sweets and chocolate, toiletries, magazines, children's playthings, and there was a cool cabinet for drinks and sandwiches from the hospital kitchen. There was also a place to buy drinks just inside the shop with a separate till, helping us to keep the money separate, and outside the shop was a sitting area designated for people to sit and have their refreshments, whilst those that wanted to, could smoke.

The new shop in the Maternity Unit, completed one month later, was a small unit but its stock was good, especially for the needs of a new mother and her baby. Both shops were open in the afternoon and early evenings. Members working in the Maternity Shop enjoyed seeing the new babies on their way home. We had a Grand Opening of both shops during the month of May with representatives from Area Office including Lennie Holmes, our new Area Organiser Elect; Margaret Spriggs, and Miss Lea the Hospital Accounts Organiser. Present from the Health Authority were Mr Tom Taylor, the Chairman for the Health Authority; Richard Sutherland, Hospital Treasurer and John Brunt, Administrator for the Hospital. Many of our members also attended.

The Corridor Shop at Bolton Royal Infirmary opened in May, its position being perfect for visitors, hospital staffs and ambulant patients. A new trolley was also ordered, larger and able to carry a better selection of goods and drinks, to operate both morning and evening.

During the course of the year the WRVS were asked to fund a complete refurbishment of the Outpatients Department at the Infirmary and we intended to refurbish the kiosk as soon as the plans were completed, however it had taken a back seat with all the other work going on. If we were to refurbish the kiosk and the whole department it would be a major project. The costings for the whole project were £25,000, but when it was completed the change would be dramatic. On seeing the competed plans, we saw the décor was to change from cream and brown – typical hospital colours – to a more tasteful pink and grey. One thing that concerned me when this project was suggested was the rumours that had been rife throughout the hospital that in the not too distant future the hospital might close down. Over the last few years, there had been much speculation. I expressed my concerns to the management who gave assurance that the hospital would stay open at least another ten years and explained that right up to closure the building would have to be adequately maintained and the refurbishment would undoubtedly give pleasure to staff and patients during that period.

It was around this time I first met Miss Thompson, who was to become a good friend to the WRVS and eventually steer the hospital, as well as us, through the exciting move from the Bolton Royal Infirmary to the new Royal Bolton Hospital, but at that time the move seemed to be a long way off.

In conjunction with the refurbishment, a Welcomer Service was organised in the Outpatients Department. This was in line with the' hospital's policy of good patient care. The Welcomer would guide patients through the departments, because often, when attending one appointment the patient would have to go to another department and whilst the layout was not as confusing at the Bolton General, to an elderly confused patient there alone, it was a daunting prospect.

Several items were gifted for the hospital this year, but by far the majority of profits made went on refurbishments for the shops and new trolleys.

During the course of 1988 Doreen Reynolds, who had been the Hospital Organiser since 1985, told us she was leaving Bolton and going to live in Southport. She had recently appointed a Deputy Hospital Organiser, Sherrill Murphy, who proved to be very efficient and was prepared to take on the role as Hospital Organiser.

Through the 1990s

The opening of the new Main Corridor Shop at Bolton Infirmary was worth the wait as it was spacious and behind the shop was a storeroom. The trolley going to Outpatients Department operated from the shop. There was great excitement felt as the refurbishment of the Outpatients Department was soon to be underway. Meetings for it had gone on through all of the previous year. The colour scheme was looking good but we soon realised the floorcovering would have to be replaced as it didn't match this lovely new scheme of pink and grey at all as it was a brown wooden floor with green lino-type squares. Miss Thompson had brought this to our attention and we asked her to get prices for new flooring. Eventually we agreed, so negotiations with a floor specialist began, and a deal was eventually struck. We were to have a grey floor with an inlay of pink. In September, work began with hope of completion for Christmas. Sherrill and Ann kept an eye on the work throughout the autumn and we saw it all ready for Christmas, a new start for the coming decade. In the early part of 1990, a presentation to the Hospital Authorities was made of the newly refurbished Outpatients Department, BRI.

Try as we did with the Hostess Service in the Outpatients Department at Bolton Royal it was not successful and was abandoned during the course of 1990.

Profits from the projects at Bolton General Hospital funded three

The opening of the newly refurbished Outpatients Department, 1990

new microscopes for Histology and Cytology. These pieces of equipment were needed because of the increasing numbers of smear tests
being done to detect cervical cancer. Early detection would improved
a patient's chances of recovery and also this equipment comple-
mented the gift of a laser in 1986.

While all this was happening, Local Resource Funding was introduced at a conference in that year, causing quite a stir, particularly
as LRF for hospitals amounted to a percentage of the takings which
was sent to Headquarters twice a year. It applied to most of the
projects in the WRVS including Luncheon Clubs but the hospital contribution was by far the larger. However, the WRVS received a grant
from the Home Office and the Home Office objected to supporting
the costs of Hospital WRVS services. All large accounts had to
be audited by Headquarters staff to comply with VAT regulations.
There was quite a complex web of legal requirements to deal with,
even though the service operated with mainly voluntary labour.
Headquarters had to employ qualified staff to deal with the large
amounts of work needed to comply with all the regulations now
required by Government.

The year 1994 brought about a most exciting change. Finally, the
hospital staff gave us space behind the Welcome desk for a WRVS
office. Work had to been done before we could occupy it but its worth
to us was immense.

Having acquired an office within the hospital meant we were able to resolve any ongoing problem immediately. A difficult situation, if not dealt with, could soon become a problem, then on occasions the problem became an emergency. Just by being there Ann was able to diffuse any niggles there might be. To eliminate the need for lots of keys for each project, a single key would be collected in the morning and then dropped in at the office at the end of a duty. We were now able to restrict the number of keys in use but before the newly acquired office, there was no other way. WRVS members rarely resign as such, they just sort of drift away, mostly with a real intention of coming back to work. This left us with keys outstanding everywhere. We were now able to have one key per project per day, to be collected and returned to the hospital office. However, there still had to be one keyholder per team for the evening/weekend shifts responsible for passing the key to another member of the team at holiday times.

We were very fortunate in our dedicated volunteers and we rarely had to close a project due to staff shortages thanks to the skills of persuasion of the rota members who did a fantastic job on the phone making sure someone would step in. Enid Swarsbrick was an absolute stalwart in keeping us fully staffed. Her job was to maintain the rotas for the Main Corridor Shop and the Mother and Baby Shop and both shops had evening duties that were by far the hardest to fill. During the early 1990s Enid hurt the tendons in her foot and had to sit with her leg up for several weeks, but she took no time off work and did the rotas whilst sitting down nursing her leg. 'I do not have to be at the hospital, and it will keep me occupied', was her comment. Instead of complaining, she sat and worked on rotas all day. Almost never did members not turn up because of bad weather and invariably at both hospitals we had at least one shop open on each Bank Holiday throughout the year.

The shop on Townleys site (L block, known as Townleys Branch) from where the trolley had gone round the wards and with comforts for patients, was to be converted from the 'hole in the wall' into a small walk-round shop. Whilst the work was in progress, members continued the service by providing a reduced service from a trolley that took provisions each day to the wards and day centres. After completion, the new L Block Shop was able to increase its hours, providing a daily service, and the trolley service also continued.

During April, Marian Hilton, after resigning as Metropolitan Organiser, took over Sherrill's position as Hospital Organiser. Sherrill was leaving Bolton after her husband had a job move. Ann Wood still having responsibilities for the new shops in both hospitals.

During this period I was the Liaison Officer for the northern part of Manchester Division, so it was down to me to look after the work in Bolton until I could interest someone in becoming Metropolitan Organiser.

I attended a meeting in August at the General Hospital with Ann and Marian. The meeting was convened because new fire regulations were being implemented at the hospital. The meeting was with the hospital architects regarding alterations to the Main Corridor Shop to comply with the new regulations. We listened to their plans but after hearing their ideas I wasn't at all happy with the way they were intending to alter the shop and the fact that plans had already been drawn up for the work without any consultation with us. At present, the entrance to the shop had a steel shutter that locked at floor level. To comply with the new laws we had to have a door from the corridor into a small sitting area for customers with drinks and then another door into the shop. If those plans had gone ahead, the sitting area would have been very small and look and felt like a train compartment. I asked why we could not have one door opening into the shop to make access easier. To do that, a special very expensive glass had to be fitted to create a firescreen able to hold any fire for one hour, allowing time for the fire brigade to be called; all part of the new regulations. Before leaving the meeting, I asked if new plans could be drawn up as I wanted to see how the shop would look using our design. I suggested we would pay for the glass if we had too. September arrived and plans were agreed for a major restructure of the shop to include a seating area inside the shop and fire safety glass incorporated into the frontage. Ann chose carpets and wallpaper for the coming work, also overseeing the refurbishment of the shop.

In October, the shop closed for a quoted seven to eight weeks for the alterations, however it did not reopen until the following January. When it did open it had all been worth the effort; there was a tremendous change and it was a huge improvement, providing us with a much brighter working environment. There was more shelf space and the seating area was an immediate success. Drinks were served from a kitchen behind the shop and the redundant Klix trolley was taken to BRI to replace their very heavy and cumbersome 'Clinics Trolley'. In March, the official opening of the shop took place.

The gifts presented to the hospital from profits this year were a cervical scanner, sound equipment, chairs and tables, a special mattress and the funding of the Welcomer scheme all amounting to a cost in the region of £20,000.

Training sessions throughout this period were held, along with

The opening of the Main Corridor Shop after the second refurbishment, 1994

several meetings to create the new Welcomer Service for the Main Entrance. Miss Thompson explained our desk would be opposite the door used by the general public. This time a hostess service with the new name of Welcomer might work. The hospital was expanding rapidly, causing sick patients confusion at the many changes taking place. Having the desk at the side of the shop would also help our profile. This time we decided to promote the service differently. Members would receive better training and they would wear a white blouse and a WRVS scarf, distinguishing them from members in tabards. We needed members of the public to be aware that we were there to help them and the only way it would be obvious was to dress differently.

The newspaper service within the hospital that had for many years been going around the wards twice each day was about to cease. At a hospital meeting with the Health Authority the WRVS were asked if we might organise a paper round. I smiled as I remembered the problems we had had all those years ago and battles we had with the paper man who took confectionery round the wards the same days that we did. By July, the Trolley Service at the Bolton General Hospital was extended to a daily service selling sweets, toiletries and the *Bolton Evening News* (previously, it operated Tuesdays and Thursdays).

By August, the afternoon Trolley Service at Bolton Royal Infirmary had also extended to a daily service with newspapers. By now, services at the hospital were completely stretched so another appeal for volunteers went into the *Bolton Evening News*, resulting in 16 new members joining. W. H. Smiths would not supply us with newspapers

The Bolton Evening News being delivered to patients by WRVS members, 1994

in our own right but suggested we sub-retail from a local newsagent and split the profit. We agreed to do this. Eventually, we were able to deliver papers to all the wards every afternoon. The morning papers except the weekends were distributed by hospital staff. The WRVS advertised for new members to work the weekends. We had a man and his wife working together and a boy called Paul who worked throughout his A levels and it all worked very well, and by November we had increased the service at Bolton Royal Infirmary to include weekends.

Signs were beginning to show that the Infirmary would soon be moving from its home of over 200 years in the centre of Bolton to its new site at the General Hospital. During 1994, the Ophthalmology Department had moved. In view of the distance it was from the existing facilities, the WRVS were approached to open a tea bar so later in the year we advertised again for volunteers and this time, for reasons unknown, the response was overwhelming. One of the people who volunteered was a member who had done Meals on Wheels in 1960s, Barbara Hurst; she had been a Councillor for many years and Mayor during the year of our 'Appeal for the Ambulances'.

The gifts to the hospital from profits that year were a scanner for the Maternity Unit and the refurbishment to the L block shop and including the Welcomer service the cost was approximately £36,000.

By 1995 the building of the new hospital was well on its way with a proposed date for opening in 1997. The Outpatients Department would need a tea bar and the WRVS was now negotiating space for that and the shop in the main foyer.

In February, the first meeting with architects regarding a shop to be opened in the new main entrance took place and the necessary space was allocated. Throughout the year, meetings regarding the new Welcomer Service for the new main entrance continued. In addition, the WRVS were asked to provide a Welcomer Service in the Ophthalmology Department. The need for this type of service was increasing and becoming necessary in almost every department. I am sure it had a lot to do with all the changes happening and the increasing need for patient care. However, a Welcomer Service in the Ophthalmology Department was not going to be quite as easy as the others had been. We had lengthy discussions with Miss Thomson regarding the training that would be needed, as one could not give the same directions to a sight-impaired person as to a sighted person.

Miss Thomson was Head of Nursing and sat in during the interviewing of proposed Ophthalmology Welcomers, and took a great interest in their training. She organised training from Henshaws, the School for the Blind, enabling them to experience at first hand what it was like to be blind. We were never going to be busy in that de-

Presentation of a scanner for the Maternity Unit

partment and some members after training found it not busy enough, but the majority stayed. Ann had attended a seminar in Blackpool with Miss Thomson regarding the setting up of a Welcomer service. Instruction was given as to how useful a system it was and they learned how much the patient appreciated having someone show him or her where to go, then it was explained how to go about organising a Welcomer service. They were both delighted with the progress made in the Bolton hospitals. Our Welcomer project was already up and running, having grown constantly from its early beginnings. It was regarded as a worthwhile gift to the hospital, providing assurance to patients as they were escorted to the various departments. The gift part of a Welcomer service was the cost of their travelling expenses, which was paid for from all the projects.

A year after the Ophthalmology Department opened the staff gave a birthday party for all WRVS members working in the Ophthalmology Department, a nice gesture of appreciation.

As the closure date came nearer for BRI, a meeting was held for all our volunteers. This was to be a difficult time for many of them, as although there were enough places to give everyone a new position at the new hospital when it opened, for many the journey would prove difficult. At this meeting, Miss Thomson kindly attended and gave us detailed information and plans of the new building and the plans for closing the Infirmary when the time came.

During the early part of 1995, Marian had to resign completely from the WRVS and Ann Wood took over the job as Hospital Organiser, with Enid Swarsbrick taking on the job of Hospital Personnel Organiser.

Ann had worked at both hospitals for some years now and because of her experience she was asked to join the Voluntary Working Group which held regular meetings to assess various issues relating to voluntary workers in the hospital. This was an excellent platform and helped her to tighten security and controls within the projects. In addition, the hospital personnel became aware of just how many volunteers the WRVS had working at the hospital. When Ann left in 1998, WRVS had over 450 members in the hospitals and 55 were Welcomers. There were other organisations working in the hospital but the WRVS was by far the larger group. Ann also met with Beverly Andrews, Operations Manager, on a monthly basis primarily to discuss gifting as by now the WRVS through Ann were receiving several requests per month, which were prioritised according to their merits. However, over all the time we both were involved with the hospitals very little in the way of gifts were refused. Ann attended the Hospital Team Briefing meetings which were held for all hospital departments to help filter information both down and up the channels. This way everyone was kept fully involved with the multitude of changes occurring daily.

The whole 'Townleys' area was being refurbished yet again, making way for a new Rehabilitation Centre to accommodate the move of that department from BRI. Another portion of the Infirmary was coming on site. We had received detailed plans of a new kiosk needed in the new Rehabilitation waiting area, to be staffed by the WRVS.

During this period, the main corridor going straight down through the hospital, from D wards to the Maternity Block had to be closed. The big difficulty for members was the trolley going to the wards, as because of the corridor closure members had to go outside the building for part of the way. This proved a big disadvantage for everyone, including Ann when she visited the Maternity Tea Bar, Women's Health Tea Bar and Ophthalmology Tea Bar or ESMI projects she said it always appeared to be raining. Members also had to go outside on their way to the hospital safe depositing their takings from projects, which was too dangerous, especially for the evening shifts, so a small safe was installed in a cupboard within the Mother and Baby Shop which Ann emptied daily.

A computer was bought for the WRVS hospital office so we could now print our own rotas and update the Welcomer 'Bible' (the book which told members at the desk where every ward and clinic was – vital information as more departments moved). However, information concerning patients who had gone home and those admitted came from the hospital computer. Regular newsletters were printed: as the number of members increased keeping them informed was difficult but necessary.

Gifts this year consisted of ward curtains, an X-ray trolley, Main Corridor Shop refurbishment, equipment for the Ophthalmology Department, linen trolleys, and the Welcomer service expenses, totalling £57,500.

In 1996, during Working Party meetings to discuss the move from the Infirmary, it became obvious that we were not to have a kiosk in the new Outpatients Department; the main problem being that the department was spread over three blocks and on two floors. Another fact we were unaware of was that the area that had been suggested as our base did not even have a water supply and despite several meetings with various 'men in suits', no solution was found. Having worked so long in the Outpatients Department at Bolton Royal I think we had envisaged the same set up. Eventually, it was

Presentation of equipment for the Opthalmology Unit

decided that a trolley was the only solution and eventually the Klix trolley came back from BRI. This wasn't an ideal solution as the new departments were now fully carpeted, making it very difficult to push trolleys, but we kept a few very dedicated ladies, Olive Pickles and Mary Ashton especially. We now needed to recruit 'strong' ladies, teach them the geography of the whole department and hope they stayed with the WRVS.

We were now selling newspapers daily, and it was time we had our own agency. W. H. Smiths were asked again and this time they agreed to deal with us in our own right so we now made the full (25 per cent) profit on all our sales and were able to offer a wider selection of publications. 'Top Shelf' magazines go to newsagents automatically and Ann had to negotiate a special dispensation not to stock them, as the hospital shop was not the place to sell *Play Boy*.

Regular meetings to keep everyone informed of the planned closure of BRI took place, however many members working at the Infirmary were upset at losing their places, despite reassurances that there would be plenty of work for them at BDG. It was quite understandable as many of these women had worked at the Royal for many years.

Tours around the new hospital

Throughout the spring and summer of 1996 with the building work coming to an end, 'tours' around the new development began for the new and existing members who were to become Welcomers. The hospital was now very large and as the new main entrance was still being constructed, it was even more confusing. It became a huge task; and one tour sometimes was not enough! Members could not always remember where they had been and often needed more instruction. Ann helped Miss Thomson with several drafts of site maps for WRVS use and for distribution by the Welcomer to patients. In the initial stages, Miss Thompson did all the tours herself, but after the Main Entrance opened, Ann and Pat Bentley took her place in guiding members around.

Ann attended the coordinating meetings relating to the imminent move of all the equipment and services from Bolton Royal Infirmary up to the Royal Bolton Hospital.

The part played at these meetings by the WRVS was very insignificant, but Ann found them constructive. It was without doubt because of the forethought of the hospital staff that the move eventually went as well as it did, especially considering it included the Accident and Emergency Department and all the relevant equipment. During this time everything was kept up and running. Miss Thomson was the co-coordinator of the whole move. She retired within months of the move, having done a spectacular job. It was a complement to the Service that the WRVS was included in these groups and meetings. However, I thought Ann's dedication to the job gained the WRVS such esteem.

In June Ann had a meeting with the members running the BRI kiosk and broke the news that there would not be a kiosk in the new Outpatients Department. This had come as quite a shock to many, not least to us. Some members volunteered for the trolley and others agreed to help at the new Rehabilitation Unit kiosk, which was due to open in the refurbished Townleys Building. However, the new hospital was too great a distance for some to travel, so sadly several members decided to retire at that time.

When the plans for the new Main Entrance Shop were revealed, it was obviously too small and not ideally suited for the needs of a busy department such as this. After much discussion and compromise, we came up with a working option. However, the architect's plans for the shop came in at 70 per cent over budget so it was back to the drawing board. Savings were made on light fittings and glass, and reusing the shop fittings from the Infirmary saved us money. We had to incorporate storage and a sink, after a request for us to sell flowers in the shop at the hospital. Eventually because of the flowers we gained the extra floor space needed, so the result was a good compromise.

On 5 August 1996 the now fully trained Welcomer Service started at the new main entrance, and the training tours had paid off, as no one got lost. Wards from the Infirmary began moving into the new hospital on a daily basis and again our newspaper trolleys were extended to cover the new wards.

The last day for the kiosk at the Infirmary was 30 August and it had been on a site in that department before the WVS took it over in 1946–47. By early September, the Clinic Trolley did its last journey and by 8 September, the Infirmary Corridor Shop closed. I am sure there were some tears from volunteers and staff alike. However, there were new beginnings to look forward to and many happy memories left behind. On 10 September the WRVS held a farewell lunch for the members who had worked at the Infirmary.

The WRVS ambulance helped to transfer the contents of the shop and kiosk and everything went up to the Royal Bolton Hospital. Nothing was wasted; the shop-fitters took the shop fittings, cleaned them and stored them ready for installation elsewhere.

Accident and Emergency moved the following day, and was the last department to go to the Royal Bolton and soon after the old hospital building was up for sale.

At the Royal Bolton, the Hospital Cashiers Department had now moved to its new home in the main entrance to the hospital. With it went the use of the night safe in the centre of the main corridor where we had deposited takings from each duty since the WRVS began working in the hospital. All the monies went now to the newly sited

The farewell lunch for BRI volunteers, with Edna Blinkhorn
receiving her Long Service Medal

safe. This meant at the end of each week when the counters arrived, money deposited each day from the night safe had to be carried down the main corridor for counting in the WRVS office, and returned to the safe after the count was completed. This obviously was not practical as money is heavy, and neither was it secure so after more discussions we obtained the use of the Pharmacy Library to do the weekly count, situated behind the new pharmacy in the new entrance. We had four members very willing, very conscientious and just one hour in which to count £8000–9000 a week. Stress was upon us again.

The Pharmacy Department wanted the WRVS to provide a Welcomer Service within their department; this time it was to greet patients and help them fill in their prescriptions. This service required one member twice per day and started in October.

The Rehabilitation kiosk also opened in October and for members working in the Townleys section more readjustments had to be made, which these members did in true WRVS spirit.

For the benefit of Welcomers, 'Deaf Awareness' training sessions started and all the Welcomers attended. This training was necessary to make WRVS members aware of hearing problems that patients might have, which could be simply hard of hearing or profoundly deaf. It had been realised how futile it would be going into lengthy explanations if the patient you were speaking to was deaf. We were encouraged to make sure the patient was facing you and could lip-read if they were not hearing what one said. It all sounded so obvious, but there are times when we all have to be aware of the obvious. Our members responded well. There was even talk of learning sign language but that never happened.

Ann now sat on the new Induction Procedures Committee that was introduced by the hospital for new members, which was to include security, ID tags and fire procedures. These were all an improvement on the old system but again took huge amounts of time.

In December, the new Main Entrance Shop opened, staffed with many members who had previously worked at the Infirmary Shop and kiosk and had remained loyal since their redundancy in September. Everyone was shocked with how small the shop was, but responded to the need for a shop in that area, and it was a very busy shop from the beginning.

After repeated burglary threats at the Maternity Clinic kiosk, the hospital staff enclosed the area. This had needed doing for years. However the increase in theft crime was becoming a problem everywhere. With the help of Ellen Knowles who had helped design the original Main Corridor Shop, we transferred the old frontage from Accident and Emergency reception area at Bolton Royal Infirmary and used it to enclose the kiosk. Until the work was completed, members served the patients from a trolley in the Maternity Department.

Members working on the Maternity Tea Bar always said how much pleasure they received from their duties. They knew the patients quite well, as many patients visited on a weekly basic, particularly if the pregnancy was a difficult one. Many times after the birth of a baby, the mother would take the baby back, showing how well her baby was, especially when the baby had been poorly at birth. I remember hearing of a father who came each week with his wife, and being profoundly deaf himself, he wept with joy on hearing his child had no hearing problems at all, and was a fine healthy baby.

During the time of the closure of the Bolton Royal Infirmary there was a great feeling amongst many of the staff who worked there to retain as much of the history of the Infirmary as was possible. As a result, many artefacts and artworks found a new home at the Royal Bolton Hospital. After they were incorporated into the décor, they made a permanent record of Bolton Royal Infirmary's long history.

Miss Thomson retired when the new hospital changes were completed: she had created a warm and wonderful friendship between herself and the WRVS, always being cheerful and optimistic. Obviously, Ann held a special place in her affections, for, on leaving she insisted that Ann take her desk as a parting gift.

This year, the gifts to the hospital were phenomenal, and had to be a record. The list of the gifts included a defibrillator, breast screen equipment, urinary flow meter, blood pressure machine, ultrasound scanner and several more major items costing approximately £52,000, and with several refurbishment projects the total was in the region of £158,000. All the work undertaken by volunteers during this period was phenomenal, and more often than not done with a great deal of patience.

Things began to quieten down and the period of activity slowed as the new projects worked well. Things did not stand completely still but despite the workload, we developed the range of magazines we sold, increasing the shelves in the Main Corridor Shop to cope. The Breast Screening Welcomer Service was increased, members attended the Deaf Awareness courses etc. and presentations of gifts were made from the WRVS to the hospital.

During the course of the year the accounts systems were being refined; all projects previously having had their own accounts were amalgamated. The intention was to make accounting easier. However, with the new system should an individual problem arise it could be more difficult to trace.

Retro Payments were under discussion by all projects throughout the country as by using the same supplier we would get better prices and WRVS Head Office would receive a payment.

The newly created Four-Core system for the work of WRVS was implemented first in hospitals. Beginning with a restructuring of Headquarters management, several positions developed. There was to be a Hospital Services Director with five Hospital Service Managers who each had three Regional Hospital Services Managers. Ann had been a superb Hospital Organiser for Bolton and was offered the position of a Regional Services Manager in July 1997. After much consideration, she took the new position.

Hospital charges were introduced to replace Local Resource Funding as the reduction of the Government grant bit hard. In the light of this LRF was not enough; this new charge was a percentage of the sales on a sliding scale. Bolton WRVS was turning over a third of a million pounds by this time and fell into the highest category of 10 per cent, therefore 10 per cent of all sales went directly to the running costs of the WRVS.

Previously the larger projects had to register for VAT and from first registering, we had to complete a patient /non-patient ratio check, for one week each year at the VAT-paying projects. Every member working on a till had to ask every customer she served in the course of a week whether the goods she had purchased were for her own use or for that of a patient. The member on duty that day recorded the results of every sale. We were exempt from paying VAT on those items bought by a patient or for a patient. More often than not the majority of the goods bought were for the patient. Obviously, this was a huge saving on the VAT payable and once the survey was done, the results could be used for the VAT returns for a year.

During a 10-year period at the hospitals, we had five VAT inspections and I think the system baffled every one of the inspectors, as it was peculiar only to the WRVS.We also took stock twice yearly and a full set of accounts, a Profit and Loss and Balance Sheet were produced. A copy went to the Health Authority and one to Headquarters.

By means of a thank you to all the voluntary organisations working in the hospital, a Volunteers Evening was held yearly. I was present at the first one given way back when I was a new Hospital Organiser and I heard tell of how they had grown in the ensuing years from approximately 50 people to several hundred. Several different voluntary organisations attended every year. In the beginning, they were held at the Health Authority offices at Churchgate but with the increase in numbers the venue changed to the hospital staff restaurant.

Varying WRVS personnel visited our hospitals over the years and several from other hospitals, including the Hospitals Department at Headquarters. We had the largest WRVS involvement in any of the north west hospitals in terms of turnover and non-trading projects, which included a large body of Welcomers. The gifts for 1997–98 covered many items of equipment for many departments at a cost of almost £75,000.

In 1998 all projects had to have a till, and scanning tills were introduced, and what's more the till had to balance – no more leaving the till drawer open because it was easier that way! Whilst some members saw this as a challenge and an achievement, it did not go down well with everyone.

Professional merchandisers came into the shops and for the wont of repeating myself again, this was not the best of times for everyone, but still compromises were reached. The official suppliers were nationwide companies who won the WRVS contract from Head Office to supply all our projects. In return, we were to get the cheapest prices available at project level and WRVS Head Office received retro payments, a percentage of the turnover to go towards the funding of the WRVS. The suppliers of course wanted to maximise our sales and sent their merchandisers into the shops to achieve the best displays. Their methods were a real science. They suggested that by displaying chocolate bars in a certain position the sales would rise.

Presentation of a platelet incubator

This was to increase profits for WRVS and extra sales for the manufacturers and was done by merchants in most large stores throughout the country. But our outlets were not in the main huge outlets. Considering the number of outlets when combined, they would be classed as a big store with a very large turnover selling goods throughout country. However, merchandisers had not allowed for our members and their scientific approach to selling and they all had one, believe me. Over the years many of our members had developed their own particular science in selling and kept the Mars bars in a certain place, other commodities also having their own place. This was fine, but other members also enjoyed re-sorting the shelves and many did it each time they arrived for duty. On some days, our merchandise was subjected to a merry-go-round ride. These members were good volunteers and enjoyed selling, along with making the shop/kiosk look good. It was almost impossible to keep solely to the merchandisers plan. Explanations of course were made as to why this had to be a certain way but many members saw it as pressure selling and 'profit' became the buzzword. Nevertheless, retro payments to the WRVS began, helping to cover some of the costs incurred in keeping the Service going.

HACCP procedures were put into operation, and stood for Hazard and Critically Controlled Points and became a legal requirement for all catering establishments. Every stage was chronicalled, from goods entering the premises. Storage was a concern and procedures for every eventuality had to be organised, charts filled in accordingly, then put up for display. It was an onerous task and many of the members wondered who looked at the completed charts. The

Presentation of a hoist, funded by the proceeds of the ESMI Trolley Shop

reasoning behind the new procedure was to help staff with the storing of goods in the right order and at the correct temperature. Ice cream was one of the commodities causing concern, sandwiches another – each had their respective temperatures and needed placing in the fridge or freezer – again this would have been easy with only one person being responsible, but we had many volunteers, who did their best to comply.

In 1998, much to my surprise, I received a special prize for work done in the community in the years I was Organiser, presented by Bolton's Women of the Year Committee for work done in the community. I was delighted when the same year Ann was a runner-up for Woman of the Year for her work at the hospital. My award came after I had left Bolton WRVS but nontheless I was thrilled and quite humbled. However, Ann received hers whilst still working there, which was wonderful. It was a great compliment to her and all the team. Ann felt she was there representing the 400-strong team of volunteers, and they all deserved praise. They did a superb job in pulling together all the challenges that took place over the months of changes that happened in the hospitals. Ann represented the WRVS at the Royal Garden Party and said that her day at the Palace was a fantastic day, one she would never forget.

Janet Fletcher became the Organiser for the hospitals after Ann left to work as a Regional Hospital Organiser and between them they organised a Hospitals Diamond Jubilee party at the hospital. The hospital provided the buffet and constructed a display of our work done throughout the hospital. In addition, the hospital did a flower display on the roundabout within the grounds with the WRVS logo and 1938–98 set out in flowers.

Ann Wood's own memories of her early years working at the hospital:

In my early days with WRVS before coming as involved as I eventually did, Rachael, my youngest daughter came to the hospital with me from being three years old. She loved playing in the cardboard boxes that the stock was delivered in and had hundred's of 'Grandma's'. She could use a pricing gun at the age of three and a half and was a good help pricing up goods. A member working in the Clothing Department made Rachael a WRVS tabard, which she wore with pride. I dropped her off at nursery in the mornings and went to the hospital, collected her two hours later in Horwich, and then went back to the hospital. Natalie, my elder daughter loved to come and help during her school holidays. They looked through the toy catalogues for items for the shop. I have an apology to make to all the little boys of Bolton as I think the stock was definitely biased to 'girlie' toys! When the girls were ill and my Mum or Garry my husband could not look after them, I stayed at home and went to the hospital in the evening. This worked well as it meant I was able to see the evening and weekend members. On one occasion, through sickness, one of the reps came to our house for his order.

When the hospital year-end returns were due, I took them home and completed them at the kitchen table whilst Rachael, still pre-school age, crayoned in a book beside me. On one occasion whilst working at the returns I had to answer the phone. On returning to my paperwork some time later, I found Rachel had 'crayoned by accident' on the completed returns. On bringing them to the office I felt quite upset and worried that I might have to do them all again. Pat persuaded me to send them in as they were, saying 'It's the Women's Voluntary Service and women have babies who grow into toddlers and enjoy copying their mothers – that is all Rachael was doing! Sometimes these things happen. Do not worry about it, I am sure no one at Headquarters will mind in the least.'

Over the years the shop came to be very professionally run, from the first early days when one lady managed to get the till key chain stuck in the till drawer – with herself attached to it, to today when we are using state of the art scanning tills! We had to comply with all current legislation, Trading Standards, Food Hygiene, and all the Health and Safety at Work Acts, Hazard and Critical Control Points Procedures – quite a story from the beginning of work in hospitals at the end of the war years to now – what a change!

Ann Wood left Bolton WRVS, and became North West Regional Hospital Manager, and was replaced as Hospital Organiser by Janet Fletcher. By the end of that year, she was to leave the WRVS and together with her husband, they opened a café in the town centre of Bolton.

This book covers the years from 1938 until the WRVS Diamond Jubilee in 1998 when members working in the hospital totalled approximately 650, with 70 of these being Welcomers.

Over all the years we have had so many extraordinary members working for the good of all the people of Bolton. Some members worked with a lot of responsibility, some doing several duties every week, and many did one duty a week. They worked in lots of different situations but all were valuable in the running of this great organisation. There have had to be changes over the years to allow us to grow, and let us hope that it continues to do so.

Remembrance Day

Bolton WRVS are present every year at the Cenotaph in Bolton Town Centre. Lillian Punchaby has for some years been leading this occasion, which is popular and many of the same members have marched for several years.

WRVS members also make a presence at the Cenotaph in London each year, ncluding members from Headquarters and volunteers from around the country. It is an honour to be invited. Betty Taylor went in the mid–1980s, Sheila went in the mid–1990s, and these are her memories.

I went to the Cenotaph Remembrance Service one freezing cold day somewhere in the mid–1990s. I have great memories of the day but also some of being frozen stiff and not at all certain that I would be able to move when it was time to march. During the morning we were drilled in the art of marching but unfortunately it was pouring with rain. Eventually we all marched onto Whitehall and the rain stopped but the temperature dropped! Finally, I did eventually thaw out but it took all night; fortunately I had my thermals on! The day however was wonderful, a very moving experience which I thoroughly enjoyed.

The Diamond Jubilee of the WRVS, 1998

During this period of change, we were approaching the sixtieth year of the Service. Unlike previous anniversaries and because of financial constraints, there was no funding for celebrations. It was left to the resourcefulness of each Division to organise whatever was possible. There was a celebration at Bridgewater Hall and members from the whole Division were invited. It was a showing of the work done by WRVS in various areas some being quite unfamiliar to other areas. There were several speeches that day but Margaret Spriggs, ex-Area Organiser for Greater Manchester gave her speech about the years up to the Golden Jubilee. She spoke well, and many who heard her that day will not forget one small part of her speech. The years up to the fiftieth anniversary, she said, were like the name of the occasion, Golden, reminding one of softness and warmth, but Diamond sounded hard and crisp, reminding one of the hardness of the time the WRVS was now in. It was a great occasion, organised in the main by Norma Gibbons. There was also a Garden Party at Chatsworth House for members organised by Lennie for the North West Division and a Royal Garden Party to celebrate the Diamond Jubilee was organised at Milton Hill. There was a special celebratory meeting and a buffet tea at the Bolton General Hospital for members working in the hospitals, also an exhibition of work, and I am sure there would have been celebrations organised for the clubs by their Leaders.

The Summing up of Sixty years' voluntary service

The WVS was initially formed as an arm of the Government and recruited its members from women of many lifestyles, its purpose being to help win a war. Many members worked across the length and breadth of the country in many situations. They worked tirelessly with refugees and evacuees, collected goods for recycling, help-, ing to conserve the nation's resources, helped in their task by several Allied countries that provided many items for their work. The mass evacuation of children, mothers and teachers was a superhuman task. The work of providing comfort to people in the bombed-out cities was phenomenal, and clothing the nation when the need arose was comforting. By 1942 there were one million members working for the WVS and by the end of the atrocities the WVS worked in many countries around the world. For the thousands of women who lost families in the tragedy of war, the companionship of other WVS members proved their salvation. Bonds were made between women that lasted for years and provided the succour by which many survived the horrors.

After the war ended and the Service wound down, many of its members were saddened. However when the promise of funding for the continuation of the WVS came from the Government in 1947, there was much relief. The Government eventually took responsibility for the basic expenses of the Service, requiring the WRVS to provide Clothing Stores and Emergency Services for the nation. This brought renewed vigour, helping put Britain back together. Welfare work started albeit slowly in some areas, then gained momentum.

As the years passed and work increased a new generation of the WVS emerged, later after Her Majesty the Queen bestowed the Royal Seal we became the WRVS in 1966. Amongst the projects that came to the fore was Welfare Work, where the WRVS worked alongside the National Health Service, which started after the war ended, and as the Welfare State emerged, they began services for the Elderly, Children and the Meals on Wheels Service, being responsible for millions of meals delivered daily. Each decade brought the changes required to keep the Service functioning and they responded to appeals worldwide as well as home emergencies, becoming very competent in their chosen fields. By the end of the 1980s, the numbers of WRVS members had risen and were at their highest since the early war years. The WVS/WRVS celebrated each anniversary in turn, culminating in the extraordinary celebrations for the Golden Jubilee in 1988.

Towards the end of the 1980s and early 1990s new Government legislation arrived and by the nature of that legislation, we saw many changes in store for the entire voluntary sector. The WRVS being the huge organisation it was, almost every field in which we worked would be affected. The Charity Commission meant that the WRVS had to become more accountable, changing our banking strategies tremendously, and changing the nature of the work many of the volunteers did. The Children Act 1989 forced us to look closer at the work we did with children. The Woodhead Report, undertaken by the WRVS for possible restructuring of the Service in line with new legislation advocated sweeping changes in its structure. Eventually we were aware the Government grant we had cherished for so many years was about to be much reduced. In turn, that eventually reduced the services we did, but we now had to look at making the services we had left sound and on a strong footing. What the future holds no one knows, but I hope the WRVS will be around for many years to come, still serving the people of Britain.

→ *Appendix* ←

Gifts from WRVS hospital profits, 1980–98

During my early years money was accumulating and not being spent. Eventually, as the message got through to the right authority, this changed. The lists were growing and we had received requests for a varied selection of goods, and we were still coming away from previously buying only comforts for patients as now equipment took priority. The WRVS did its purchasing through the Health Authority Trust and by doing this saved some tax. During these early years, the Authority requested an amazing array of goods: comforts, equipment and some refurbishment for all three hospitals in Bolton.

I have included some photographs of the presentations of comforts and equipment we bought through profits. There were so many however during these first five years from all three Hospitals, the list was as follows.

Bolton General

Two defibrillators
Three TVs
Blood pressure monitor
Funding a schoolroom for sick children
Funding the furnishings of a room for the relatives of sick patients, including special beds
Funding for the CCU Rest room
Stair trolley
Air compressor

Hulton Lane Hospital
Lifting gear for patients
Garden furniture
Piano
A donation to the Centenary Fund

Bolton Royal Infirmary
Special beds (including tilt and turn bed)
Water bed for sick patient care
A donation for BRI Centenary Fund
Part funding of a childrens' holiday scheme
Funding of training for a dog for the deaf

1986–90
In this period the list grew tremendously:
Furnishings for a ward at Hulton Lane
Laser for cervical cancer from all the projects
Donation to Great Ormond Street Hospital
Keyboard for Hulton Lane
Computer printer for the Children's Unit
Refurbishing of a Post Operative Intensive Care Room
Nebulisers
2 cupboards
2 TVs
2 Highchairs
Blood pressure machine
Donation to Lady Tonge Clinic

1987–88
The Main Corridor Shop and the new Princess Anne shop refurbishment took place with the WRVS covering most of the cost.

1988–89
Donations to all three hospitals for a variety of goods.

1990
Donations for a collection of items for all three hospitals.

During the decade to follow, the gifts from profits were phenomenal:

1991

A Chiropody chair
Refurbishing the Pharmacy waiting area
Children's crockery
Outpatients Department refurbishment
2 Care monitors
Donation to the refurbishment of the porter's reception area
A birthing bed

1992

Cytology microscope
Lego play table
Children's crockery
Noticeboards for the Main Corridor
An Ultrasound diagnostic scanner
Fittings for the Main Corridor Shop
Mekolifts

1993

The Welcomer Service expenses were in the way of a gift
Cervical scanner
Chairs and tables
Pegasus mattress
Sound equipment
High chairs

1994–95

Scanner
Welcomer expenses
The refurbishment of L Block
Noticeboards

1995/6

Cubicle curtains for Churchill Ward BRI kiosk
An X-ray trolley
BRI ward trolley
A hoist for patients
ESMI Trolley
Second Main Corridor Shop Upgrade, Main Corridor Shop

A Humphrey Field Analyser for Ophthalmology (BRI Shop). This
piece of equipment helped in the treatment of Glaucoma.
Linen trolleys for theatre (BRI kiosk)
Expenses for the Welcomer Service

1996–97
Patients' information folders, Women's Healthcare
Refurbishment at Hulton Lane
Hulton Lane trolley
Resuscitation practise dolls
Chapel furnishings, L Block shop
A urinary flow meter, Main Corridor Shop
The fitting out of the Main Entrance Shop
An autoscope for Urology
A plasma thawing bath to help previously frozen blood to be thawed
    out for traumatised patients
A draught lobby
Breast screening equipment for the Breast Clinic
A defibrillator
A Dinamap blood pressure machine
Ultrasound scanner
A camera for Ophthalmology
A TV for E3 Ward
Welcomer expenses
Refurbishments that year included
Women's Health and Ophthalmology
Princess Anne kiosk
A storeroom in Maternity

1997–98
Urology table
Digital camera for medical illustration
A treadmill for Rehabilitation
ECG machine for Rehabilitation
Food trolley for K Wards
Television sets for 3 wards
A syringe pump for diabetics
Videos for the Discharge Lounge
Wheelchairs for the Minerva Daycentre
A foetal heart monitor
C Ds for Ante-Natal Department

County Borough Organisers 1938–74
Mrs. Clara Kay
Mrs. Evelyn Warr
Mrs. Madeline Wadsworth

Metropolitan Organisers 1974–98
Mrs. Margaret Sydall
Mrs. Pat Cox
Joint Organisers, Mrs. Marian Hilton and Mrs. Dorothy Todd
Mrs. Sheila Leyland

Bolton Local Organisers
Mrs. Pat Cox
Mrs. May Fielding
Mrs. Freda Clunie
Mrs. Sheila Leyland

Farnworth Local Organisers
Mrs. Wynn Shaw
Mrs. Dorothy Ellison
Mrs. Pat Bentley
Mrs. Joyce Armitage

Horwich Local Organisers
Mrs. Lillian Rawlinson
Mrs. Jane Whitehead
Mrs. Mickey Hale
Mrs. Sheila Johnson

Printed in the United Kingdom
by Lightning Source UK Ltd.
9737700001B/148-204